The Hermeneutic Spiral and Interpretation in Literature and the Visual Arts

This collection brings together fourteen of the author's original papers, previously published in a variety of academic journals and edited collections over the last three decades, on the process of interpretation in literature and the visual arts in one comprehensive volume. The volume highlights the centrality of artistic texts to the study of multimodality, organised into six sections each representing a different modality or semiotic system, including literature, television, film, painting, and architecture. A new introduction lays the foundation for the theoretically based method of analysis running through each of the chapters, one that emphasises the interplay of textual details and larger thematic purposes to create an open-ended and continuous approach to the interpretation of artistic texts, otherwise known as the 'hermeneutic spiral.' Showcasing Michael O'Toole's extensive contributions to the field of multimodality and on research on interpretation in literature and the visual arts, this book is essential reading for students and scholars in multimodality, visual arts, art history, film studies, and comparative literature.

Michael O'Toole is Emeritus Professor of Communication Studies at Murdoch University in Perth, Western Australia.

Routledge Studies in Multimodality
Edited by Kay L. O'Halloran,
Curtin University

The Discourse of YouTube
Multimodal Text in a Global Context
Phil Benson

The Semiotics of Movement in Space
A User's Perspective
Robert James McMurtrie

Mapping Multimodality Performance Spaces
Edited by Maria Grazia Sindoni, Janina Wildfeuer, and Kay L. O'Halloran

The Discourse of Physics
Building Knowledge through Language, Mathematics and Image
Y. J. Doran

Advancing Multimodal and Critical Discourse Studies
Interdisciplinary Research Inspirited by Theo van Leeuwen's Social Semiotics
Edited by Sumin Zhao, Emilia Djonov, Anders Björkvall and Morten Boeriis

The Materiality of Writing
A Trace Making Perspective
Edited by Christian Mosbæk Johannessen and Theo van Leeuwen

Designing and Implementing Multimodal Curricula and Programs
Edited by J. C. Lee and Santosh Khadka

The Hermeneutic Spiral and Interpretation in Literature and the Visual Arts
Michael O'Toole

For more information about this series, please visit: www.routledge.com

The Hermeneutic Spiral and Interpretation in Literature and the Visual Arts

Michael O'Toole

NEW YORK AND LONDON

First published 2018
by Routledge
711 Third Avenue, New York, NY 10017

and by Routledge
2 Park Square, Milton Park, Abingdon, Oxon OX14 4RN

Routledge is an imprint of the Taylor & Francis Group, an informa business

© 2018 Taylor & Francis

The right of Michael O'Toole to be identified as author of this work has been asserted by him in accordance with sections 77 and 78 of the Copyright, Designs and Patents Act 1988.

All rights reserved. No part of this book may be reprinted or reproduced or utilised in any form or by any electronic, mechanical, or other means, now known or hereafter invented, including photocopying and recording, or in any information storage or retrieval system, without permission in writing from the publishers.

Trademark notice: Product or corporate names may be trademarks or registered trademarks, and are used only for identification and explanation without intent to infringe.

Library of Congress Cataloging-in-Publication Data
Names: O'Toole, L. M. (Lawrence Michael), 1934– author.
Title: The hermeneutic spiral and interpretation in literature and the visual arts / by Michael O'Toole.
Description: New York : Routledge, 2017. | Series: Routledge studies in multimodality ; 22 | Includes bibliographical references and index.
Identifiers: LCCN 2017061288 | ISBN 9781138503779 (hardback : alk. paper) | ISBN 9781315145525 (ebk)
Subjects: LCSH: Arts—Philosophy. | Hermeneutics.
Classification: LCC BH39 .O865 2017 | DDC 700.1—dc23
LC record available at https://lccn.loc.gov/2017061288

ISBN: 978-1-138-50377-9 (hbk)
ISBN: 978-1-315-14552-5 (ebk)

Typeset in Sabon
by Apex CoVantage, LLC

For Leela and Janek for their love and support.

Contents

List of Plates ix
Acknowledgements x
Charts xii

Introduction 1

PART 1
Literary Narrative 7

1 Structure and Style in the Short Story: Chekhov's "The Student" 9

2 Narrative Structure and Living Texture: Joyce's "Two Gallants" 34

3 Analytic and Synthetic Approaches to Narrative Structure: Sherlock Holmes and "The Sussex Vampire" 50

4 Dimensions of Semiotic Space in Narrative: "Joseph and His Brethren" and James Joyce's "Eveline" 75

PART 2
TV Narrative 93

5 Art versus Computer Animation: Integrity and Technology in *South Park* 95

PART 3
Film 107

6 Eisenstein in *October* 109

viii Contents

  7 Structural Interpretation of a Film: Eisenstein's *Strike*   115

  8 The Revolution in Techniques and Human Values:
Early Soviet Cinema   125

PART 4
Painting   137

  9 Towards a Systemic-Functional Semiotics of Painting:
Frank Hinder's *The Flight into Egypt*   139

10 Captain Banning Cocq's Three Left Hands: A Semiotic
Interpretation of Rembrandt's *The Night Watch*   158

11 Word Pictures and Painted Narrative. Longstaff's
Breaking the News: The Systemic-Functional Model
Relating the Analysis of Pictorial Discourse, Verbal
Discourse and Narrative Form   168

12 Pushing Out the Boundaries: Designing a
Systemic-Functional Model for Non-European
Visual Arts: A Chinese Landscape Painting   187

13 Exploiting Famous Paintings: The Canon Colour Wizz
Photocopier and Picasso's *Girl Before a Mirror*   199

PART 5
Architecture and Language   205

14 The Presentation of Self in Everyday Architecture
and Language   207

References   223
Index   227

Plates

1. Frank Hinder: *Flight into Egypt* (1952). Oil and tempera on hardboard. State Art Collection, Art Gallery of Western Australia. Gift of the Friends of the Art Gallery, 1953. Photographer: Bo Wong

2. Rembrandt: *Night Watch* (1642). Oil on canvas. Rijksmuseum, Amsterdam

3. John Longstaff: *Breaking the News* (1887). Oil on canvas. State Art Collection, Art Gallery of Western Australia. Purchased with funds from the Hackett Bequest Fund, 1933. Photographer: Bo Wong

4. Gong Xian: *Landscape Scroll* (1682). Inks and colour wash. Honolulu Museum of Art

5. Pablo Picasso: *Girl Before a Mirror* (1936) and the Canon Colour Wizz Photocopier. *The Australian Magazine*, May 2–3, 1992

Acknowledgements

1. "Structure and Style in Chekhov's Student" was published in *The Slavonic and East European Review*, vol XLIX, No 114, Jan 1971. Courtesy of Cambridge University Press.

2. "Narrative Structure and Living Texture: Joyce's 'Two Gallants'" was published in *PTL: A Journal for Descriptive Poetics and Literature*, vol 1, No 3, Oct 1976. Courtesy of The Porter Institute for Poetics and Semiotics, University of Tel Aviv.

3. "Analytic and synthetic approaches to narrative structure: Sherlock Holmes and 'The Sussex Vampire'" was published in Roger Fowler (ed), *Style and Structure in Literature*, 1975. Courtesy of Basil Blackwell, Oxford.

4. "Dimensions of semiotic space: the story of Joseph in the Bible and James Joyce's 'Eveline'" was published in *Poetics Today*, vol 1, No 4, Summer 1980. Courtesy of The Porter Institute for Poetics and Semiotics, University of Tel Aviv.

5. "Art vs. Computer Animation: Integrity and Technology in *South Park*" was published in Kay L. O'Halloran & Bradley A. Smith (eds.) *Multimodal Studies*, 2011. Courtesy of Routledge.

7. "Eisenstein's *Strike*: a structuralist interpretation" was published in J. Andrew (ed.) *Essays on Poetics*, 1994. Courtesy of Ryburn Publishing.

8. "Early Soviet Cinema: The revolution in techniques and human values" was published in University of Exeter Tapes (*).

9. "A systemic-functional semiotics of art: Frank Hinder's *The Flight into Egypt*" was published in Peter H. Fries & Michael Gregory (eds.) *Discourse in Society: Systemic Functional Perspectives*, 1995. Courtesy of Ablex Publishing Corp.

10. "Captain Banning Cocq's three left hands: a semiotic interpretation of Rembrandt's *The Night Watch*" was published in *Russian Literature LIV* (2003). Courtesy of Elsevier.

11. "Word Pictures and Painted Narrative" was published in A. Archer & E. Breuer (eds.) *Multimodality in Writing*, 2015. Courtesy of Brill.

12. "Pushing out the boundaries: designing a systemic-functional model for non-European visual arts. A Chinese landscape painting: Gong Xian: *Landscape Scroll* (1682)" was published in Linguistics and the Human Sciences, 2005, vol 1.1. Courtesy of Equinox.

13. "Exploiting famous paintings: the Canon Colour Wizz Photocopier and Picasso's *Girl Before a Mirror*" images published in *The Australian Magazine*, May 1992.

14. "The presentation of self in everyday architecture and language: *Fawlty Towers*" was published in Carlos A. M. Gouveia & Marta Filipe Alexandre (eds.) *Languages, metalanguages, modalities, cultures*, 2013. Courtesy of Lisbon: iLteC.

Charts

Rank \ Function	IDEATIONAL — Experiential	IDEATIONAL — Logical	INTERPERSONAL	TEXTUAL
CLAUSE	TRANSITIVITY types of process, participants and circumstances (identity clauses) (things, facts and reports)	condition addition report POLARITY	MOOD types of speech function modality (the WH-function)	THEME types of message (identity as text relation) (identification, predication, reference, substitution)
Verbal GROUP	TENSE (verb clauses)	catenation secondary tense	PERSON ('marked' options)	VOICE ('constrastive' options)
Nominal GROUP	MODIFICATION epithet function enumeration (noun classes) (adjective classes)	classification sub-modification	ATTITUDE attitudinal modifiers intensifiers	DEIXIS determiners 'phoric' elements (qualifiers) (definite article)
Adverbial (including prepositional) GROUP	'MINOR PROCESSES' prepositional relations (classes of circumstantial adjunct)	narrowing sub-modification	COMMENT (classes of comment adjunct)	CONJUNCTION (classes of discourse adjunct)
WORD (including lexical item)	LEXICAL 'CONTENT' (taxonomic organization of vocabulary)	compounding deviation	LEXICAL 'REGISTER' (expressive words) (stylistic organization of vocabulary)	COLLOCATION (collocational organisation of vocabulary)
INFORMATION UNIT			TONE intonation systems	INFORMATION distribution and focus

Spanning the IDEATIONAL column: PARATACTIC COMPLEXES (all ranks) — co-ordination, apposition; HYPOTACTIC COMPLEXES OF CLAUSE, GROUP AND WORD.

Spanning INTERPERSONAL and TEXTUAL (top): COHESION ('above the sentence'; non-structural relations) — reference, substitution and ellipsis; conjunctions; lexical cohesion.

Chart 1 Functions and systems in language (Halliday, 1973)

Unit \ Function	REPRESENTATIONAL	MODAL	COMPOSITIONAL
WORK	Narrative themes Scenes Portrayals Interplay of episodes	Rhythm Modality Gaze Framing Light Perspective	Proportion Gestalt: Geometry Frame Line Horizontals Rhythm Verticals Colour Diagonals
EPISODE	Actions, events Agents–patients–goals Focal/side sequence Interplay of actions	Relative Prominence Scale Centrality Interplay of Modalities	Relative position in work Alignment Interplay } of forms Coherence
FIGURE	Character Object Act/Stance/Gesture Clothing components	Gaze Contrast: Scale Stance Line Characterization Light Colour	Relative position in episode Parallelism/Opposition Subframing
MEMBER	Part of body/object Natural form	Stylization	Cohesion: Reference (Parallel/Contrast/Rhythm)

Chart 2 Functions and systems in painting (O'Toole)

Units \ Functions	EXPERIENTIAL	INTERPERSONAL	TEXTUAL
BUILDING	Practical function: Public/Private; Industrial/Commercial/Agricultural/ Governmental/Educational/Medical/ Cultural/Religious/Residential; Domestic/Utility Orientation to light Orientation to wind Orientation to earth Orientation to service (water/sewage/power)	Size Orientation to neighbours Verticality Orientation to road Chthonicity Orientation to entrant Facade Intertextuality: Cladding reference Colour mimicry Modernity contrast Exoticism Opacity Reflectivity	Relation to city Relation to road Relation to adjacent buildings Proportions Rhythms: contrasting shapes, angles Textures: rough/smooth Roof/wall relation Opacity Reflectivity

FLOOR	Sub-functions:
	    Access
	    Working
	    Selling
	    Administration
	    Storing
	    Waking
	    Sleeping
	    Parking
		Height Sites of power
		Spaciousness Separation of groups
		Accessibility
		Openness of vista
		View
		Hard/soft texture
		Colour
			Relation to other floors
			Relation to outer world
			Relation to connectors; stairs/lift escalator (external cohesion)
			Relation of landing/corridor/foyer/room (internal cohesion)
			Degree of partition
			Permanence of partition

ROOM	Specific functions: Access Study Foyer Entry Toilet Restaurant Living room Laundry Kitchen Family room Gamesroom Bar Kitchen Retreat Bedroom Bathroom En suite Bedroom Servery	Comfort Lighting Modernity Sound Opulence Welcome Style: rustic, pioneer, colonial, suburban 'Dallas', working class, tenement, slum Foregrounding of function	Scale Lighting Sound Relation to outside Relation to other rooms Connectors: doors/windows/hatches/intercom Focus (e.g. hearth, dais, altar, desk)
ELEMENT	Light: window, lamp, curtains, blinds Air: window, fan, conditioner Heating: central, fire, stove Sound: carpet, rugs, partitions acoustic, treatment Seating (function/comfort) Table (dining/coffee/occasional/desk/computer/drawing board)	Relevance Functionality: convention/surprise Texture: rough/smooth Newness Decorativeness 'Stance' Stylistic coherence Projection (e.g. TV)	Texture Positioning: to light/heat/other elements Finish

Chart 3 Functions and systems in architecture (O'Toole) (See Chapter 14)

Introduction

This archive is a collection of 14 original papers from academic journals and book chapters published between 1971 and 2015, exploring the process and nature of interpretation in literature, film and the displayed visual art of painting. Running through all of them is a search for methods of analysis which can be (and have been) shared by students, other researchers and ordinary readers and viewers.

The whole collection stresses the centrality of artistic texts in the study of multimodality. It combines close detailed analysis of literary texts and films (art forms that unfold in time on the one hand) and paintings, which are simply "displayed," out of time.

The book articulates a theoretically based and consistent method of analysis relating artistic texts in three different modalities (or semiotic systems). It argues for a coherent and consistent process of interpretation, linking pre-existing knowledge and attitudes in the reader/viewer with patterns discovered in the process of detailed analysis. Each chapter stresses the labile and open-ended process of interpretation ("the hermeneutic spiral"). Most of the works analysed are well known and have attracted a wide range of literary and art-historical commentary, but it is my contention that the hermeneutic spiral, with its detailed and multi-layered analysis makes new interpretations possible and provable.

The German literary theorists Hans-Georg Gadamer (1768–1834) and Wilhelm Dilthey (1833–1911) drew on a tradition of biblical scholarship which related linguistic detail in a text to overall meanings discovered in the process of interpretation: "Hermeneutics." This notion of "seeing both the forest and the trees" was exemplified in the Austrian Leo Spitzer's approach to French texts in his attempt to marry linguistics and literary history in what he termed "the philological circle" (1948). The present author, armed with a powerful contemporary linguistic model and an education in literature, film and the visual arts, prefers the metaphor of a "hermeneutic spiral" where the interplay of textual details and the larger thematic purposes of the text leads to an open-ended and continuing "spiral" of interpretation.

2 Introduction

Hermeneutics and *Explication de texte*

It was at the age of 15 that I was introduced by my French teacher, Eric Smedley, to the method of study of literary texts then currently popular in France known as "explication de texte." This involved confronting a school student with a page or so of one of their "set books"—a novel or short story or play that they were studying for their national examinations. The student would have half an hour or so to pick out features of the text which seemed to stand out and reflect the larger thematic purposes of the literary work.

As an illustration of this process I want to look at a short English text, the poem **"The Road Not Taken,"** by Robert Frost, as I have approached the hermeneutic process through my teaching career in stylistics and semiotics, which is roughly traced in the course of this book.

The columns in italics alongside the text of the poem represent two stages in the analytical process: **NS (Narrative Structure)** recognises the story line in the poem and—as a first stage of the hermeneutic process—pinpoints features of Setting (in space and time), Character and PV (Point of View) which we visualise.

The *Tense/Modality* column focuses on the linguistic structures of verb tense and modal auxiliaries and comments which cast doubts on the poet's resolve: (*sorry, could not, as far as I could, as just as fair, perhaps, as for that, about the same, no step, I doubted if I should ever, somewhere ages and ages hence*)

"The Road Not Taken"	NS	Tense/Modality
1 Two roads diverged in a yellow wood	*Setting*	*Past*
2 And sorry I could not travel both	*Char + PV*	*Modal (Fut)*
3 And be one traveller, long I stood	*Time*	*Past*
4 And looked down one as far as I could	*PV*	*Modal*
5 To where it bent in the undergrowth;	*Setting*	*Past*
6 Then took the other, as just as fair,	*Char + Action/ Choice*	*Past*
7 And having perhaps the better claim,	*PV*	*Modal*
8 Because it was grassy and wanted wear;	*Setting + PV*	
9 Though as for that, the passing there	*PV + Setting*	*Modal*
10 Had worn them really about the same		*Modal*
11 And both that morning equally lay	*Time*	*Modal*
12 In leaves no step had trodden black.	*Setting (Neg)*	*Modal*
13 Oh, I kept the first for another day!	*Char + Decision*	
14 Yet knowing how way leads on to way,	*Doubts + PV*	*Modal*
15 I doubted if I should ever come back.		*Modal (Fut)*
16 I shall be telling this with a sigh	*Prediction + PV*	*Modal*
17 Somewhere ages and ages hence:		*Vague*
18 Two roads diverged in a wood, and I—	*Setting/self-quote*	
19 I took the one less travelled by,	*Char/Action*	
20 And that has made all the difference.	*Result + Ambiguity*	

My first pass through this text tended to focus on its narrative structure (**NS**), noting the complex shuttling between the Setting, the Character of the narrator, and the progress of his decisions about which road to choose (all overshadowed by the poem's title: *The Road **Not** Taken*. The verbs describing the Setting are mainly Intransitive (*diverged, stood, bent, wanted wear*), while those describing the narrator involve Mental Process (*sorry, looked down, knowing, doubted*) or Verbal (*shall be telling*).

The second pass focussed on the prevalence of various degrees of Negativity: e.g., Not existent (*no step had trodden black*); Not other: (*could not travel both/And be one traveller; looked down one; for another day; one less travelled by*); Negative modulation/ ability (*I could not; as far as I could*) and negative modalities (*sorry, just as fair, perhaps, wanted wear, as for that, really about the same, how way leads on to way, doubted if I should ever, with a sigh, somewhere ages and ages hence, has made all the difference*). The lack of resolve reflected in these modalities, of course, culminates in the ambiguity of his sigh (*Oh!* in line 13; and *with a sigh* in line 16) and the total lack of resolution of the last line of the poem: *that has made all the difference*, which is—in normal speech—the celebration of a good outcome.

I was discussing this play with modality and the lack of resolution in the grammar and word choices in Frost's poem with a phonetics specialist in my department and he immediately homed in on what he saw as a patterned lack of resolution in the sound structure of the poem. (Often it takes two or more readers to develop the Hermeneutic Spiral.) The sound structure includes rhyming schemes, alliteration and metre and this is more like the non-verbal patterning in paintings or films which was beginning to attract my attention after years of focussing on the lexical and grammatical patterning of short stories. Andrew (the phonetician) pointed out that the rhyme scheme of "The Road Not Taken" was **a—b—a—a—b** (**wood—both—stood—could—growth**) and that this delay in resolving the rhyme pattern was sustained throughout the poem until the last stanza where the stressed monosyllable of **hence** (line 17) is "resolved" (or not!) by the polysyllables of **all the difference** (line 20), the most ambiguous phrase in the whole poem.

Similarly with the metre. The dominant pattern is iambic: |short Long|, but certain lines include an anapaest: |short short Long|

and That| has Made| all the Diff |erEnce

Here the boundaries of metrical feet are marked with a vertical line, while stressed syllables begin with a capital and unstressed syllables with lower case. But this "regular irregularity" is compounded (another twist in the Hermeneutic Spiral) by the fact that nearly all the anapaests involve syllables from at least two words and have a preponderance of half vowels (y or j) and unstopped consonants (l, r, s. z, n, ng, f, th, w):

1 |in a Yell| ; 2 |ry I could| ; 3 |veller Long| 4 |as i Could| ; 5 |in the Un-|;

4   *Introduction*

6 |ther as Just| ; 7 |ing perhaps| ; 8 |it was grass| y and Want| ; 9 | as for That| ; 10 |ly a Bout|

11 |qually Lay|; 13 | for an Oth| ; 14 | wing how Way|; 15 |ted if I|;. |ver come Back|;

16 |shall be Tell| ; | with a Sigh| ; 18 | in a Wood| ; 20 | all the Diff |.

It is very satisfying when a pattern from one semiotic system (e.g., sound patterning) matches patterns we have discovered in the narrative structure and lexicogrammar of a work. As our analysis of short stories by Chekhov, James Joyce, Conan Doyle and from the Bible in Part I shows, visual elements of Setting, Character and Narrative Structure often match or enhance the verbal plot.

Parts 2 and 3 of this collection argue that in the case of cartoons and classic films the basic plot is carried by caricatured participants and the silent (or subtitled) conflicts of montage. The early Russian masters of silent cinema had to make their moving visual images tell the story. It helped, of course, that they had an important historic story to tell and that they commanded a remarkable repertoire of cinematic tricks to create both continuity and conflict.

My multimodal analysis of painting and architecture from the 1980s onwards (Chapters 9 to 13) was made feasible by my adaptation of Michael Halliday's distinction between the semantic "metafunctions" of the Experiential, Interpersonal and Textual, so that a clause of language was expressing not only facts and processes in the real world (Experiential meanings), but moods and attitudes to that reality and between speaker and listener (Interpersonal meanings). These were then realised through the Textual meanings which make speech coherent and situationally appropriate. Halliday's chart of systems and functions in language (Chart 1) inspired a similar chart (my Chart 2) of systems and functions in painting, where the painter Represents some aspect of the real (or imaginary) world, varies the Modality of that reality to engage the viewer, and incorporates both the Representation and the Modality into a coherent Composition.

Frank Hinder's painting *The Flight Into Egypt* (Chapter 9) was the winner of the 1952 Blake Prize for Religious Art in Sydney. Its award aroused a storm of criticism from both conservatives and modernists among the critics and followers of art of that period. I have tried to show how quite small features in the three functions are at interplay with each other to create a hermeneutic spiral that reflects the social semiotic of both parties at that time.

There was no such controversy over the social semiotic of one of the world's great paintings, Rembrandt's *The Night Watch* (Chapter 10). The Amsterdam dignitaries who "sat" for the painting fell over themselves and paid good money to have their representation recognised, and in fact a whole room next to the gallery in the Rijksmuseum where the painting hangs is dedicated to proving their identity. Most visitors—and even the gallery guards—regard this aspect of the Representational function as paramount and fail to complement their hermeneutic spiral by noticing the way the painter has framed and lit his figures and (Modally) depicted the central figure's left hand in three distinctive ways and the way this has fixed the Compositional structure of the whole work.

The story-line of John Longstaff's (1887) painting in the Art Gallery of Western Australia *Breaking the News* is fairly easy to reconstruct—and I have reconstructed it as the thought processes of the young woman to whom the "news" of the mine disaster is being broken (Chapter 11). It was fortunate that this disaster at Bulli in New South Wales was also recounted verbally in a contemporary newspaper report and a historical account nearly a century after the event, so that we have contrasting modes of discourse for comparing their representation of the scene, the emotional involvement of the participants and the way they are composed verbally and pictorially. My claim is that this juxtaposition of verbal and pictorial records offers a powerful educational tool and that the close analysis of the linguistic and visual details contributes to our hermeneutic spiral rather as the interplay of narrative structure and sound patterning does in our analysis of Robert Frost's poem.

After some ten years of writing about paintings, sculptures and buildings within various European traditions, I felt that the launch of the new journal *Linguistics and the Human Sciences* in 2005 would be a good opportunity to educate myself about another set of painting techniques and cultural assumptions by studying a seventeenth-century Chinese landscape scroll by Gong Xian (1689), Chapter 12. This was also a good time to celebrate Michael Halliday's lifelong commitment to Chinese language and culture and to recognise the fast-growing interest in systemic-functional linguistics and semiotics among Chinese academics and students.

A favourite genre of multimodal studies is the analysis of the simultaneous discourses of verbal and pictorial texts in commercial advertisements (Chapter 13). By good fortune I happened upon an advert for Canon Photocopiers which incorporated a famous painting by Picasso, his *Girl Before a Mirror* (in *The Australian Magazine*, 2–3 May 1992). By less good fortune, although the reproduction of this painting in the advert is excellent, the digital image of the page on which it is printed can no longer be traced, so readers will have to manage (as they would in a dentist's waiting room) with a scan of the page of the magazine. The interplay of the painting in full colour with the design and verbal text of the advert is still clear and very revealing about the intentions of both Picasso and Canon Photocopiers.

If Chapters 12 and 13 deliberately juxtapose the codes of verbal and pictorial texts, my final chapter (14) is an analysis of the opening of a sequence in the TV comedy series *Fawlty Towers*, where the participants' *movements in architectural space* are interplayed with the codes and dialects of their speech. The chapter concludes with a series of images of Basil Fawlty, Sybil Fawlty and a guest engaged in spatial interaction simultaneously with their verbal interaction. I have also added two pages of the script of the episode, pinpointing the simultaneous play with verbal discourse and architectural space.

Interpretation in all the arts should be fun. Most of the works studied employ elements of humour or irony, and so do my analyses. (I would not presume to compare my work with that of Viktor Shklovsky, the great pioneer of Russian Formalism, but I believe his humour and lively style made him immensely readable and very accessible, even when discussing serious works and complex theoretical issues.)

I would like to express my warmest thanks to Kay O'Halloran, editor of Routledge's Multimodality series, for persuading me to republish these chapters in the series, and for her patience and careful reading of drafts. Also to Elysse Preposi and Allie Simmons, Routledge editors, who were unstinting in their friendly professional advice.

Part 1
Literary Narrative

My model for the analysis of narrative form in short fiction was derived from concepts and methods expounded by the Russian Formalists (1917–1929), the Prague School Structuralists in the 1930s and French semioticians of the 1960s, enriched at the level of text by Halliday's systemic-functional linguistic stylistics, of which I was an early proponent. The fullest demonstration of this model at work was published in my book *Structure, Style and Interpretation in the Russian Short Story* (Yale University Press, 1982), which is still in print and used in university courses on Russian literature. None of the papers collected here are used in that book, and most of them involve the analysis and interpretation of English literary texts.

It also led to me founding the Neo-Formalist Circle, a group of Slavic and other international literary scholars who met twice yearly from 1970 to 2005. Other spin-offs were the series I started and ran with Dr Ann Shukman, *Russian Poetics in Translation* (12 vols., 1975–1982; now available on line through Amazon) and a series *Essays in Poetics* founded and run by Joe Andrew and Chris Pike of Keele University (1974–2006). My original paper on "The Student" was republished with a (self-)critical 'Post-script' in a book devoted to articles on Russian literature by colleagues using my method of analysis (1984, eds. J. Andrew & C. Pike).

1 Structure and Style in the Short Story
Chekhov's "The Student"

(NB: The analysis below is preceded by a complete translation of the original Chekhov story.)

Introduction

The early sections of this chapter outline the approaches to the analysis of narrative structure by key scholars of the group of scholars writing in the newly established Soviet Union generally known collectively as The Russian Formalists (1916–1932). Although they have been regarded as new and revolutionary, both at home and in the West, their theories and modes of analysis were founded on classical models from Aristotle and the ancient and mediaeval rhetoricians. My claim is that Narrative Structure and Point of View are in interplay in the shape of Fable, Plot, Character and Setting. Each of these components of a well-made narrative can and should be analysed in their own right, but they work together in different ways in the course of a story. The later sections of the chapter discuss in detail the workings of Style in literary narratives and the linguistic methods for describing style in relation to all the structural categories.

I have provided an English translation of the whole story to provide a clear context for each stage of the analysis. The quotations of the text in Russian used in the original publication in a Slavonic academic journal have been preserved in English transliteration because the linguistic forms are crucial for the contextual study of style. Style and structure are inseparable, as I have claimed throughout this book—and as was established by the Russian Formalist scholars and their successors.

Translation of "The Student"

The weather at first was fine and calm. Thrushes were singing and in the marshes nearby something alive was hooting plaintively as if someone was blowing into an empty bottle. A solitary woodcock took flight and a shot in its direction rang out echoing and cheerful in the spring air. But as darkness fell in the wood a chill penetrating wind blew up from the east and silence fell. Icy needles stretched over the puddles and the wood became uncomfortable, muffled and lonely. There was a smell of winter.

Ivan Velikopol'skii, a seminary student and son of a church deacon, returning home from a shoot, made his way along a path through the water-meadows. His fingers had grown numb from the cold and his face felt hot from the wind. He felt that this sudden cold snap had upset the order and harmony in everything, that even nature was threatening and so the evening gloom had descended more quickly than it should. All around was deserted and somehow particularly gloomy. Only in the widows' market-gardens down by the river a fire glimmered; but far around and where the village lay, some four versts away, everything was plunged in the cold evening gloom. The student recalled that when he had left home, his mother, sitting barefoot in the porch, had been cleaning the samovar, and his father lay on the stove and coughed; because of Easter Friday nothing was being cooked at home and he was dying to have something to eat. And now, hunched up from the cold, the student thought that just such a wind was blowing in the time of Prince Ryurik, of Ivan the Terrible, and of Peter the Great, and in their day there was just the same kind of terrible poverty and starvation; the same straw roofs full of holes, the same ignorance and melancholy, the same emptiness, gloom and feeling of oppression—all these horrors had been, were now and would continue, because another thousand years might pass and life would not improve. And he didn't feel like going home.

The market gardens were known as "the widows'" because they were kept by two widows, mother and daughter. The bonfire burned warmly and crackled, lighting up the ploughed earth all around. Widow Vasilisa, a tall plump old woman, dressed in a man's jacket, stood nearby and gazed meditatively at the fire; her daughter Luker'ya, small and pock-marked, with a rather stupid face, was seated on the ground washing the cooking-pot and spoons. Obviously they had just had some supper. Men's voices could be heard, it was the local labourers watering their horses down by the river.

"Well, here's winter back for you," said the student coming up to the bonfire. "Greetings!"

Vasilisa jumped, but recognised him at once and smiled in greeting.

"I didn't recognise you, God be with you. May you grow rich."

They talked for a bit. Vasilisa, a worldly wise woman who had once worked for the landowners as a wet-nurse and later as a children's nurse-maid, expressed herself delicately and all the time a soft staid smile never left her face; while her daughter Luker'ya, a peasant wench abused by her husband, merely squinted at the student and said nothing, and her expression was strange like that of someone deaf and dumb.

"On just such a cold night as this the apostle Peter warmed himself by a bonfire," said the student, stretching his hands out towards the fire. "So even then it was cold. Oh what a terrible night that was, granny! An extremely dismal, long night!"

He looked around at the twilight, shook his head convulsively and asked: "I don't suppose you've been at the service for the twelve apostles?"

"I have," answered Vasilisa.

"If you remember, on Good Friday Peter said to Jesus 'I'm ready to go to prison with Thee, even unto death.' And the Lord replied unto him: 'I say unto thee, Peter, the rooster, that is, the cock shall not have crowed today when you deny me thrice and claim that you do not know me.' After the Good Friday gathering Jesus grieved mortally in the garden and prayed, and poor Peter was worn out and weakened and there was no way he could fight off sleep. He slept. Then, you've heard, Judas that very night kissed Jesus and betrayed Him to the torturers. They led Him bound to the high priest and beat him. But Peter, worn out by anxiety and fear because he hadn't slept, you know, sensing that any moment something terrible was about to happen on this earth, followed after ... He passionately, forgetting everything, loved Jesus, and now from afar saw them beating Him...."

Luker'ya put down the spoons and stared motionless at the student.

"They came unto the high priest," he continued. "They began to cross-examine Jesus, and meanwhile the workmen spread the fire around the courtyard, because it was cold and warmed themselves. Among them by the bonfire stood Peter and also warmed himself, like me now.

"One woman, catching sight of him, said 'This man was also with Jesus' that is to say, he too should be cross-examined. And all the workmen who were there around the fire must have stared suspiciously and angrily at him because he got confused and said 'I know Him not.' A little later someone again recognised in him one of Jesus' pupils and said: 'You too are one of them.' But he again denied it. And a third time someone turned to him: 'So wasn't it you I saw in the garden with Him?' A third time he denied it. And after this moment a cock crowed at once, and Peter, glancing at Jesus from afar, remembered the words that He had spoken to him on Good Friday ... He remembered, came to himself, left the courtyard and cried bitterly. In the Gospel it says: 'And going out from there, he cried bitterly.' I can just imagine it: a quiet-quiet, ever so dark garden and in the silence you can barely hear muffled sobs...."

The student sighed and grew thoughtful. Still smiling, Vasilisa suddenly sobbed and big, gushing tears began to run down her cheeks, and she shaded her face from the fire with her sleeve, as if ashamed of her tears, while Luker'ya, gazing fixedly at the student, blushed, and her expression became heavy and tense like someone suppressing a strong pain.

The workers were returning from the river, and one of them on horseback was already nearby and the firelight flickered on him. The student wished the widows goodnight and went on his way. And again the twilight descended and his hands began to freeze. A cruel wind was blowing, winter really was coming back in earnest, and it didn't feel as though the day after next was Easter Sunday.

Now the student thought about Vasilisa: if she burst into tears, then everything that had happened on that terrible night to Peter had some relevance to her.

He looked back. The solitary bonfire winked calmly in the darkness and there was no longer anyone to be seen nearby. The student again had the thought that if Vasilisa had burst into tears and her daughter had got embarrassed, then obviously what he had been telling them about, what had happened nineteen centuries before had some relation to the present—to both the women, and probably to this village out in the wilds, to himself and to all mankind. If the old woman had burst into tears, then it wasn't because he could tell a touching story, but because Peter was close to her and because she was concerned in the depths of her being with what had occurred in the soul of Peter.

And joy suddenly welled up in his heart and he even halted for a moment to draw breath. The past—he thought—is joined to the present by an unbroken chain of events flowing one into the next. And it seemed to him that he had just glimpsed both ends of this chain; he had simply touched one end and the other one shook.

And when he was crossing the river on the ferry and then as he climbed the hill beyond looked over towards his home village and towards the west where a cold crimson dawn shone in a narrow strip, he thought how the truth and beauty governing human life back there in the garden and in the court of the high priest had continued unbroken to this very day and evidently had constituted the main thing in human life and on earth in general; and a sense of youth, health and strength—he was only twenty-two—and the inexpressibly sweet expectation of happiness, of an unknown mysterious happiness gradually overwhelmed him, and life seemed delightful, wonderful and full of the highest meaning.

The Student: Narrative Structure

I

The aims of this chapter are twofold: to provide a framework for the structural analysis of short-story form, and to illustrate that this framework works by applying it to a short story by Chekhov.

The question of terminology is a basic problem for the student of narrative fiction. The student of poetry has recourse to a fairly precise set of descriptive terms based on a clear theory of poetry elaborated primarily by the Russian Formalists and American New Criticism and tested over a wide range of poetic genres and styles. For narrative prose genres from the anecdote to the novel no such firmly-based and widely-accepted terminology exists, although the basis of a theory can be pieced together from essays by such Formalist and like-minded critics of the 1920s as Tomashevsky, Eikhenbaum, Shklovsky, Petrovsky, Propp, Vinogradov[1] and others. This has been re-elaborated by Wellek and Warren in their *Theory of Literature* and it underlies many of the admirable, if sometimes over-simplified, textbooks on practical criticism for American college students. For some of the terms in the present article the author is indebted to H. Oulanoff, who, in his book on the Serapion Brothers, has understood the seriousness of the problem and has taken pains to define his terms as he introduces them. The most important terms as used here will be briefly defined.

II

"The Student" (1894) was one of Chekhov's own favourites among his stories and one, according to his brother Ivan and the writer Bunin, that he considered to be structurally most perfect. This story suits the purpose of the present study well since it is sufficiently short for a detailed analysis in several dimensions, followed by a reintegration, or synthesis, of observations in terms of the whole work. The dimensions of analysis are separate yet interrelated and include: Theme, Fable, Plot, Narrative Structure, Setting (in time and place), Point of View, Characterisation and Language.

The story will be analysed in one dimension at a time, and some of the devices a writer may use and those which Chekhov does use to produce particular effects will be examined. Only after completion of this analysis will general statements be made about the work or comparisons with other works be justifiable. For example, a study of "The Student" in each dimension will provide explicit examples of the different ways in which Chekhov relates setting and point of view, will clarify the function of setting in the story as a whole, and will make it possible to compare the use of setting in "The Student" with its use in any other story by Chekhov or another writer analysed in similar detail. Whether or not the author was consciously using the devices examined in order to create atmosphere is not relevant here. While the hearer of the spoken word merely recreates the speaker's meaning, the job of the linguist is to analyse the utterance itself. Readers recreate intuitively the thoughts and emotions of the inspired artist, but critics must analyse the medium of this intuitive communication, knowing that the mature artist uses his skills for the most part unconsciously.

III

The theme should be stated as briefly as possible and the accuracy of this tested by checking that "the axis that maintains the unity and consistency of meaning in the work" (H. Oulanoff, 1966) has been determined.

The theme of "The Student" is the power of tragedy to move and inspire—in a word, 'catharsis.' The story (within the story) of Peter's denial of Christ has all the elements of tragedy in the Aristotelian sense of the word: it has universality and inevitability; a fatal *hubris* in the tragic hero, Peter, leads him to ignore divine warnings; the archetypal pattern—prophecy, triple denial, fulfillment and recognition—is as powerful as the emotional content: this tragedy has the power simultaneously to arouse pity and fear and to purge these emotions. By embodying these concepts in the artistic form of the short story, Chekhov does not state them: he shows them in action.

It might be objected that Chekhov is concerned with the impression made by the story of Peter's denial of Christ on three Christians as much from the religious point of view as the aesthetic. The choice of a Christian myth rather than, say, a classical Greek myth is certainly vital to the story, but more in terms of setting and character than for the essential theme. The fact that the story is set on Good Friday, the fact that the bonfire provides both a stage for the narration of the drama and a point of reference for its origins, the fact that a theology student would know the gospel story almost verbatim and would comprehend its significance, the fact that his audience of simple believers would have foreknowledge of the end of the tragedy, would sense its inevitability—all these facts make the tragedy of Peter more relevant for Russia in the 1890s than would the tragedy of Orestes—and, above all, they all add to the story's structural and thematic coherence. Nevertheless, the essential theme is not the power of faith, but the power of tragedy.

The reason for attempting to state the theme first, before analysing the structure in several dimensions, is that it seems important to capture one's first reaction to the work, partly because one thereby gains a point of reference for the analysis which follows. On the other hand, there is nothing sacrosanct about this initial statement of theme, and it may need to be restated later in a much more complex way after consideration of narrative structure and other dimensions of analysis. The method is dialectic, the ultimate statement of theme—a synthesis. As Tomashevsky (1925) put it: "The concept of theme is a summarizing concept!"

IV

The terms Fable, Plot and Narrative Structure are closely related and might all be said to belong to one analytical level of structure or plot. They are, however, three distinct concepts and the interplay of contrast between them may be extremely significant in a work of narrative fiction.

The Fable shows what actually happened. It is the raw material of situations or events in their original chronological sequence. In certain genres, where the narrative element is weak, such as stories and novels which are based on dialogue or are in the form of internal monologues of the 'stream of consciousness' type, the fable may be so suppressed that it takes a considerable effort of the imagination on the reader's part to reconstitute it. This, of course, is one of the charms of this type of fiction.

Although all the significant 'events' in "The Student" are psychological events, there is no such problem here. A student returning home in a sad mood one evening stops to talk to two women; he tells them the story of Peter's denial of Christ, is heartened by their reaction to it, and continues his journey home in an optimistic frame of mind. The sequence in life and the sequence in the narrative coincide.

M. A. Petrovsky makes a useful distinction here between the 'dispositional sequence' (events as they 'occur in life,' i.e., according to our reconstruction of the 'reality' behind the narrative) and the 'expositional' (or 'compositional') sequence. He observes, quite rightly, that the 'disposition' of events, the fable, is of no great interest except as a point of reference for the 'exposition,' a term which includes both plot and narrative structure.

Plot may be defined as the causal unfolding of the narrative, the selection and arrangement of events in such a way that they form a logical sequence. This still only provides the raw material for the work of art: all detective stories have plot; only those with a coherent and aesthetically satisfying narrative structure qualify for consideration as literature. Oulanoff (1966, p. 35) defines plot as "the selection of those reciprocally conditioned and motivated events logically necessary to impel the action."

The essential plot of "The Student" is as follows: because the evening has turned unseasonably cold and gloomy, the student feels uncomfortable; physical discomfort induces a mood of melancholy and pessimism which makes him recall the miserable condition of his parents as he last saw them. From the particular scene of human misery his thoughts extend in time and space to a contemplation of the misery which he sees as a general condition in Russia since her beginnings. Because of these thoughts he feels disinclined to go straight home, so he pauses to warm himself physically and spiritually beside a bonfire and through human contact. Because it is Good Friday, the student of theology recalls a similar bonfire on the night of the first Good Friday. The centre of attention at that bonfire had been Peter, so it is his particular drama that the student retells. (The story itself, of course, has its own plot, or chain of causes and effects, which it is unnecessary to analyse here—though clearly there are a number of intertextual references.) Since Peter's is a human tragedy, it moves the widows (who also understand loss) more deeply than the central, superhuman, tragedy of that night which, after nineteen centuries of re-enactment and retelling, tends to evoke stock responses. The student is himself moved, but, being an intellectual, he can rationalise this grief, can relate it to the general abstract concept of the continuity of human experience and can give this abstraction concrete form in the image of a continuous chain, stretching from the first Good Friday to the present. Having re-established, intellectually and imaginatively, the order and harmony which he had previously thought were lacking in the world, because of his own physical discomfort, he continues his way homeward full of joy and optimism.

This outline of the plot, although fairly detailed, only takes account of the main patterns of motivation in the story. With a writer as complex and subtle as Chekhov, there is an almost infinitely detailed chain of cause and effect running through the story, which it would be difficult to treat exhaustively and which might not add greatly to this structural analysis. Since no level of analysis can, or should, be wholly separated from the other levels—the subject of analysis being still a coherent whole. However rigorous the method, some of the subtler details of cause and effect can be examined most productively through other categories. For instance, the precise effect produced by the story on Vasilisa and Luker'ya respectively can best be examined on the level of Character; the effect of landscape and weather on the student (under the heading of Point of View); the interplay of the details of this landcape (under Setting); the growth in intensity of the student's thoughts about the misery of the human condition, or the emotive power of the story of Peter (under Language). What is important to the argument is that all the above-mentioned details of cause and effect in the plot structure are psychological events, that the sensations and emotions and thoughts of the story are the products of one psyche. It is the change that takes place in this psyche that represents the *peripeteia* and—as already shown—the overall theme of the story.

An aspect of the plot of "The Student," which is as crucial at the level of syntax as it is in the structure of the story as a whole, is the relationship between sensation and thought for the central character. In the second paragraph the alternation of sensation and thought is almost schematic in its regularity (Figure 1.1):[2]

Sensation	Thought
had become numb, had grown red;	it seemed that the cold had broken;
desolately, somberly, shone;	remembered…mother…father;
was sinking in the darkness	
hunched up from the cold	thought

Figure 1.1

Even the student's thoughts at this point seem to alternate between miseries which are felt (wind, poverty, hunger) and those which are seen or apprehended mentally (roofs with holes, ignorance, melancholy) and felt (desolateness, gloom, feeling of oppression). The passive reactions to external phenomena seem to alternate with attempts at active rationalisation on the student's part. As the paragraph progresses, he succumbs more and more to physical sensation until the mind despairs:

> all these horrors were, are and will be, and just because another thousand years will pass life won't get better.
>
> (p. 367)

In the pattern of the story as a whole, the student is initially the victim of his physical sensations, which induce his melancholy thoughts. The warmth of the fire and of human contact reminds him of the approaching festival and of the story which he then tells. Sensation, to which he responds passively, is dominant throughout the first half of the story. In the second half, the physical discomfort is just as bad:

> And again twilight had begun, and his hands had begun to freeze. A cruel wind blew....
>
> (p. 369)

But now the sensations are dismissed with a rationalisation:

> Winter was indeed returning, and it didn't at all seem that Easter was the day after tomorrow
>
> (p. 369)

By this time an active intelligence is dominant; it can consider abstract and ennobling thoughts and dismiss mere physical sensations. The landscape—the cold crimson sunset which he glimpses in the west as he climbs the hill—is coloured by the student's own mood of optimism and confidence in the power of truth and beauty.

V

The clear symmetry of the two halves of the story in terms of the power of sensation and intellect to motivate human moods and actions brings us to the problem of Narrative Structure. The term *narrative structure* signifies the actual form whereby the reader learns the story; it implies the formal arrangement of all the devices and motives of the story. If the story succeeds artistically, then the artist has found the most powerful sequence for their arrangement. As Oulanoff says

> The narrative structure is none other than the totality of motives presented in the very sequence which appears in the book. What consequently matters is the introduction of a given motive at the moment when this motive achieves the greatest aesthetic effect.
>
> (1966, p. 14)

It was primarily the analysis of narrative structure that such Formalist critics as Propp and Petrovsky were attempting to put on a scientific basis in their morphological studies of particular genres of narrative prose.

A fundamental characteristic of the short story as a genre is the tightness, unity and coherence of its structure. Because the short story is composed to be read uninterrupted at a single sitting, it aims at a unified effect and every element in its structure should point to this effect. As Edgar Allen Poe put it in a famous review of Hawthorne's *Twice Told Tales* (1842):

> A skilful literary artist has constructed a tale. If wise, he has not fashioned his thoughts to accommodate his incidents; but having conceived, with

deliberate care, a certain unique or single *effect t*to be wrought out, he then invents such incidents—he then combines such events as may best aid him, in establishing this preconceived effect. If his very initial sentence tends not to the outbringing of this effect, then he has failed in his first step. In the whole composition there should be no word written of which the tendency, direct or indirect, is not to the one pre-established design.

(1965, p. 153)

A more concise, if less elegant, way of expressing this idea would be to suggest that while both the novel (apart from the chronicle genre) and the short story have a centre (e.g., a relationship, a character, a state of mind or a philosophical idea), the novel tends to be *centrifugal* while the short story tends to be *centripetal*. Considerations of theme and plot have already suggested that this is true for "The Student": an examination of the narrative structure of the story should reveal the tendency most clearly.

Oulanoff is probably right in claiming that narrative structure "implies all the artistic devices at play. These artistic devices are understandable only within the framework of the narrative structure" (1966, p. 15). For this analysis, however, a narrower definition of narrative structure will be used (viz. the grouping of episodes and motives around the central situation), while agreeing with Oulanoff—and Aristotle—in relating the other artistic devices to this grouping or framework.

In considering the cause-and-effect patterns of the plot, it was demonstrated that the story's aesthetic effect depends on a reversal, or *peripeteia* (the student's complete change of mood). The narrative structure of "The Student" meets all the requirements of Aristotle's definition of a 'complex action' in tragedy:

A complex action is one in which the change is accompanied by reversal, or by recognition, or by both. These last should arise from the internal structure of the plot, so that what follows should be the necessary or probable result of the preceding action.

(Butcher, 1932, pp. 142–143)

The relevant consideration here is not tragedy as such, but Aristotle's preoccupation with whatever produces the most powerful aesthetic pattern. In "The Student" the reversal in the mood of the central character depends on his recognition of the power of Peter's story to move. The central episode starts with a memory of the original Good Friday and develops in such a way that the power of the story completely overwhelms the immediate personal discomforts not only of the audience but of the student himself. A crucial element in Chekhov's creation of atmosphere in the story is that at the emotional peak of the tragedy which the student narrates the author interrupts to show us the reaction of the least emotional and demonstrative character, the almost bovine Luker'ya:

> "He loved Jesus passionately, to distraction, and could now see from afar how he was being scourged...."
> Luker'ya put aside the spoons and stared fixedly at the student.
>
> (p. 368)

Chekhov reveals a similar artistic restraint, using the same device of juxtaposition, and even the same key word *fixedly* when his own story reaches its emotional climax:

> The student sighed and became pensive. Still smiling, Vasilisa suddenly sobbed and tears, large and abundant, began to flow down her cheeks and she hid her face from the fire with her sleeve as though ashamed of her tears, while Luker'ya, fixedly looking at the student, blushed, and her expression became heavy, strained, like that of someone stifling severe pain.
>
> (p. 368)

For the plot and narrative structure what is important here is that Vasilisa wept and Luker'ya blushed; the peculiar and very powerful ambiguity of the scene stems from the smile that remains on Vasilisa's face and her gesture of shame as she weeps, and from the heavy impenetrability of Luker'ya's emotion. The student does not react emotionally. He has ceased to function as an artist-narrator now, so he sighs and falls silent. But he falls to thinking, and it is this thought that leads to the dénouement which follows, where the power of reason and the intellect prevails.

The dénouement matches symmetrically the initial complication, before the student meets the widows, where he is motivated wholly by sensations. (The, Russian terminology for the central elements in narrative structure as used by Petrovsky: *zavyazka—uzel—razvyazka* ('binding'—'knot'—'unbinding') expresses the relationship between them far more vividly than the clumsy 'Complication'—'Crisis'—'Dénouement' of our own criticism.) These central elements are framed by elements of *prologue* and *epilogue* (These terms are ambiguous and are only used provisionally. Here the essential secondary levels of character, setting and point of view are established, each contributing in its own way to the unified impact of the structure.)

The inner part of this frame (specific prologue) gives the immediate setting for the complication (a theology student walking home from a snipe-shoot on a cold and gloomy evening), and the dénouement is framed by a specific epilogue (continuing his journey across the river and up the hill to face the sunset). As Petrovsky shows,[3] the specific prologue and epilogue are usually framed, if only implicitly, by a general prologue and epilogue which allow a glimpse of the more distant past and future and lend the central episode a perspective in time analogous to spatial perspective in painting.

The symmetry and chronology of this structure are clear from his diagram (Figure 1.2):

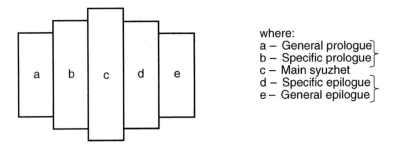

where:
a – General prologue
b – Specific prologue
c – Main syuzhet
d – Specific epilogue
e – General epilogue

Figure 1.2

The reader responds in a particular way to those 'slice-of-life' short stories whose main structural characteristic is that they lack the outer elements of this framework. Any re-ordering of the elements also affects our response. In "The Student" Chekhov adopts the common device of starting with the *b* element of the immediate setting and state of mind of the central character and introducing the *a* element through his recollections (flashback). The motivation for the Complication is thus far stronger, since this memory of the miserable condition in which he last saw his parents is introduced at the peak of his physical discomfort: "everything around was sinking in the cold evening gloom." It is consistent with the logic of the plot and the theme that there should be no re-ordering of the elements in the epilogue. The student's happy thoughts and feelings in the last paragraph lead naturally to his expectations for the future. The hope expressed in the final two paragraphs matches perfectly the despair of the first two paragraphs of the story.

The moment of Complication occurs where the student joins the two widows in the circle of firelight, the warmth of human contact offering some possibility of resolving his despair. The Peripeteia will be the beginning of the reversal of this mood, and the Dénouement, marking the growth of hope, occurs where the student takes leave of the widows. The choice of these two particular moments as Complication and Dénouement is not arbitrary: later examination of setting and language will reveal that Chekhov has marked these moments quite deliberately.

In trying to establish the actual moment of the Peripeteia, however, it is necessary to reconsider the original statement of the Theme. If the theme is merely 'catharsis,' then the narrative structure revolves around the peripeteia at Vasilisa's sob in response to the completed narration of the Peter tragedy. If the theme is the essential link between the past and the present, then the peripeteia may occur at the moment of Luker'ya's first response to the story, i.e., when she lays down the spoons and stares fixedly at the student. This argument is borne out by the language, since the two paragraphs of the narration differ quite markedly in narrative manner, in the proportion of narrator's interpolations to pure gospel text, in the degree to which he refers, consciously or unconsciously, to his audience. Since the language and manner of his narration change when Luker'ya starts to pay attention, the student is already aware unconsciously of how these past events relate to the present. Vasilisa's sob makes this relationship emotionally explicit and the student's later musings make it intellectually explicit.

Thus the two interpretations of theme and narrative structure are not necessarily incompatible, since catharsis is itself a bridge between two dimensions of time and is presumably a growing process which may be triggered off on different levels of consciousness by different moments in the tragedy, rather than by a single moment of revelation on any one level. The apparent ambiguity may be deliberate: Chekhov is here seeing human consciousness as having many layers which exist in a sort of hierarchy from the unconscious mind, through the emotional to the conscious, intellectual mind. Thus the central and most essential peripeteia is at the level of the unconscious mind (which Luker'ya symbolises, since she is, purposely, not equipped to react at any other level). The process thus set in motion by this reversal, i.e., the dénouement, includes two other moments of reversal nearer the surface: an emotional peripeteia (a sob and tears, which Vasilisa is best equipped to represent, and an intellectual one (the student's recognition of what has happened), as the student is the only one capable of reaction on the conscious level.

This is not to say that the student ceases at any moment to be the 'sentient centre' of the story. It is the change in his mode of narration which shows us that a reversal on the unconscious level has already taken place. To this extent Luker'ya and Vasilisa may be seen as projections of the unconscious and emotional planes of the student's psyche, even though, on another plane of the story's reality they are real persons in their own right. It may be that Chekhov is here making an interesting disclosure about the relationship between actor and audience, and the interdependence of their response to reality and to the myth of the drama.

Petrovsky's morphology is probably suitable for anecdotes or stories from the *Decameron*, but it seems scarcely adequate for analysing an art form as complex and varied as the true short story which tends to have a multiplicity of narrative structures which relate and interpenetrate in various ways: a kind of meta-patterning which cannot be reached through the application of a standard formula, but will emerge through the dialectic process by which the individual critic relates such dimensions as theme and narrative structure.

VI

The *Setting* of "The Student" enriches the atmosphere which, as shown, stems partly from the structure. It also parallels the symmetry of this structure. The low-lying water meadows by the river seem to impede the student's progress as they collect the cold, damp mist of twilight. After symbolically crossing the river (during the 'intellectual peripeteia'), he ascends physically, as well as spiritually, to breast the hill from where a narrow but bright strip of sunset still defies the twilight. The East, whence an icy wind blows, reducing him to such a passive despair, is juxtaposed to the West, lit-up by a hope-inspiring glow. Since the triumph of reason in the latter scene contrasts so dramatically with the triumph of sensation in the former, perhaps Chekhov was juxtaposing the notions of the West, where will-power and reason are supposed to be dominant, and the East, where passive acceptance, the surrender of will and the world of sensation prevail. (This East/West opposition was, of course, taken for granted by a number of Russian philosophers and the Symbolist poets among Chekhov's contemporaries. Similarly, nearly a century later, Claude Levi-Strauss stresses the mythical and structural significance of this opposition in his challenging analysis of Indian folk-myths from the North Canadian Pacific Coast in his paper 'La geste d'Asdiwal').

Throughout the story light contrasts with darkness. The darkness in the first paragraph ("but when it grew dark") confirms hints of a change in the weather. In the second paragraph visual impressions predominate over the aural impressions of the first. The bonfire, first glimpsed as a spot of comfort in the darkness, becomes a focal point for the two dramas, a symbol of warmth and togetherness in the face of a hostile world, with the added paradox that in the narrated tragedy it was the scene for the bystanders' betrayal of Peter and Peter's betrayal of Christ. Finally the dénouement in the student's consciousness takes place between the pin-point of firelight and the crimson sunset.

Most characteristically Chekhovian in this symbolic and 'atmospheric' use of setting are the workmen watering their horses in the river. They exactly frame the central episode of the student's whole conversation with the widows. After the scene has been set with Vasilisa standing and Luker'ya sitting by the bonfire, and before the student greets them, these anonymous and somehow mysterious figures are heard, human, yet a part of the unseen and unknown world beyond the circle of firelight:

> Men's voices could be heard; it was the local workmen watering their horses at the river.
>
> (p. 367)

After the climax, and another visual description of the widows—this time reacting to the tragedy—and before the student takes his leave, we catch a glimpse of one of these men with the firelight flickering on him:

> The workmen were returning from the river, and one of them on horseback was already near, and the light from the bonfire flickered on him.
>
> (pp. 368–369)

The world beyond the firelight has begun to be visible (through catharsis), and this stranger seems to summon the student to continue his journey home and his life in the world. There is nothing conventionally symbolic about this image. What could be more prosaic than a gang of farm workers taking their horses to water? Yet in giving them such a precise role as a bridge between juxtaposed episodes and as a frame in the overall narrative structure, Chekhov establishes an essential mood in the reader. A modulation passage in music may be quite banal and yet, in its setting, as a structural element in a whole movement, it may become noble or sad or tender or gay. It is the structure and the orchestration that count.

It is the same with Chekhov's imagery. Of the two similes in "The Student," one is positively (and purposely) anti-poetic: "Nearby in the marshes something living moaned plaintively as if someone was blowing into an empty bottle" (p. 366).

Its vagueness (something living), the impersonal quality of the Russian neuter verb (it was blowing), its prosaic flatness, sum up the desolation of a whole scene and the loneliness of its observer. The other image (which Chekhov attributes to the student) is a monumental cliché:

> The past, he thought, is connected to the present by an unbroken chain of events which have flowed one from another. And it seemed to him that he had just seen both ends of this chain: as he touched one end, the other end quivered.
>
> (p. 369)

He makes it worse by mixing his chain metaphor with one about water flowing. Yet this poor image summarises the high point of the student's elation at having restored order and harmony to his world. In any case, Chekhov hates the reader to identify too closely with his intellectuals. For all their deep experiences and noble aspirations, his Trofimovs and Astrovs are all a shade ridiculous.

VII

It all depends on the *Point of View*. The slightest unexpected shift of focus may create irony. A consistency of point of view will tend to strengthen a particular atmosphere.

Ever since Percy Lubbock's examination of this particular problem of novel structure in *The Craft of Fiction*, a majority of critics and literary theorists have assumed that the application of a closed-ended label, such as 'first person narrator,' 'third person, omniscient' would be an adequate substitute for analysis of point of view. But these labels provide only the broadest indication of what we need to know. At least three-quarters of Chekhov's stories use the 'third person, limited omniscient' point of view which has been neatly defined as follows: "The author narrates the story in the third person, but chooses one character as his 'sentient centre' whom he follows throughout the action, restricting the reader to the field of vision and range of knowledge of that character alone" (Abrams, 1957). But how much more is learnt about one of these stories by applying this label? The necessary information is not who held the camera, but his angle and distance from the subject at any particular moment, his 'aperture' (receptiveness), 'focus' (clarity of vision) and 'shutter speed' (intelligence). The author may adjust any of these at different points in the story and the pattern of his adjustments will probably bear some relation to the pattern of elements in the narrative structure.

A careful examination of the opening paragraph of "The Student" will show that this is not just a piece of objective description of nature providing the setting for the story. *At first* and *when it grew dark* show an awareness of the passing of time. *Nearby, in the marshes, in the wood, from the east* and *across the lakes* show an awareness of position in relation to the surrounding world. The sounds: *sang, moaned, rang out, fell silent,* and the physical sensations: *a penetrating cold wind began to blow, inhospitable, remote,* are apprehended by a specific human consciousness which, moreover, responds emotionally to this rather threatening world with a mournful image and highly subjective words such as *plaintively, boomingly, merrily, inopportunely, empty of people.* With the steady growth in emotional intensity through a so far anonymous point of view, by the end of the paragraph with its despairingly brief final sentence: *It smelt of winter*, the identification and characterisation of this human consciousness becomes an urgent necessity. Chekhov has fulfilled Poe's requirement that from the very first sentence everything should tend to the outbringing of the preconceived effect.

In the second paragraph a single sentence tells, from the narrator's objective point of view, all the facts of the student's biography and present situation that are vital for the story, but which could not convincingly or economically be presented through his musings or recollections. From this point forward everything is revealed via the consciousness of the character whom Chekhov has chosen to embody in the story's title: physical sensations, visual impressions, memories, historical and philosophical thoughts; moods and emotions. Since the theme and the peripeteia of the story concern the change that takes place in the student's own psyche when he sees how his audience reacts, it is important that the characterisation of the two widows is conveyed through his appraisal of their appearances, gestures and speech. Vasilisa's deferential smile and Luker'ya's stupid, unwavering stare are revealed, as we will show, through the student's consciousness. The awesome universal tragedy of Peter's betrayal is given immediacy and a human scale through the student's comments and explanations. As already seen, the vision of history as a chain, the touching of one end of which will stir a response at the other end, is the student's own. It does not matter that the image is unoriginal (the student is an interpretive rather than a creative artist); what matters is the force of the student's realisation of this truth. The denouement and epilogue, matching the prologue and complication, are bound by the whole logic of the story to be the product of the student's point of view. The atmosphere of the story depends partly on the tension and interplay between the student's awareness of himself and his awareness of the world around him, between his present and his past, between the clear focus of his immediate surroundings, the blurred focus at the edges and the darkness of what lies beyond. The lens-angle widens and narrows like a zoom device. There is a consistency of atmosphere in "The Student" because there is a consistent point of view.

As has often been pointed out, the choice of 'third person, limited omniscient' point of view enables an author to combine the virtues of subjectivity (an authentic and deeply felt emotional response) and objectivity (the power to analyse and generalise). That the 'sentient centre' of this point of view coincides with the consciousness in which the story's essential reversal takes place, strengthens in "The Student" the two prime virtues of short-story form—unity and economy.

VIII

The foregoing examination of plot and point of view leaves little need for a detailed analysis of the creation and function of *Character* in the story. As already seen, knowledge of the student himself is built up from a complex pattern of sensations, visual impressions, memories, thoughts, emotions, gestures and language. Because of his central function in theme, plot and narrative structure, it is important that he has strong sensations, a sense of history and a sense of justice, that he can pity as well as criticise. As a student of theology he knows the Good Friday story almost by heart, as a humane person he can be moved by the affective power of the tragedy, as an intellectual he can rationalise this power, and as an idealist he can gain hope from his rationalisations.

As we have noted, the most effective aspect of the characterisation of the two widows is their juxtaposition. Vasilisa's height and girth and presence contrast with Luker'ya's littleness, ugliness and subjugation; the one knows the world and the gentry and has learned a little of the arts of social hypocrisy, the other is limited in outlook and unresponsive; the one responds actively, the other with mute passivity. The reader, like the student, has some contact with and sympathy for Vasilisa, and yet, by a nice paradox which Chekhov clearly engineered, it is the very negativity of Luker'ya's emotional reaction which is moving:

> her expression had become heavy and strained, as with a person holding back a strong pain.
>
> (p. 368)

26 *Literary Narrative*

Luker'ya is unaffected by physical discomfort and pain: could it be that Peter's tragedy and resulting grief give her more pain than anybody? Chekhov strengthens the atmosphere of the story by leaving the reader to decide.

IX

Schools of literary scholarship disagree upon methods of approaching the *Language* of a text. One tends to give greater weight to inspiration, while another undertakes a maximum of hard work hoping that inspiration will follow. The first approach, which has proved congenial to a majority of critics, claims that the trained creative reader will respond to the inspiration of the creative artist and recognise intuitively the significant linguistic details which will then illustrate or illuminate some general thesis about the work. At its rare best, this type of stylistics is both inspired and illuminating; when it is, as commonly, mediocre or bound to a narrow thesis, it belongs more to the fields of chiromancy or propaganda than to literary criticism.

Proponents of the second approach very properly believe that literary study can be a science as well as an art and that meaningful generalisations will only emerge from classifications based on theoretically validated categories.

Modern linguistics offers a theory and a system of classifications which can adequately describe some of the patterns of non-literary utterances. Since the literary work itself represents a coherent pattern, some critics have proposed the attractive formula: 'a patterning of patterns' to describe the relation between the whole work and the linguistic units of which it is composed. In the very few attempts which have been made to apply this formula, a preoccupation with the (micro-) patterns has obscured the (macro-) patterning: most exhaustive analysis and classification has yielded a mass of data whose significance is either obscure or trivial. A partial reason for this may be that the individual's preoccupations have been more linguistic than literary, but the major reason must be that, with the linguistic sciences in their infancy, linguistic stylistics is embryonic. No convincing bridge has yet been built between an analysis of the formal properties (phonological, grammatical and lexical) of words and structures within a sentence and their structural and thematic properties in the whole work. And since the unity and consistency of the whole work is more essential in literature than in any other kind of linguistic utterance, this gap must be bridged before statements about the 'style' of a particular work can be made. Unfortunately, even in post-Firthian linguistics, which at least recognises that language 'events' take place in a context, the semantic and contextual levels of the analytical framework still lack the systematic theoretical and descriptive foundation that can now be taken for granted for the formal levels of phonology and grammar.

The concept of cohesion, which has also been developed by M.A.K. Halliday and other post-Firthian linguists, appears to have far more potential

Structure and Style in the Short Story 27

as a systematic, economical and illuminating approach to the study of style. The term 'cohesion' implies the total system of relationships between the units of an utterance. Within a sentence these relationships can be formally defined. Grammatically, there is a major cohesion (e.g., the relationship between bound-clauses and free clauses) and a minor cohesion (where one element of the structure of a clause or group may 'correspond' to an element in another clause or group). Lexically, the feature of lexical repetition or of collocation, or of substitution may provide a cohesive force. Phonologically, the relationship of units of sound to the intonation pattern is cohesive, together with the more specifically literary devices of rhyme, pun, assonance and alliteration. As one moves outside the sentence to study the paragraph, the cohesion will inevitably become less formal and more contextual. Lexical and semantic cohesion and the relationships between the themes and ideas of individual sentences will be the most significant, although formal features, such as the use of parallel or contrasting syntactic patterns and the use of linking or contrasting adjuncts, may still play an important role, and it should be possible to describe in fairly formal terms the rhythm, intonation and other phonological patterns of a whole paragraph as one can, of course, do for a whole verse or stanza in poetry.

The linguist's nerve fails when he tries to venture beyond the limits of the paragraph and he realises that the patterns he can so exhaustively describe and enumerate up to this point are themselves patterned but until he knows how, he cannot talk significantly about the whole work. The formal links susceptible to linguistic analysis at sentence or paragraph level are all too tenuous for this vast jungle of semantic and thematic associations.

Nonetheless, the structural critical apparatus applied here so far has some of the formal rigour that the linguist hopes to apply in a stylistic analysis and is concerned with those patterns of association and cohesion that elude him. What is proposed is a fusion of the linguist's and the literary critic's notions of context. The structural analysis outlined and illustrated here will provide a 'patterning' of contexts which linguistic analysis is competent to describe; the patterns which emerge from the linguistic description will acquire a relevance to the theme and structure of the whole work. This fusion will demand both the epistemological clarity of our second school of literary criticism and the bold creative imagination of our first. At its best, it may produce generalisations about individual literary works which are both inspired and proven.

X

There is no such thing as an exhaustive study of the style of even the shortest literary work. Even where an author has a markedly individual style, the totality of syntactic patterns is too complex to be comprehended as a unity; the semantic associations of the vocabulary are so various and, often, ambiguous. The contribution of patterns of intonation and rhythm in literary prose to the aesthetic power of the work has hardly been noticed by linguists or critics in the Russian field, despite Tomashevsky's rigorous pioneering essay on prose rhythm.

Selection is unavoidable in illustrations of style. At least the concept of cohesion, linking the 'microstylistics' of the clause and sentence with the 'macrostylistics' of the whole work, permit confidence in making selection. We will therefore examine a few of the patterns of language in "The Student" which bear a marked relation to the patterning elements of the structural analysis: theme, plot, narrative structure, point of view, character and setting.

The language in which the tragedy of Peter is narrated probably provides the best microcosm to illustrate the theme of the short story. As already seen, Chekhov juxtaposes the archaic but monumentally simple language of the gospel account (Church Slavonic), which his hero can quote verbatim, with the student's own comments and interjections. This provides the juxtaposition and interaction of two extreme registers: the formal, archaic, literary, and the informal, modern, colloquial; and the syntax, vocabulary and rhythm of these two registers could be examined in detail in so far as they interact or cohere. It is possible to demonstrate that the proportions of these two components vary according to the narrative structure of this story within the story as well as to the overall narrative structure. As he sets the scene for his narrative, only the dialogue comes direct from the gospel text, although the student's own words have some of the archaic flavour of that text:

> "vo vremya tainoi vecheri, smertel'no toskoval, istomilsya dushoi zamuchennyi toskoi i trevogoi, shel vsled."

but are lightened by his own colloquial comments:

> "Yesli pomnish, A gospod' yemu na eto, to yest' petukh, byednyi Petr, on nikak ne mog poborot' sna. Spal. Potom, ty slyshala, ponimayesh' li, vot-vot na zemlye proizoidet chto-to uzhasnoye, bez pamyati."

Once he reaches the central episode, the student gives both the narrative and the dialogue in the elliptical, harshly objective language of the gospels (mainly according to St. Luke) and only an occasional explanatory phrase 'stirs the chain' and reminds his audience and the reader of their relationship to the events narrated:

> "Kak vot ya teper,' to yest' chto i yego, mol, nuzhno vesti k doprosu. I vsye rabotniki, chto nakhodilis' okolo ognya, dolzhno byt,' podozritel'no i surovo poglyadeli na nego."

The climactic end of the narration reveals the student as a superb interpretive artist. After a short, but significant, pause (three-dot pauses are always significant in Chekhov), he resumes in his own words:

Structure and Style in the Short Story 29

Vspomnil, ochnulsya, poshel so dvora i gor'ko-gor'ko zaplakal. V yevangelii skazano: "I isshed von, plakasya gor'ko." Voobrazhayu: tikhii-tikhii, temnyi-temnyi sad, i v tishine yedva slyshatsya glukhiye rydaniya....

(p. 363)

The student gives his subjective account of Peter's emotions with the double adverb *gor'ko-gor'ko*, juxtaposes with it the stark gospel statement, then reintroduces and intensifies the emotion with the double adjectives: *tikhii-tikhii, temnyi-temnyi,* which themselves sound like muffled sobs. Throughout the tragedy one end of the chain of time, embodied in the archaic, yet majestically economical Church Slavonic of the Gospels, is repeatedly linked to the other end, with the emotionally involved modern everyday speech of the student. One of the story's themes is conveyed in the interplay of the styles as much as in the message.

Our section on the plot has already drawn attention to one important aspect of the story's style. The alternation of verbs of sensation and verbs of thought in the second paragraph, which reflects perfectly the larger patterns of cause and effect, continues throughout the narrative, with thought gradually ousting sensation as a motivating force, the rationality of intellectual man conquering the weakness of the flesh.

Are there any patterns of language which reflect the patterning of the narrative structure? An analysis of the syntax of every sentence would be a Herculean labour whose results could scarcely justify the amount of work involved. The 'average' sentence, consisting of two or three linked or bound clauses, as V. V. Gurbanov discovered but did not admit, shows syntactic variations of somewhat limited significance, although examination of the language in relation to character and setting reveals some interesting patterning on the smaller scale of the paragraph. In "The Student," as, one suspects, elsewhere in Chekhov, it is the short and long sentences, as distinct from those of average length, which carry the main weight of the narrative structure.[4]

The short sentences, i.e., those consisting of a single clause or, at most, two verbs linked by a single subject, crop up like milestones at significant moments in the narrative, summarizing the tenor of the previous or, occasionally, the following sections. "*Pogoda vnachale byla khoroshaya, tikhaya*": the brief résumé of nature's mood already hints at a disappointing change; "*Zapakhlo zimoi*" sums up the tendency of the previous sensations, while "*I yemu nye khotelos' domoi*" summarises the student's emotions at the point of complication. The visual presentation of the widows is completed by: "*Ochevidno, tol'ko chto otuzhinali. Pogovorili*" introduces the student's awareness of their social characteristics. Dialogue and commentary in the story-within-the-story sometimes consist of short sentences, but these have the special linguistic characteristics already noticed and do not belong to the overall narrative structure. The only two remaining short sentences are:

"Student vzdokhnul i zadumalsya," which is a frame to the internal narrative, and *"On oglyanulsya,"* which, at the point of peripeteia, bridges the two physical and temporal planes of the story. (Gurbanov points out the importance of this verb *oglyanut'sya* in another article on Chekhov's style, but in the context of a general article covering some thirty-two stories he is not able to examine its precise structural significance in any one of them.)

Nearly all of the remainder of the story after this verb consists of long sentences, i.e., four or more clauses, and the last paragraph is a single sentence containing eleven complex and interwoven clauses. As Gurbanov points out—again with examples out of context—Chekhov very rarely uses long sentences in his narrative prose, and where he does so, he strives for extreme simplicity of syntax. Clauses are linked (especially with the 'simplest' conjunction *'i'*) rather than bound in a system of subordination and conditioning; often, halves of a long sentence are linked with a semi-colon or juxtaposed with a colon. Chekhov helps the reader to keep the thread of what he is saying with repetition or anaphora. This is true of all the long sentences in "The Student" except the last. Apart from the three long sentences referring to Vasilisa and Luker'ya, which will be considered briefly under character, all the long sentences convey the student's thought. Being an intellectual, he can rationalise in longer periods, though while the order in the world seems to be threatened by the impersonal and irrational forces around him he keeps a tight hold on his syntax: *"Yemu kazalos,' chto ... chto ... i ottogo ...; Student vspomnil, chto ... yego mat' ... a otets...."* and, after a semi-colon, the summary of their condition. Two key sentences are the long ones representing the student's thoughts about the continuity of human experience, the first in the passage leading up to the complication at the end of the second paragraph, the other in the third paragraph from the end, leading down from the dénouement. These sentences are parallel, not only by virtue of their positions in the narrative structure and in the explicit ideas they contain, but also in their marked use of anaphora to convey the intensification of an emotion. In the first of these, *"tochno takoi zhe ... i pri ... i pri ... i pri ... i pri ..., tochno takaya zhe ... takiye zhe ... takaya zhe"* express the student's growing despair which reaches its climax in: *"vsye eti uzhasy byli, yest' i budut."* In the second sentence the *"yesli ... to ... to ..., o chem ... chto ... k ... k ... k ... k ... ko"* express his growing relief and joy at having seen some kind of order restored in the world. A clear continuity is perceptible between linguistic cohesion within the sentence and structural and thematic cohesion in the whole work. In the last paragraph reason and hope have triumphed and the student can trust himself to the logical tight-rope of complex and interpenetrating clauses without needing mechanical linguistic aids such as anaphora to help him keep his balance.

In considering character in the story, we found that for structural and emotive reasons Chekhov systematically juxtaposes the figures of Vasilisa and Luker'ya. Just how neatly he does this will be immediately apparent if the descriptions of each of them in the relevant three paragraphs are placed side-by-side instead of consecutively (Figure 1.3):

1. Visible characteristics
Vdova Vasilisa,
vysokaya, pukhlaya starukha
v muzhskom polushubke,
stoyala vozle
i v razdum'ye glyadela na ogon'

yeyo doch' Luker'ya,
malen'kaya, ryabaya,
s glupovatym litsom,
sidela na zemle
i myla kotel i lozhki.

2. Social characteristics
Vasilisa
zhenschina byvalaya,
sluzhivshaya kogda-to u gospod
v mamkakh a potom v nyan'kakh,
vyrazhalas' delikatno
i s litsa yeyo vsyo vremya ne skhodila
myagkaya stepennaya ulybka

doch' zhe yeyo Luker'ya
derevenskaya baba,
zabitaya muzhem,

tol'ko schurilas' na studenta
i vyrazheniye u nyeyo bylo
strannoye, kak u glukhonemoi.

3. Response to Narrative
Prodolzhaya ulybat'sya
Vasilisa
vdrug vskhlipnula,
slezy krupnye, izobil'nye
potekli u nyeyo po schekam,
i ona zaslonila rukavom litso ot ognya,
kak by stydyas' svoikh slyez.

a Luker'ya,
glyadya nepodvizhno na studenta
pokrasnela,
i vyrazheniye u nyeyo stalo
tyazhelym, napryazhennym,
kak u cheloveka, kotoryi
sderzhivayet sil'nuyu bol'.

Figure 1.3

The setting, as introduced in the first paragraph of the story, has been examined in some detail already, but the relationship we noted between the natural phenomena described and the 'sentient centre' of the narration is reflected even in the parallel linguistic patterning of the two halves of the paragraph. The change in the weather and the change in the mood of the a-yet anonymous psyche begins with the words: "*No kogda stemnelo v lesu,*" and around this miniature peripeteia the clauses match. The similarity of the two halves intensifies their thematic contrast. While it is fine the student is aware of the sound of animate forces in his environment which act in personal verb forms; when it turns miserable, he is aware of the lack of sound in nature where inanimate forces, working through impersonal verb forms, prevail. Each pair of clauses reflects this contrast (Figure 1.4):

Transition
(*No kogda stemnelo v lesu*)

Pogoda vnachale byla khoroshaya, tikhaya
Krichali drozdy
protyanul odin val'dshnep
prozvuchala v vesennem vozdukhe
raskatisto i veselo

Nekstati podul s vostoka kholodnyi,
pronizyvayuschii veter
vsyo smolklo
Protyanulis' ledyanye igly
stalo v lesu neuyutno, glukho
i nelyudimo

Summary
(*Zapakhlo zimoi*)

Figure 1.4

(*The symmetry, rather than parallelism, of these clauses increases the force of the contrast: personal-verb/subject begins a sentence with a note of noise and optimism, while neuter-pronoun-subject/impersonal verb closes a sentence on a note of silence and passive despair.)

In this compact paragraph is the patterning, in miniature, of the first third of Turgenev's *Bezhin lug* (1852), where an active narrator perceives and enjoys the sights and sounds of pleasant, active, often animised natural phenomena and then, as it grows darker, succumbs passively to the power of unpleasant impersonal forces which assume a supernatural and threatening character. The shift in the relationship between a human consciousness and its environment sets the atmosphere for that most 'atmospheric' of Turgenev's stories, where the forces of light and reason are constantly threatened by the forces of darkness and irrationality. There is no suggestion here that Chekhov was, even unconsciously, influenced by Turgenev's creation of atmosphere in *Bezhin lug*, but a comparison of the two stories makes it clear that the particular combination of structural, stylistic and thematic features which both Chekhov and Turgenev have used contributes very powerfully to the creation of atmosphere.

XI

The analytical apparatus which we have discussed and tested in the foregoing study may seem a rather complex and ponderous method of reaching conclusions about a short story four pages long. It is considerably less ponderous, of course, if analysis can be carried out at the various levels directly, without the need for the definition of terminology and the arguments elaborated here in justification. The critical method is validated, however, on two main grounds: (1) its rigorous application almost inevitably inspires new intuitions about the theme, structure and language of a work (a hermeneutic spiral); (2) it reduces the possibility (as well as the respectability) of making inspired subjective statements about a work without the support of detailed and objective evidence from the text.

This is not playing with patterns for their own sake: it is not killing the organic qualities of a work of art for the sake of pseudo-scientific schematisation and classification: this deep study of the work itself is the minimum necessary prerequisite for a serious approach to the historical, the sociological and the comparative study of literature.

Notes

1. V.I. Propp, *Morfologiya skazki*. Leningrad, 1928. (An important review of Propp's work is: Claude Lévi-Strauss, 'L'analyse morphologique des contes russes,' *International Journal of Slavic Linguistics and Poetics*, Vol. 3, 1960).

2. This, of course, is a recurring motif in Chekhov's stories, which he frequently uses to signal that the *zavyazka* is about to begin, i.e., some change is due to occur in the central psyche due to the appearance of a new character. Cf. Nadya's thoughts just before the appearance of Sasha in *Nevesta*.
3. Petrovsky, disappointingly, uses the German terms *Vorgeschichte* and *Nachgeschichte*.
4. A statistical study of clause patterning in "The Student" carried out by D. Hamblyn at the University of Essex substantiates this intuitive hypothesis.

2 Narrative Structure and Living Texture
Joyce's "Two Gallants"

Introduction

This paper, with which I launched the Neo-Formalist Circle, in February 1975, as a section of BUAS (the British Universities Association of Slavists), is an attempt to synthesise and integrate the results of a group analysis of James Joyce's story "Two Gallants" from his *Dubliners* (1905–1906). This was held at a symposium on "Structures in Literary Texts" organised jointly by the Department of Language and Linguistics at the University of Essex and the Neo-Formalist Circle in a country house in the village of Thaxted in Essex. One of the distinguished literary theorists taking part was Benjamin Hrushovski, founder of a new journal in Israel, *PTL: A Journal for Descriptive Poetics and Theory of Literature* who commissioned a fully developed paper from our group analysis for the opening volume of this journal (*PTL* Vol. 1, No 3, October 1976, pp. 441–458). The published paper was used in literature teaching courses in schools and universities in several English-speaking cultures.

While the author is indebted to his fellow participants in the discussion for many acute and valuable insights and interpretations, he must accept the main responsibility for the shortcomings of their synthesis into an integrated view of the story's theme, narrative structure and linguistic texture. "Collective analyses" of short stories and poems became a regular feature of our twice-yearly meetings of the Neo-Formalist Circle.

Theory and Analysis: "Two Gallants"

Structuralist critics are frequently accused of "reductionism." They are motivated apparently by a simple-minded neo-positivist urge to reduce the complexities of the organic literary text to a unitary theme, a rigid compositional structure and an unconvincing one-to-one relationship between meaning in the text and the units of language which bear that meaning.

Some structuralists have certainly made rather exaggerated claims for their methods. The discovery of binary oppositions of meaning in a literary text and their structuring into four-term homologies (A : B :: X : Y) does not necessarily produce more insights than an intuitive recognition of relationships between two characters or two situations in the text. A painstaking analysis of a work level by level does not of itself lead to a coherent interpretation; it may, indeed, make a unified interpretation seem strained and improbable. The recognition of a linguistic pattern, say, a recurrent sentence structure, a lexical or phonetic patterning, will not alone be sufficient to account for the author's attitude to his subject and his characters.

The point is that the structuralist is inclined to equip himself for the task of literary study with a wide range of relatively precise, describable and repeatable techniques, logical, classificatory and linguistic, any of which may prove useful and insightful for a particular stage of the total analytic-synthetic process. What the anti-structuralist dislikes is the technical complexity of the procedures, necessitating a whole range of techniques and a new vocabulary to learn with each. What he fails to appreciate is the virtue of explicitness: any critic imposes a model of some sort on the literary text, whether it be derived from the author's biography, the social or political history of his age, some assumptions about his psychological disabilities or political intentions or from a theory about language and text structure. Only the latter type of model is required, however, to be fully explicit about the terms it adopts and the way the categories of the model relate to elements of the subject studied.

What the structuralist himself often fails to recognise is the interplay between the abstract model and the concrete textual fact, the degree to which the theory is constantly under pressure from the data. It can account explicitly for only a certain amount in the thematic and linguistic structuring of the text and then must yield to intuition, The excitement of the structural study of an art form—perhaps that of any human institution—is in the dialectic tension between creative insight and methodological rigor: having read the short story (or novel or poem or play) one postulates a theme (intuition): one tests this interpretation by analysing the work as systematically as possible on a number of levels (technique); but the analyses can only be reintegrated or synthesised by a new, more complex, statement of theme (intuition); the revised interpretation may then be further tested against an analysis of linguistic patterning or against more pervasive elements such as interplay of characters point of view or symbolism, etc. At every stage of this "hermeneutic spiral" the student of the text is conscious of the degree to which he can or cannot rely solely on the application of technique and he has a way of describing the role which intuitive leaps play in his unravelling of the texture and meaning. He has a vocabulary and an explicit set of assumptions and procedures on which he may base discussion of any literary work. Dialogue becomes possible: literary discourse becomes a secular and democratic activity. The initiation of student novitiates by a high priesthood of "Literature" begins to seem a rather disreputable process.

A theme which appears to relate many elements of Joyce's "Two Gallants" satisfactorily is that of exploitation. The story is an account of how

Corley exploits a young servant girl, seducing her in order to get her to steal money from her employer. Analysed in purely linear terms of fable and plot, the story yields a rather sparse synopsis. Reconstructed in the time sequence in which the original events took place (*fable*), the story reads: Corley, the unemployed son of a Dublin police inspector, is accustomed to picking up working girls, seducing them and abandoning them—in one case, to prostitution. He meets a slavey from Baggot Street, takes her on a tram to Donnybrook and makes love to her. At their next meetings she brings him cigarettes and cigars and pays for the tram. He tells his friend Lenehan, also an unemployed Dubliner, of this latest conquest as they walk to a new rendezvous with the girl. Lenehan persuades Corley to let him walk past them in order to have a look at the girl. They make an appointment to meet later in the evening and Corley goes off with the girl. Lenehan kills time by walking round Dublin, eating a meal, chatting with acquaintances and smoking until the appointed time, when he stands in the shadow of a lamp on the corner of a street where the slavey lives. The couple return, the girl runs down into the area entrance to the house and re-emerges a few moments later with a coin which she hands to Corley. Corley walks away, pursued by Lenehan and eventually shows him the coin.

A reconstruction of the basic story line in temporal sequence is not of great interest in itself. The act of reconstruction, however, reveals four essential ways in which the actual story differs from the fable: changes in sequence, the disposition of the events through the text, the mode by which we learn of the events, and the amount of the text which is left out. The essential background of Corley's life is narrated by the narrator *after* the introduction of Lenehan and after Corley's own flashback to his previous meetings with the young woman, while the still earlier history of Corley's other affairs (pluperfect, as it were) is conveyed after this in a dialogue between Corley and Lenehan. The little we learn of Lenehan's earlier life emerges early on from the narrator's account of the reputation Lenehan enjoys among other people, notably his drinking companions, and later in the story from his own rather disconsolate musings after the meal in the café. In other words, the information we need to know about the characters prior to Corley's exploitation of the young slavey are spread out atemporally through at least two-thirds of the story and are conveyed from four different points of view: the narrator's own account (Corley), his references to other people's views (Lenehan), direct speech (Corley) and free indirect speech in soliloquy (Lenehan). Thus all we learn of Corley is conveyed in a direct, unmediated way, while our information about Lenehan is all refracted through the consciousness of either Lenehan or his drinking companions. This has important implications, as we shall see, for the levels of plot, narrative structure and point of view. Finally, we scarcely need to point out that the essential sequence of events comprising the fable actually accounts for a very small portion of the whole text of "Two Gallants."

Much the same is true of the plot. The causal relationships are for most of the story implicit in Corley's and Lenehan's assumptions about the purposes of the seduction. As in most detective and mystery fiction—almost by definition—there is a mismatch between the temporal and the causal sequence: some essential causal factor (the identity of the murderer, the explanation of the mystery) is withheld until the last moment. So too here: Corley's seduction of the girl seems to imply a rather brutal kind of sexual exploitation and we interpret the recurrent references to Corley's ultimate purpose in this light: "Well, *that* takes the biscuit!"; "you'll be able to pull *it* off?"; "Is she game for *that*?"; "I know *the way to get round her*, man"; "But you can bring *it* off all right? You know *it's* a ticklish job. They're damn close *on that point*"; "I'll pull *it* off. Leave *it* to me, can't you?"; "Are you trying to get inside me?"; "Work *it* all right now"; "and sat for some time thinking of Corley's *adventure*"; "He wondered had Corley managed *it* successfully. He wondered if he had asked her yet or if he would leave *it* to the last"; "He was sure Corley would pull *it* off all right"; "tried to read *the result* in their walk"; "An intimation of *the result* pricked him like the point of a sharp instrument"; "Well?" he said "Did *it* come off?" "Did you *try* her?" the final revelation of the gold coin which the young woman has stolen for Corley necessitates a complete reinterpretation of the nature of this exploitation of her. Joyce has given us several clues, to be sure: from Corley's first account of his latest conquest it is clear that he has already made love to her and that this was not her first sexual experience. Moreover, his rewards increase in value: first, cigarettes, then tram-fares, then "two bloody fine cigars—O, the real cheese, you know, that the old fellow used to smoke"(54). Lenehan's aspirations, too, inextricably link sex and domesticity with money: "He might yet be able to settle down in some snug corner and live happily if only he could come across some good simple-minded girl with a little of the ready" (62). Like well-trained readers of detective stories, however, we insist on ignoring these clues and are surprised by the cynical twist at the end.

What takes us by surprise is Joyce's definition of seduction and prostitution. Corley's rather ungallant account of his earlier conquests makes it clear that conventionally one pays a girl for her favours:

> "I used to take them out, man, on the tram somewhere and pay the tram or take them to a band or a play at the theatre, or buy them chocolate and sweets or something that way. I used to spend money on them right enough," he added, in a convincing tone, as if he was conscious of being disbelieved. But Lenehan could well believe it; he nodded gravely. "I know that game," he said, "and it's a mug's game!"
>
> (Joyce, 1954: 56)

But the new "game" involves a switching of roles which may be seen clearest in transactional terms:

1. prostitution is an exchange of sex for money; in which
2. female uses sex to acquire cash
3. male uses cash to acquire sex

We are shocked by Corley's adoption of the female role in this transaction: there is something particularly ungallant about a gigolo. Yet perhaps we are too inured by custom and prejudice to perceive the usual male purchase of sex as exploitative. Clearly the outcome of the story does not focus on the girl's role in the mutual exploitation in the same way as it focuses on Corley's role, but there is a clear hint in the description of the girl, as seen through Lenehan's eyes, that she is a willing partner in the transaction. The first impression from a distance is of a gay and rather innocent figure in a blue dress and white sailor hat swinging an umbrella, executing half turns on her heels and laughing coyly. But in close-up she hardly sustains the image of a helpless and unwitting victim:

> Frank rude health glowed in her face, on her fat, red cheeks and in her unabashed blue eyes. Her features were blunt. She had broad nostrils, a straggling mouth which lay open in a contented leer, and two projecting front teeth.
>
> (59–60)

The story is indeed about a sort of sexual-financial exploitation, but the exploitation is mutual.

This raises some questions about the interpretation of the harp symbol in the story. The harp in Kildare Street symbolises, as most commentators have shown (see, for example, Tindall, 1960; Litz, 1969), a fallen Ireland, a rural, poetic, traditional, sometime glorious Ireland, now being plucked "heedlessly" by a harpist whose only live concern is to draw money from passers-by. Her song ("Silent, O Moyle") is of a slumbering Erin, "Lir's lonely daughter" (a child of the sea: a girl in a sailor hat), waiting to be released (a slavey dishonoured in a market place). It is less clear that the girl, like the harp, is "heedless that her coverings had fallen about her knees" or "seemed very weary alike of the eyes of strangers and of her master's hands." Possibly this rather painful piece of anthropomorphism is less crucially symbolic then the hands which pluck the harp: one hand playing the bass melody (Corley—heavy British-style police oppressor) and other careering (like Lenehan—rootless, feckless, verbose Dubliner) in the treble after each group of notes.

Narrative Structure

If analysis of the linear structure of "Two Gallants" in terms of fable and plot supports the notion of the theme of the story being exploitation in sexual and financial terms with a parallel sub-theme of political oppression and exploitation carried out by the symbol of the harp, analysis of the story paradigmatically in terms of narrative structure and point of view reveals two other dimensions of exploitation, Narrative structure may be defined as the pattern of *complication—peripeteia—dénouement* which the writer has imposed on the temporal and causal sequence of events to give them meaning. It is equivalent in text structure to the process-participant relationship conveyed by a transitive verb in sentence structure. But this essentially ideational content is refracted through a point of view which imposes a personal interpretation on the meaning, as do patterns of modality within the sentence. The crucial thing about the narrative structure of "Two Gallants" is that it is virtually concentrated in the last half-page of the story and that it is transmitted to us, not directly, but through the perceptions of Lenehan. The complication established early on, is Corley's much-mentioned but unspecified plan to use this rendezvous with the girl for a new purpose. The bulk of the story then describes the various manifestations of Lenehan's anxiety about the outcome culminating in the "silent film" sequence in which he observes Corley and the girl returning and her fetching something from the house and giving it to Corley. This anxiety is resolved only in the last line. But Corley plays his moment of triumph for all it is worth, first avoiding Lenehan, who he knows is waiting for him, desperate to know the outcome, then:

> Corley halted at the first lamp and stared grimly before him. Then with a grave gesture he extended a hand towards the light and, smiling, opened it slowly to the gaze of his disciple [...]
>
> (65)

In a sense, then, Corley exploits his friend as audience to the drama and as disciple, gaining power and a sense of worth for himself from Lenehan's perceptual and emotional dependence. But as in the prostitute-client relationship, the exploitation involved between actor and audience or between master and disciple also cuts both ways. As the old psychoanalytic joke has it, "the definition of a sadist is 'someone who is kind to a masochist.'" There is repeated stress in the story on Lenehan as a kind of satellite to Corley, walking on the verge of the path and at times stepping into the road out of the latter's unswerving path, observing Corley and the girl from his orbit, timing his pace to theirs and always responsive to the ponderous swivel of Corley's massive round head. But Lenehan, the man of words, needs Corley, the man of action for his own fulfilment. Only capable of vicarious satisfaction, all his tension, we assume, is released once Corley's success is revealed. But the action in the narrative is not just any quest; it is a sexual quest, the reader has assumed. And Lenehan is not just a spectator; he is a voyeur. As he hurried to his rendezvous with Corley he hears many "couples bidding one another goodnight" (63). The intensity of his anxiety is psycho-sexual: "hurrying for fear Corley should return too soon." His stance is classically that of the "Peeping Tom": "he took his stand in the shadow of a lamp and brought out one of the cigarettes which he had reserved and lit it. He leaned against the lamppost and kept his gaze fixed on the part from which he expected to see Corley and the young woman return." Even more explicitly:

"he suffered all the pangs and thrills of his friend's situation as well as those of his own" (63). The reader's view of what is happening during the silent sequence is obstructed, like Lenehan's, by the shadows, the position of the area and front-steps and by Corley's burly body; the tension which he shares with Lenehan is psychosexual.

Just as we only learn at the very end that Corley's quest was for money by way of sex, so we simultaneously learn, perhaps with even greater revulsion, that Lenehan's voyeurism has had money as its focus of vicarious gratification, not sex. For, at a third level of exploitation, Joyce has cheated us. Through his manipulation of point of view, through his stress on the sexual aspects of Lenehan's thoughts and behaviour and through the verbal camouflage, he has managed to conceal from us until the last few words of the story the nature of Corley's triumph and the reason for Lenehan's anxiety. The last sentence is both peripeteia and dénouement for us as well as for Lenehan. While for Lenehan the result of the quest is in doubt, for us its very nature is obscure until the gold coin reveals all. Not that we have cause to complain at being exploited in this way; the reader reads to have his knowledge and emotions manipulated in some way and the writer uses all kinds of devices to create tension in us. Joyce's favourite device is an "epiphany." This is not simply one of those mechanical "twists" of plot merely reversing the action which O. Henry and Maupassant are often accused of (though Maupassant's endings are usually much more like epiphanies), but "a sudden spiritual manifestation, whether in the vulgarity of speech or of gesture or in a memorable phase of the mind itself." (The definition is Joyce's own, voiced by Stephen Daedalus in *Stephen Hero* [1944: 188].) Like the spiritual manifestation of the infant Jesus to the Magi on the Feast of the Epiphany, some neutral thing may acquire a sudden radiance which illuminates everything that relates to it: "We recognise that it is *that* thing which it is. It's [sic] soul, its whatness, leaps to us from the vestment of its appearance. The soul of the commonest object, the structure of which is so adjusted, seems to us radiant. The object achieves its epiphany" (Joyce, 1944: 189–190).

The small gold coin shining in Corley's palm in the final sentence casts its radiance back over the whole story and reveals everything in a new light. Corley's quest, the young woman's downfall and Lenehan's voyeurism all shift from a sexual to a financial meaning. Ireland's downfall symbolised by the harp is transformed by the tyranny imposed from the outside by the brute military strength and insensitivity of such as Corley to a much deeper degradation where spirituality has been replaced by venality. Tindall refers to a common theme running through the *Dubliners* stories of "paralysis or living death" and quotes Joyce's wish, expressed in a letter of 1904 (a year before he wrote "Two Gallants") "to betray the soul of that ... paralysis which many consider a city"; to write "a chapter of the moral history of my country and a first step toward its spiritual liberation" (Tindall, 1960: 24).

Setting

If this is typical of Joyce's attitude to Dublin during the period in which he wrote "Two Gallants," does it affect our perception of the story's setting? At first reading we are struck by the sheer quantity of names of streets and squares and institutions: what could be more neutral and colourless than this litany of proper names: Rutland Square—Trinity College—Nassau Street—Kildare Street—Stephen's Green—Hume Street—Shelbourne Hotel—Merrion Square—Duke's Lawn—Grafton Street—Rutland Square—Capel Street—City Hall—Dame Street—George's Street—City Markets—Grafton Street—College of Surgeons—the Green (Stephen's?)—Merrion Street—Baggot Street—Stephen's Green—Ely Place. But in the light of the final epiphany the merely geographical acquires moral overtones. Even without a street map of Dublin we sense a circularity here: we encountered the two men in Rutland Square and it is to Rutland Square that Lenehan returns for his solitary meal; on his route from Merrion Square where he loses sight of Corley and the girl to the corner of Merrion Street where they reappear he twice passes Grafton Street and Stephen's Green. The aimless, hopeless circularity of Lenehan's route within the story seems to plot the map of the mind of this "sporting vagrant" with his "brave manner of coming up to a party of them [friends] in a bar and holding himself nimbly at the borders of the company until he was included in the round" and whose "name was vaguely associated with racing tissues" (53). Most vacuously circular of all is Lenehan's conversation with two friends as he makes his way, revived by his meal, back to the rendezvous. The placing of this conversation in the story and the minute detail of who said what to whom makes it particularly significant. Yet it is so empty of content that only the names (Westmoreland Street, Egan's, Mac and Holohan) emerge from the limbo with any suggestion of meaning or permanency. Circles of drinkers, the racing circuit, the round of Dublin's streets, the terrifying circularity of voyeurism—Lenehan is a satellite looking for an orbit. Not that his chosen sun, Corley, he of the "large, globular and oily" and "slowly revolving" head, exactly defies gravity. He plucks girls off the South Circular, shuttles out to Donnybrooks on the tram to seduce them, then back to plod the Dublin round once more. Yet at least the action of the story represents a break with routine; the latest trip to Donnybrooks is quite a new venture.

The motif of circularity recurs time and again throughout the story and each time acquires new significance in the light of the gold coin at the end: the mild warm air circulates the streets (like the vagrant heroes we are about to meet). Lenehan's biscuits, whether figurative ("that takes the biscuit!—uttered three times [53]) or comestible ("which he had asked two grudging curates to bring him" [61]) begin to suggest the disc of the host of the Mass. The large faint moon circled with a double halo is the focus of the "poet" Lenehan's attention ("he watched earnestly the passing of the grey web of twilight across his face" [55]) while Corley turns to smile at passing girls, but the moon and the girls are linked a little later when Corley recalls the one girl (now a prostitute) that he ever got any money out of: "The recollection brightened his eyes. He, too, gazes at the pale disc of the moon, now nearly veiled, and seemed to meditate" (56). In the course of a short dialogue linking sex and money, the pure, round moon has been almost obscured; by the end of the story, the vivid, dynamic personality of the young woman is all but obliterated by Corley's massive round head and outshone by a small gold coin. Echoing the rhyme of circularity through the story are clock faces on famous buildings (Trinity College, the College of Surgeons, Waterhouse's) which, with illuminated dials, become fixed spatial and temporal beacons in the endless odyssey round Dublin: round plates bearing cut round hams and light plum puddings in a lighted shop window; round coins paid for round peas. Certainly one should not take the symbolism too far and I am inclined to doubt whether Lenehan's meal of peas, seasoned with pepper and vinegar, is really the "mess of pottage" for which he has sold his birthright, as has been suggested (Tindall, 1960: 24). Yet such fanciful associations are not to be ruled out entirely with an artist endowed with Joyce's eye for a symbol and ear for a pun. It is hard to avoid relating the gleaming coin shown to his disciple by Corley (who aspirated the first letter of his name) to "base betrayer" (said with a tragic gesture) and Lenehan's "last supper," though this link is the betrayal of an ideal rather than an identification with roles in the Christian drama.

The other crucial aspect of setting is the interplay of light and darkness anticipated from the very first paragraph: "Like illuminated pearls the lamps shone from the summits of their tall poles upon the living texture below." The source of light is usually above (street lamps, moon) and it casts circles of illumination on the baser deeds of man in the streets and squares below. As we have seen, its main function is to limit Lenehan's point of view, but it also related at times to his mood: "[he] felt more at ease in the dark quiet street, the sombre look of which suited his mood" (61).

Character

It must be admitted that in our analysis so far we have still not really "got inside" Lenehan. The theme of "exploitation," which we took as our starting point, proves quite adequate on the levels of fable and plot and, in another sense, when we analysed point of view in the story Yet virtually all the narrative structure is concentrated in the last eighth of the story and even then is refracted through Lenehan's consciousness. By far the larger proportion of the text is taken up with the narrator's descriptions of Lenehan and Corley, with dialogue between them, with Lenehan's circumambulations and meal, his thoughts and musings, his aspirations and anticipations. The idea of exploitation accounts for very little once we begin to analyse the character of the protagonists. Here more of a clue is offered by the multiple irony of the story's title. Corley and Lenehan each represent certain aspects of the traditional code of gallantry and, like the three musketeers, they contrast strongly with each other.

In the tradition of courtly love the gallant is free and independent in his life style, bold and decisive in action, eloquent and subtle in speech, handsome and charming in manner, gaily and even exotically dressed, with Italy or Spain as the model for his finery. He is loyal in friendship and chivalrous in love and owes allegiance to a freemasonry of gallants rather than any institutionalised community or leader. His typical modes of action—preferably by moonlight in romantic settings—are fighting, making eloquent and witty speeches and love-making, all three activities frequently combining in the rescue of some pure and beautiful damsel in distress. Victory is celebrated with feasting and drinking and speech-making in good company, a natural break in the cycle of quest and conquest for celebration and renewal. Money, if it appears at all, is a means to an end through the purchase of gifts, bribery or gambling, and is always gold.

Well, the title of Joyce's story suggests gallantry and comradeship and the story ends with the revelation of a small gold coin; one gallant is referred to as "a gay Lothario" and aspirates the first letter of his name "after the manner of Florentines" (55) while the other "sporting vagrant" (53) slings his coat over his shoulder "toreador fashion" (52) and enjoys a certain gift of the gab. Otherwise every detail of the character, plot and setting subverts or ironically reverses some aspect of this code of gallantry.

Far from being free and independent, both gallants are parasites. Lenehan is by common consent "a leech" (53) with no known means to support other than, perhaps, gambling on horses and scrounging drinks in public houses. In the wet city of Dublin he is a creature of the gutter, half on the pavement and half in the road. Not only do his clothes betray his watery habitat—yachting cap, rubber shoes and waterproof—but his whole body seems to be in the power of aqueous forces: "the narrative to which he listened made constant waves of expression break forth over his face from the corners of his nose and eyes and mouth [drains?]. Little jets of wheezing laughter followed one another out of his convulsed body ... his face, when the waves of expression had passed over it, had a ravaged look" (52). Stylistically, this passage stresses Lenehan's passivity as well as his wetness. Not a single verb ascribed to him is transitive: he is the passive subject of the power of amusement and of Corley. If the latter appears free and independent when the story opens, by the end his financial parasitism (on the girl) and his emotional parasitism (on his "disciple," Lenehan) have become clear. For all his power of decision he seems trapped inside his bulbous, globular head and the frame and gait he has inherited from his father.

Our first impressions of Lenehan's verbal virtuosity soon fade. The lively colloquialness of his opening words: "Well! [...] That takes the biscuit!" and their elaboration into the rhythmic and exotic "That takes the solitary, unique, and, if I may so call it, *recherché* biscuit!" is offset by a voice "winnowed of vigour" by a humour "to enforce his words" (53) by being

44   *Literary Narrative*

repeated yet a third time to close a section of their dialogue, and by our later awareness of the real biscuits he had had to scrounge that morning—Joyce leaves us in no doubt about the cynicism with which Lenehan exploits his verbal skills.

> his adroitness and eloquence had always prevented his friends from forming any general policy against him. He had a brave manner of coming up to a party of them in a bar and of holding himself nimbly at the borders of the company until he was included in a round. He was a sporting vagrant, armed with a vast stock of stories, limericks and riddles.

and, later,

> A shade of mockery relieved the servility of his manner. To save himself he had the habit of leaving his flattery open to the interpretation of raillery.
> (55)

Having exploited his full repertoire of smiles, head-shaking, winks and tragic gestures,

> Lenehan said no more. He did not wish to ruffle his friend's temper, to be sent to the devil and told that his advice was not wanted. A little tact was necessary.
> (57)

So far all we know of Lenehan is through the narrator's observations. Once he is alone, however, we get a glimpse behind the public mask of tame buffoon. The emphasis is on his anxiety, listlessness, moroseness and boredom. He does not even enjoy the blarney which had seemed to be his raison d'être:

> He walked listlessly round Stephen's Green and down Grafton Street. Though his eyes took note of many elements of the crowd through which he passed they did so morosely. He found trivial all that was meant to charm him, and did not answer the glances which invited him to be bold. He knew that he would have to speak a great deal, to invent and to amuse, and his brain and throat were too dry for such a task.
> (60)

He makes no verbal contact with the other customers in the café, apart from adjusting his mask ("He spoke roughly in order to belie his air of gentility" [61]) and the thought of "Corley's voice in deep energetic gallantries … made him feel keenly his own poverty of purse and spirit" (62). When he does meet up again with his friends, though apparently revived by his meal, the conversation is totally vacuous, as we have seen, as devoid of elegant form as of meaningful content.

Like many a word spoken in jest, "base betrayer," accompanied by a tragic gesture, has serious implications for the whole code of morality of our two "gallants." Explicitly it refers to an earlier seduction of a girl by Corley (who has a snake-like habit of "moistening his upper lip by rubbing his tongue along it"), but with tragic irony it points forward to the betrayal of Corley's latest conquest. On the other hand, the phrase arises out of a dispute about whether Lenehan can believe Corley:

> "You know you can't kid me, Corley," he said.
> "Honest to God!" said Corley. "Didn't she tell me herself?"
> Lenehan made a tragic gesture.
> "Base betrayer!" he said.
>
> (56)

Lenehan's later anxiety in the story hinges not only on whether Corley can "pull it off all right" (63), but on whether he would "give him the slip" (64). In a final tense moment the full lack of trust between them is unmasked for a moment: "He was baffled, and a note of menace pierced through his voice. 'Can't you just tell us?' he said" (65). Not that Corley trusts Lenehan either:

> Lenehan grew lively.
> "Let's have a look at her, Corley," he said.
> Corley glanced sideways at his friend and an unpleasant grin appeared on his face.
> "Are you trying to get inside me?" he asked.
>
> (58)

So much for the gallants' code of honour. If Corley owes allegiance anywhere it is not to a freemasonry of fellow gallants, but to an alien, highly institutionalised and repressive force, as brutally oppressive to the "real Ireland" epitomised in the harp playing "Silent, O Moyle" as Corley is to the slaveys from the South Circular and Baggot Street. If there was one thing a true gallant could never be, it was a copper's nark.

Gallantry Reversed

Corley's account of his encounter with the young woman reads like a black parody of a traditional gallant courtship pattern: from the first magic encounter ("Where did you pick her up, Corley?") with a vision of beauty ("I spotted a fine tart") and a fond farewell ("and said goodnight, you know"), via a first idyllic stroll ("We went for a walk round by the canal") and intimations of affection ("I put my arm round her and squeezed her a bit that night"), to the ecstasy of love-making ("We went out to Donnybrook and I brought her into a field there"), not, we might note, with a pure and unsullied dairymaid but with a slavey who "told me that she used

46   *Literary Narrative*

to go with a dairyman" (53)—all this at *Donnybrook* which is a synonym for bedlam or a beer garden. As we have seen, the presentation of gifts was by her to him (i.e., in reverse), the fine hospitality was second-hand ("two bloody fine cigars—O, the real cheese, you know, that the old fellow used to smoke" [54]) and the ultimate dream of marriage and family bliss thwarted:

> "I was afraid, man, she'd get in the family way. But she's up to the dodge!"
> "Maybe she thinks you'll marry her," said Lenehan.
> "I told her I was out of a job," said Corley.
> "I told her I was in Pim's. She doesn't know my name. I was too hairy to tell her that. But she thinks I'm a bit of class, you know."
> (54)

This blunt recital of anti-gallantry is conveyed in short, inelegant sentences linked only by simple coordination and punctuated by crude slang and the repetition of "fine," "you know" and "man." (It is intriguing that Joyce adopts a similar blunt style, heavy in coordinate structures for his descriptions of Corley, while the descriptions of Lenehan, like the man's own speech, are vivid, complex and involve more elaborate subordination.)

It is clear from Corley's story that the object of his "love" is not exactly a helpless maiden. Nor does she seem to be in much distress. As we saw in discussing the nature of their transaction, Lenehan's initial impression of a gay, almost fragile figure turns out on close inspection to be blunt, unabashed and leering contentedly: a match, indeed, for Corley. Even Lenehan's dream of warm domesticity and marital bliss at the café turn sour for the reader through the chiasmus Joyce exploits to reintroduce the waitress and get Lenehan out into the street once more:

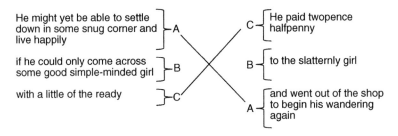

Figure 2.1

Finally, the convivial feasting and drinking which should set the seal on each deed of gallantry here becomes a plate of grocer's hot peas, seasoned with the bitterness of pepper and vinegar, and a bottle of ginger beer which serves only to confirm Lenehan's loneliness and foreshadow the "base betrayal."

Joyce has thus reversed a whole code of gallantry in the distorting mirror of contemporary Dublin, and we must reconsider our original theme of "exploitation" as one facet of the more pervasive theme of "gallantry unmasked." This means that there is no conflict over whether to define the story as a "tale of action" or as a "character portrait." For all the suspense the plot may hold for the reader on a first reading, it is essentially an actualisation of a complex of character traits. Corley's quest for money via love which form the narrative structure is a dynamic realisation of the knight errant theme of gallantry and Lenehan's anxious voyeurism, through which we perceive so much of the action, is a case study of the poet-vagabond whose eloquence has turned to mere verbosity and neurosis.

Style

We are left with the problem of style. It was assumed at the Thaxted symposium where this story was studied that "Structures in Literary Texts" would include linguistic structures and that one of the major problems facing us—as it faces all those currently working in the fields of text-grammar and discourse analysis—would be to relate a writer's lexical and syntactic (sometimes even phonological) choices to the way he structures his text. In our analysis so far we have frequently pointed to elements in the language of the story which were significant for a particular level of narrative: metaphors of wetness, a stress on passivity or complex subordination in the delineation of Lenehan's character; globular or military metaphors, crude slang, simple coordination short sentences, heavily interspersed with phatic "you know" and "man" in the portrayal of Corley; deliberate inexplicitness for the sake of plot suspense in the use of pronouns "it" and "that" or dummy-nouns like "adventure" or "result" unmotivated by any clear antecedent; a recurring pattern of semantic choice which made paragraphs open full of hope and close with disillusion (the description of Lenehan moves from youthful jauntiness to aged enervation, that of the young woman from gay innocence to leering complicity), the vacuous repetitiveness of Lenehan's conversations with his friends after the meal and the recurrent pattern of questions in free indirect speech marking his mounting anxiety as his rendezvous with Corley draws near; the scrupulous indication of place names which constructs for us a moral geography of the setting: words recurring throughout the text which carry echoes of "gallantry" forward from the title.

All of these stylistic choices are "integrative" rather than "distributional"; if we extend Roland Barthes' categories of narrative functions down to the selection of linguistic options, it is true to say in each of these cases that "in order to understand what purpose an index (*indice*) or indicator serves, one must pass to a higher level (actions, of the character or narration), for only there can the 'index' be clarified ... the sanction of indices is 'higher-up' ... it is a paradigmic sanction. By contrast, the sanction of (distributional) 'functions' is always 'further on,' it is a syntagmatic sanction" (Barthes, 1975:

48 *Literary Narrative*

247). One stylistic detail we noted which is simultaneously integrative and distributional is the chiasmus relating to the "snug corner" to Lenehan's "wandering," "the simple-minded girl" to "the slatternly girl" and "a little of the ready" to "he paid twopence halfpenny." This is both an "index" of narrative structure, point of view and character and a "function" which serves to get Lenehan out of the café into the street.

The syntagmatic relation between linguistic units performing only as "functions" is necessarily much harder to map. The nature of the relationship may be extremely tenuous and, except for words denoting purely sequential action, far less clearly motivated than units which integrate via the higher levels of structure. Yet it cannot be denied that our sense of a "well-formed" text depends at least as much on our subconscious perception of these distributional relationships as on the integrative ones. "Understanding is based on a process of *linking* elements in the text, whether they are connected syntactically or not, and combining, readjusting and specifying their semantic potentials into a complex meaning or, usually, *chains of meanings*" (Hrushovski, 1974: 15).

By good fortune, a systematic syntagmatic analysis of the first paragraph of "Two Gallants" has been attempted by van Dijk (1971: 281–283). He succeeds in relating semantic representations in successive "sentoids" by rigorously applied rules of repetition (warm = warm), inclusion (evening ∩ air), synonymy (streets ⊂ city) and inductive entailment (warm summer → dress → gaily coloured). Yet this valuable and systematic technique misses such crucial elements as semantic **oppositions of: up (A) : down (B) :: permanency (X) : ephemerality (Y)** in:

```
         A    B            X           Y                              X
of: up : down : : permanency : ephemerality in "Like illumined pearls
                                                          A
(precious, fixed and permanent) the lamps shone from the summits of
     A   X                         Y          B
their tall poles (fixed) upon the living texture below, which, changing
        Y                              A
shape and hue unceasingly, sent up into the warm grey evening air an
                     X
unchanging, unceasing murmur
```

The single word "unceasing" reverses its meaning as it moves from the context "changing" to "unchanging." And are we to dismiss as accidents the phonological choices such as the reversal of "grey warm" in the first (subject) clause to "warm grey" in the final (adjunct) phrase or the choice of "swarmed" (rather than, say, "seethed" or "were full") in a sentence framed by sentences in which the syllable "warm" occurs three times? How can we avoid the elegiac connection between "a *memory* of summer" and "*shuttered* for the *repose* of Sunday" in a story which is itself an elegy to Dublin and to gallantry?

To map such linguistic patterning adequately for a whole story would be a lengthy, complex and, perhaps, self-defeating task. It seems worthwhile to remind ourselves, however, that a structural analysis, for all the wealth of insights it may provoke, will tend only to account for "integrative" features of style and that the reader's reconstruction of the meaning of the text as he reads depends at least as much on the "distributional" linguistic choices. Some attempt to describe both will unite the endeavours of structural poetics and New Criticism, and will do much to blunt the accusation of "reductionism."

3 Analytic and Synthetic Approaches to Narrative Structure
Sherlock Holmes and "The Sussex Vampire"

Introduction

In 1972 I was invited to contribute to an international conference on Style and Structure in Literature at the University of East Anglia. I was keen to test some of the analytical methods for prose narrative which I had been evolving with the Neo-Formalist Circle, which I had founded in the previous year. I had recently returned from a two-month research visit to Moscow, where I met one of the younger leading Russian structuralists, Alexander Zholkovsky, who, with his colleague Yurii Scheglov, was developing a very powerful model for generating narrative and dramatic texts from an underlying theme through a series of 'expressiveness devices.' Set to work on a Sherlock Holmes story, this made many points of comparison with my analytical approach.

Selections from the conference proceedings were published by Roger Fowler, the convenor of the conference, in a volume *Style and Structure in Literature: Essays in the New Stylistics*, Oxford: Basil Blackwell, 1975.

Writings of the Russian 'Structuralist Poetics' movement began to appear in the Soviet Union in the early 1960s, during the relatively liberal Khrushchev era. The movement gathered momentum throughout the decade in spite of increasing opposition from the academic 'lit. crit.' establishment who wielded a disproportionate amount of power in the institutes of the Academy of Science and on editorial boards.

Almost hermetically sealed off intellectually from the world outside the Soviet Union for more than twenty years, literary scholars with a commitment to 'poetika,' the close study of the literary text, were unable to keep in touch with—still less contribute to—the exciting developments of the 1930s and 1940s represented by 'Prague School' Structuralism and American 'New Criticism.' The debts they readily acknowledge is to the Russian Formalists of the 1920s who laid the foundations for new systemic ways of analysing literary texts and accounting for literature as a psychological and social phenomenon. In the study of the structure of narrative fiction the key Formalist figures were Shklovsky, Eikhenbaum, Propp and Tynyanov, with Vinogradov and Bakhtin active outside the movement proper. By its opponents, Formalism was seen as at once too radical (wedded as it was to the Futurist movement in poetry) and too reactionary (with a subtlety and flexibility in its approach to aesthetic and linguistic problems which betrayed the culture of its proponents as that of the pre-Revolutionary bourgeois intelligentsia rather than that of the emergent proletariat), and was virtually stamped out by 'proletkult' obscurantism by the end of the decade. In a similar way—but, perhaps, for less respectable ideological reasons—Russian Structuralism, too, has been seen as being too radical and even insidious by the conservative academic and literary establishment of the 1960s. This situation might seem to be exactly parallel to that of the French structuralists during the same period. In both countries a degree of academic notoriety has given the movement the moral advantage of being small, close-knit, relatively united ideologically and read avidly by younger students of literature. But there is a crucial difference in that individual structuralist critics in the Soviet Union have suffered the practical disadvantages of difficulties and delays in publishing their writings and in keeping in contact with fellow structuralists abroad, as well as having their books or symposia published in such absurdly small editions by state-owned publishing houses that they become bibliographical rarities as soon as they appear. If they operate from a rather restricted—and sometimes unexpected—range of university departments and research institutes, the best structuralists explore a vast range of related disciplines with impressive authority: general semiotics, the semiotics of literary forms, statistical literary studies, structural analyses of actual texts (usually from Russian literature and especially poetry, but happily encompassing Asian and African myths and even such exotica as the *Kama Sutra* and English limericks), the problems of versification, linguistic problems of style, the cinema and the visual arts, mythology and folk-lore. The Formalists of the 1920s have often been criticised for the excessive preoccupation some of them (notably Shklovsky in his more provocative early articles) showed with purely formal aspects of literary structure which they deliberately opposed to content and meaning. This may have been a necessary exaggeration at the beginning of the 1920s as they strove to propound a new way of looking at literary work, but it has given rise to an absurd amount of acrimonious and ill-founded disputation since that time and, more seriously, tends to mask the degree to which form and content are indissolubly linked. Just as linguistics can not limit itself for long to the study of syntax alone, but must constantly refer back to semantics, so poetics, studying the phenomenon of literary art where, by definition, meaning and form reach their highest degree of integration, must analyse not merely the formal patterns but what is being expressed by those patterns. Vice versa, the Formalists were right in insisting that for too long literary scholarship had concerned itself with nothing but content. As we shall see later, one definition of the literary work of art might be that it is the syntactic (formal) expression of a deep semantic opposition (in content).

Analysis

The way structuralist theory (from the Prague School onwards) improved Formalism by adding a semantic component may be illustrated by the case of the folk-tale. Vladimir Propp, in his seminal work *The Morphology of the Folk Tale*, deliberately strove to isolate the syntactic features of the folk-tale: only a characterisation of the thirty-one basic 'functions' and their interrelationship would produce a model abstract enough to be universally valid. To this extent Propp was right: the most complex attempts by his predecessors at cataloguing folk-tales in terms of the character of their participants had contributed little. But, as Claude Lévi-Strauss was quick to point out when the English translation of Propp's book appeared in 1958,

> while he is able to define primary functions by exclusively morphological criteria, for the sub-divisions Propp is obliged to introduce certain aspects of content so that the function 'treachery' has 22 sub-divisions which reintroduce actual situations and characters ... rather than surreptitiously reintegrate content into form, form has to be kept at such an abstract level that it almost loses significance. Formalism reduces its own object to nothing ... Before Formalism we certainly did not know what these tales had in common. After it we are deprived of all means of knowing how they differ. We have passed from concrete to abstract and can not get back ... Propp discovered (magnificently) that the content of tales is permutable. He came to the odd conclusion that the permutations were arbitrary and had no laws of their own.

Propp's model for the structure of the folk tale might be characterised as constituent structure grammar of narrative, consisting, as it does, of a series of functions, some obligatory, some optional, which 'slot in' to the text in a prescribed sequence. Victor Shklovsky proposed a similar 'constituent structure grammar' of the Sherlock Holmes detective story a few years before Propp's book appeared. As our discussion of analytic and synthetic approaches to narrative will be illustrated with reference to a Sherlock Holmes story, it would be appropriate to list Shklovsky's functions in detail:

I. Waiting, discussion of earlier cases, analysis.
II. Appearance of client. The story proper begins.
III. Narrated evidence. The crucial secondary facts given in such a way that the reader fails to notice them. Also material for false surmises.
IV. Watson interprets evidence wrongly.
V. Journey to the site of the crime: as this has often not yet been committed, the narrative is enlivened and the lines of the criminal's story and the detective's story merge. Evidence on the spot.
VI. An official police detective, if there is one, guesses wrongly, otherwise a newspaper, the victim, or Holmes himself, makes the wrong guess.

VII. An interval: Watson, not understanding Holmes's line of reasoning, tries to work things out. Holmes smokes or plays music. Sometimes he assembles groups of facts together without reaching any firm conclusion.
VIII. The denouement, usually sudden. Often an attempt to commit the crime is made at this point,
IX. Holmes' analysis of the facts.

Two of the Soviet structuralists, Alexander Zholkovsky and Yuri Scheglov, have paid tribute to Shklovsky and their other Formalist precursors in a paper given at one of the early conferences on structural poetics in 1961, but in their own work have rapidly moved away from the 'constituent structure grammar' of narrative and are regarded as the main exponents of the 'generative' model. As linguists they were well aware of the significance of the 'transformational-generative' revolution in linguistics, and their rather extreme stand in a semi-popular literary journal in 1967, *Structural poetics—generative poetics* (where the dash means 'is,' but implies 'should be,' not only upset many pillars of the establishment, but nettled some of their more moderate allies by its strident tone and a number of exaggerated claims). In a number of articles since, they have explored the implications of this new approach and experimented with mapping the 'transformational history' of narrative texts and episodes much as the generative linguist maps the transformational history of a sentence.

Theme

The starting point for such a process must be some kind of 'kernel' in the deep structure and the kernel of the literary work is what Zholkovsky and Scheglov call the 'theme.' This is not the theme in the popular meaning of the word, some kind of 'digest' of the plot, but a scientific abstraction, a formulation in a more or less abstract 'metalanguage' of the irreducible meaning of the text. In their most recent article they discuss the concept of 'theme' in some detail, seeing it as a 'primary element' out of which the whole literary text is expanded, via a variety of devices or processes ('priyomy'—a favourite word of the Formalists) such as plot-building and realisation in terms of the character, setting, properties, etc. 'The theme is linked to the text not by an "equals" sign, but by an inference arrow, or, seen the other way round, "the theme is the text minus the devices," or, more precisely—if ponderously, "the theme is that invariant of which everything in a work is a variation but which can not itself be represented as a variant of any more abstract invariant."[1]

How near to the work itself will our exploration of the generation of a given sequence of textual elements out of some highly abstract theme actually take us? Although Zholkovsky and Scheglov have so far confined themselves largely to illustrating how elements of plot, character and the object world are generated through various operations on the theme, there need be no reason in principle why this process should not be extended all the way to the generation of actual linguistic structures in the text. Some of these will relate directly to (be generated directly from) the deep 'theme' while others will relate directly to intermediate stages in the process 'theme → text.' As we hope to show, it will be possible in this way to account adequately for many features of the style of a work.

The theme itself is not discovered through the generative process. Zholkovsky and Scheglov are not very explicit about how one arrives at the statement of the theme, but imply that a combination of analysis and intuition enables one to make a provisional statement, a hypothesis which can then be tested through the process of synthesizing the text (a 'hermeneutic spiral'?). With certain types of narrative genre the analysis needed to arrive at a satisfactory theme may be extremely complex. In order to focus the discussion primarily on the synthesis we have chosen a short, highly integrated, almost schematically simple, example of a highly stylised genre. "The Sussex Vampire," one of Conan Doyle's later stories, from *The Case-Book of Sherlock Holmes*, is so neat in its structure, and so mannered in its style that one is tempted to suspect Conan Doyle of mocking his readers (and himself) with a piece of self-parody. We have chosen it above all because it is a whole story: up to the 1970s Zholkovsky and Scheglov tended to experiment in their articles with synthesizing only fragments of whole works, short anecdotes or individual episodes. Scheglov's (1968) description of detective story structure deals in detail only with the 'outer story' or prelude to Sherlock Holmes stories, i.e., the coming together of Holmes, Watson and the client and the initial narration of the problem situation before the investigation proper begins. Although this restriction is deliberate, and, perhaps, necessary in the first stages of testing a new model, the full generative potential needs to be demonstrated at every stage in the synthesis of a complete work.

An analytic approach will help us at this stage to explore the structure of the story in sufficient detail to arrive at a provisional statement of the theme. This framework which I have been testing using a number of categories proposed by the Formalists has proved useful in the analysis of more complex types of short story. This analytic approach also starts from a provisional and very flexible statement of theme, testing it against various structures in the work represented by the labels: *Fable, Plot, Narrative Structure, Points of View, Character* and *Setting*. This approach is analogous to the kind of functional models in linguistics developed by the Prague School linguists and by M.A.K. Halliday in that it starts with an examination of features and relationships in the surface structure of the text and systematically penetrates to deeper and more subtle ones. While dealing with formal syntactic categories, it treats form and meaning as inseparable, every formal choice (by language-user or literary artist) inevitably involving a semantic decision.

Something we have to take into account in stating the theme of any single Sherlock Holmes story is that it is one of a vast series of a very highly stylised and conventionally structured type. The five books of short stories contain no less than fifty-six stories and one has, therefore, to think simultaneously in terms of an underlying theme for the individual story that should be consistent for the whole series. A formula which seems to me to offer an axis that maintains unity and consistency of meaning, not only in "The Sussex Vampire" but through all the Sherlock Holmes stories is *the triumph of reason over the irrational*. The stories were written, like most popular works of suspense, detection and fantastic adventure, to titillate the reader's imagination with irrational fears and superstitions which they then reassuringly allay with rational, down-to-earth explanations. Sherlock Holmes, Conan Doyle's epitome of the rational, is explicit about this when he reacts to the various terrifying legends about vampires by demanding: "But are we to give serious attention to such things? This Agency stands flat-footed on the ground, and there it must remain. The world is big enough for us. No ghosts need apply." If there is one phrase that sums up Holmes for every Englishman, even if he has never read any of the stories, it is "Elementary, my dear Watson." Here this is elaborated to:

> [Ferguson said,] "It must be an exceedingly delicate and complex affair from your point of view."
> "It is certainly delicate," said my friend, with an amused smile, "but I have not been struck up to now with its complexity. It has been a case for intellectual deduction, but when this original intellectual deduction is confirmed point by point by quite a number of independent incidents, then the subjective becomes objective and we can say confidently that we have reached our goal."
>
> (p. 1189)

Fable

The Fable ('fabula' in Formalist theory) is the raw material of situations and events in their original chronological order. It is not a synopsis of the story in the sequence in which events occur from page to page. How does "The Sussex Vampire" look if we see all the events in their chronological order? Certainly very different, because many of the vital elements are only seen in 'flashbacks.' Quite often the reconstruction of the Fable is not a particularly interesting part of the analysis of a short story, except that it provides a point of reference for the order of events as actually narrated. In the detective story it is very important because every stage in the *present* of the story is designed to throw further light on certain aspects of the past (except where the author lays false clues which obscure or confuse the significance of past events). The typical Sherlock Holmes story, in fact, involves two time sequences: that lived by the detective (in this case Holmes and Watson together), and that lived by the client whose past has its own distinct chronology. The two chronologies merge once the investigation gets under way, except that it is important if tension is to be sustained, for the detective to be felt to be one step ahead of his client (with us, the readers, perhaps, half a step between them, half-conscious of the way his deductions are leading, pleasantly mystified, yet gratified by our superiority over the client and the stooge, Dr Watson). Each new stage of the investigation then fills in some more important details about the past of the client and his problem.

I have attempted in Figure 3.1 to map out these two chronologies in detail. The horizontal axis represents the time sequence of the events which we experience with, and through, Watson and Holmes. Here the major 'functions' are boxed and in heavy type. Each of these leads on to some disclosure which fulfils its detective story role by simultaneously revealing some extra information and deepening the mystery (at least for Watson and us, the readers). The first three 'functions' are used to provide necessary background knowledge to the case. They therefore have no content in themselves except as acts of reading or conversing. Their factual content lies along the vertical axis, the time sequence of the client, Ferguson. As will be clear if we compare the columns A, B and C, each successive stage of the contact with the client gives us a more detailed knowledge of the period anterior to the opening of the story. Yet the details only mystify.

With the 'Visit' to the scene of the crime the two time-axes merge and the events are experienced simultaneously (though not, of course, with equal understanding) by Ferguson, Watson and Holmes. Retrospectively, i.e., above the horizontal, there is a further focus on those facts about the past which may provide a vital clue.

The 'Explanation' naturally only consists of past events illuminated in a crucially new way. With the 'Epilogue' the two time sequences continue along their separate dimensions.

Plot

The nine functions which Shklovsky distilled from the Sherlock Holmes corpus are not pure Fable, since they include flashbacks in the form of narrated evidence at several points. They are rather components of *Plot*, which may be defined as the *causal* unfolding of the narrative. The interplay between temporal and causal sequence, between *Fable* and *Plot*, varies widely with different genres of prose narrative. If the Fable is temporality as perceived by the characters, Plot is causality only partly (and sometimes not at all) perceived by the characters, but gradually reconstructed by the reader. In our classic detective story we create chains of cause and effect out of interlocking patterns of motive and material, spatial and temporal evidence; the Plot is partly perceived through our reconstruction of the Fable. Holmes tantalises his client and us with some partial reconstruction of this kind. Time becomes a crucial aspect of causality:

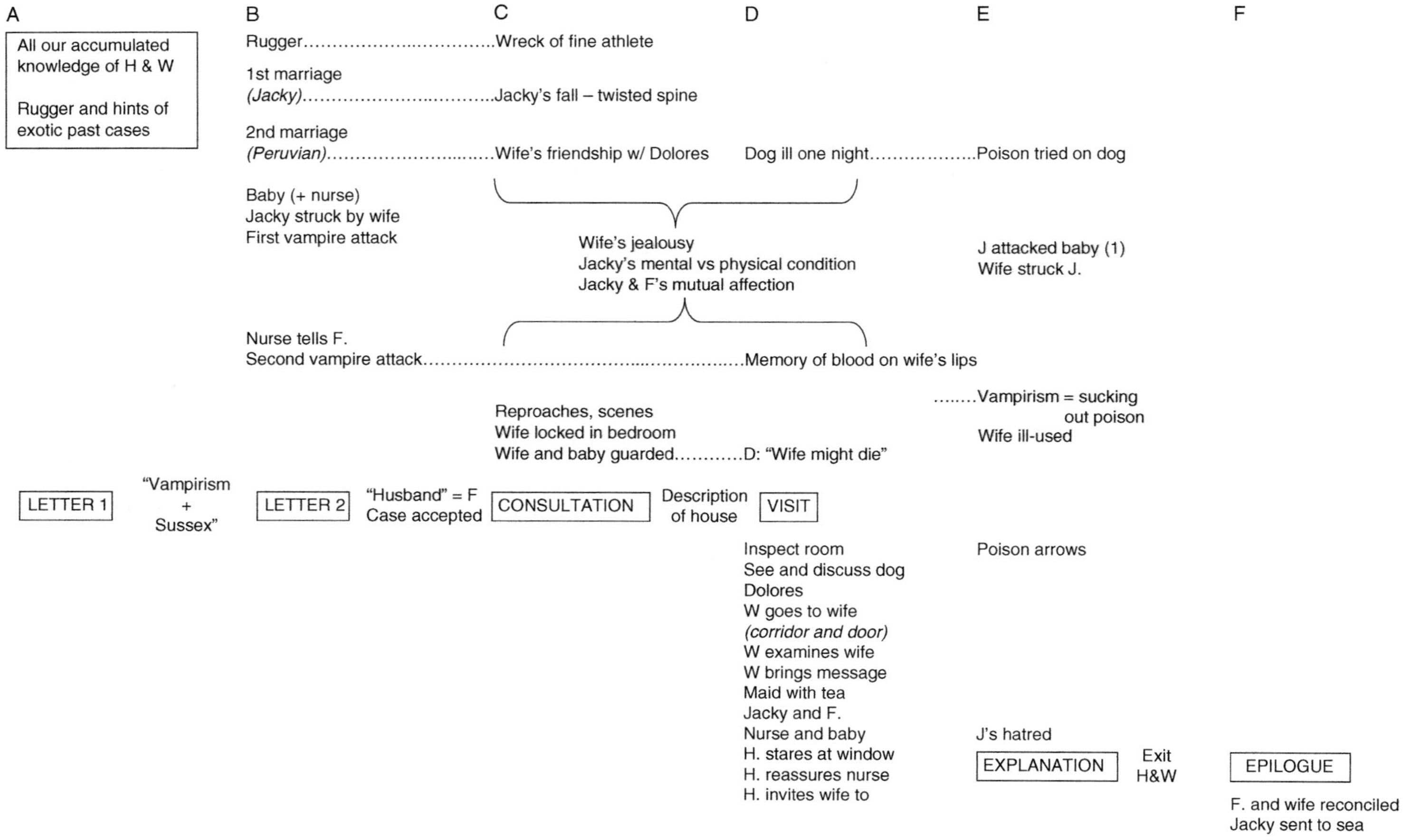

	A	B	C	D	E	F
	All our accumulated knowledge of H & W	Rugger............	....Wreck of fine athlete			
		1st marriage (*Jacky*)............	....Jacky's fall – twisted spine			
	Rugger and hints of exotic past cases	2nd marriage (*Peruvian*)............	....Wife's friendship w/ Dolores	Dog ill one night............	....Poison tried on dog	
		Baby (+ nurse) Jacky struck by wife First vampire attack	⎫ ⎬ Wife's jealousy ⎬ Jacky's mental vs physical condition ⎭ Jacky & F's mutual affection		J attacked baby (1) Wife struck J.	
		Nurse tells F. Second vampire attack............	....Memory of blood on wife's lips			
			Reproaches, scenes Wife locked in bedroom Wife and baby guarded............	....D: "Wife might die"	....Vampirism = sucking out poison Wife ill-used	
"Vampirism + Sussex"			Description of house	VISIT		
LETTER 1	LETTER 2	"Husband" = F Case accepted	CONSULTATION	Inspect room See and discuss dog Dolores W goes to wife (*corridor and door*) W examines wife W brings message Maid with tea Jacky and F. Nurse and baby H. stares at window H. reassures nurse H. invites wife to	Poison arrows	
					J's hatred	
				EXPLANATION	Exit H&W	EPILOGUE
						F. and wife reconciled Jacky sent to sea

Figure 3.1 Detection Timeline

58   *Literary Narrative*

"What is it, Mr. Holmes?"
"The dog. What's the matter with it?"
"That's what puzzled the vet. A sort of paralysis. Spinal meningitis, he thought. But it's passing. He'll be all right soon—won't you Carlo?" ...
"Did it come on suddenly?"
"In a single night."
"How long ago?"
"It may have been four months ago."
"Very remarkable. Very suggestive."

Narrative Structure

Fable and Plot, then, are interacting chains but they do not make a story. This is the function of the Narrative Structure which builds events into an easily perceived and graspable pattern. The fundamental pattern for Narrative Structure in the short story and in chapters or episodes of the novel is that of Complication—Peripeteia—Denouement, where the Complication represents some kind of disturbance of a previously prevailing inertia, the Peripeteia a switch from this disturbed state to the state which prevails finally, which may be the same as that before the story opened or some new state. We may define the short story as an idea given dynamic form; dynamic involves movement and this movement may be physical or psychological. We formulated the theme of "The Sussex Vampire" provisionally as a semantic opposition: the Irrational/Reason. If we replace the oblique stroke by an arrow we have the bare bones of narrative structure, perhaps best summed up in a word by the *verbal noun* 'rationalisation.'

The point at which the Peripeteia occurs is crucial to our understanding of the theme: indeed, in many subtly complex modern short stories initial statements of theme are frequently proved wrong or inadequate by the discovery of new peripeteia. In our detective story this point of change occurs very near the end, although, if the author has played fair, it should have been anticipated by certain deductions that we and the detective can make on the strength of what we learn earlier. The complication, then, is the mystery, the irrational terror of apparent vampirism in the heart of the Sussex weald, which is resolved with a perfectly reasonable explanation in the denouement, as Holmes' hypothesis is borne out by the glimpse of the hatred on Jacky's face seen reflected in a shuttered window.

With most types of short story it is useful to follow Petrovsky in setting the basic narrative structure of Complication—Peripeteia—Denouement within a framework of Prologue and Epilogue, in each of which we can usually distinguish two phases, the general and the specific. The General Prologue here consists of all the relevant facts from beyond the past of the story—all we already know of Holmes and Watson, their earlier cases which are mentioned, their relations with the machinery firm (the kind of exquisite irrelevance with which Conan Doyle frequently embellishes his prologues) and what we learn of Watson's youthful encounters with Ferguson on the rugby field. Some detective stories use vital aspects of the General Prologue as clues or motives in the main plot, but this is not the case in "The Sussex Vampire." The Specific Prologue is the way Holmes and Watson get involved in the case of the Sussex Vampire: the two letters and Ferguson's visit to fill in the details of the case. As Scheglov demonstrates, such prologues in the Sherlock Holmes stories are all variations on a pattern. Conan Doyle has to get his heroes acquainted with the background of each new case and the victim-hero. Usually they are at home in Baker Street when they get a startling letter followed by an interview (as here), or a coach pulls up, a ring at the doorbell is followed by a clattering up the stairs and the visitor is shown in to tell their story. There are all kinds of permutations of the details: Watson or Holmes may be preoccupied with something else when the interruption occurs; stormy weather outside increases the air of tension and expectancy; the visitor is variously greeted and welcomed to the fireside by Holmes; the latter makes various deductions about the client's job, way of life, recent activities, or state of health from his minute observation of his/her clothes, fingernails, hair etc. But basically all of the details are embellishments of the crucial mechanism of getting Holmes and Watson in on a new case.

The Epilogues may be similarly divided into Specific (the immediate future) and General (the longer term future) and may also be embellished to a greater or lesser degree. Here, however, there is no longer the need to transmit a lot of basic facts, to leave clues, or lay false trails, so the Epilogues are quite brief and factual—enough to dispose of the characters whose future is insufficiently resolved by the denouement: Ferguson and his wife are left embracing, Holmes and Watson tiptoe out of the bedroom with the ever-faithful maid, Dolores, and Jacky, we presume, will soon be packed off to the Merchant Navy for a spot of discipline. Finally (General Epilogue), back at the famous apartment, Holmes writes a letter in answer to the enquiry with which the story opened—a nice gratuitously circular touch, restoring the reassuring inertia of life with its 'feet firmly on the ground' as lived in the Edwardian image of London. Meanwhile, Watson, we presume, sits down to write up his latest case for the famous Case-Book.

Point of View

The most intriguing level of analysis is *Point of View*. There are so many subtle variations in the type of narrator who may be chosen and in the way he or she stands in relation to the events and the other characters that the possibilities are virtually infinite.[2] It is simply not enough to attach a label marked 'First-person narrator' or 'third-person omniscient' as some textbooks do. Many modern short stories since Chekhov have used the 'third person, limited omniscient' point of view, which has been defined as follows: 'The author narrates the story in the third person, but chooses one character as his "sentient center" whom he follows throughout the action, restricting

60 *Literary Narrative*

the reader to the field of vision and range of knowledge of that character alone.' But how much more is learned about such a story by applying the label? The necessary information is not who held the camera, but his angle and distance from the subject at any particular moment, his 'aperture' (or receptiveness), his 'focus' (or clarity of vision) and 'shutter speed' (or intelligence). The author may adjust these at different points in the story and the pattern of his adjustments will probably bear some relation to elements in the Narrative Structure, as well as affecting the linguistic texture. (See Chapter 1 on Chekhov's story "The Student.")

Now Conan Doyle uses Watson as a first person narrator of distinctly limited omniscience. Everything we learn is first distilled via his own down-to-earth, literal-minded perception (in a sense he is the epitome—or reduction ad absurdum—of the 'Reason' pole of our thematic opposition; Holmes, although he reintroduces reason into wildly irrational situations, usually relies on a flash of the irrational inspiration of the creative genius for making all the facts and motives fall into place). Watson is the perfect stooge for the brilliant, mercurial Holmes, plodding along after a trail of clues, many of them false, missing the vital things that Holmes takes in at a glance and noticing irrelevant things which will lead us astray for a while:

> "Of course I remember him," said I, as I laid down the letter. "Big Bob Ferguson, the finest three-quarter Richmond ever had. He was always a good-natured chap. It's like him to be concerned over a friend's case."
>
> Holmes looked at me thoughtfully and shook his head. "I never get your limits, Watson," said he. "There are unexplored possibilities about you. Take a wire down, like a good fellow. "'Will examine your case with pleasure."'
>
> "*Your* case!"
>
> "We must not let him think that this Agency is a home for the weak-minded. Of course it is his case. Send him that wire and let the matter rest till morning."

Holmes' explicit irony at Watson's expense—Watson, with his 'unexplored possibilities' is the only one who might be suspected of weak-mindedness—is carried implicitly by reference to their 'Agency,' something much too official and institutionalised to represent adequately Holmes' approach to detection.

Watson's interpretations of what Holmes is up to also confuse the situation very conveniently and allow Conan Doyle to lay the beginnings of a trail without giving the secret away before Holmes can produce his final conjuring trick with the complete explanation:

> It was at this moment that I chanced to glance at Holmes, and saw a most singular intentness in his expression. His face was set as if it had been carved out of old ivory, and his eyes, which had glanced for a moment at father and child, were now fixed with eager curiosity upon

something at the other side of the room. Following his gaze I could only guess that he was looking out of the window at the melancholy, dripping garden. It is true that a shutter had half closed outside and obstructed the view, but none the less is was certainly at the window that Holmes was fixing his concentrated attention.

We do not, of course, discover until later that this is Holmes' crucial glimpse of Jack's look of jealousy and hatred that solves the mystery, but we are alerted by the very explicit restrictions on Watson's point of view: "fixed upon something…," "It is true that…," "none the less is was certainly…," and even by Watson's rare, if rather mundane, flight of fancy about the old ivory.

One of the other delights of the problem of Point of View is that modern authors can very rarely resist drawing our attention to what they are doing, to the relationship between the assumptions operating within the framework of the story and those of the real world outside. This is taken so far in some cases that a whole story becomes a kind of dialogue between the narrator's view of the world and the view of the world the author assumes us to have, In a way, the author invents his reader as well as his narrator. Even in the relatively straightforward Sherlock Holmes stories we find a little of this interplay. The way Holmes teases Watson and casts doubts on his reliability as an observer and chronicler of events (where he is the only observer and chronicler we, as readers, have available), is an example of a temporary break in the Point of View framework: the created character, Holmes, is talking over the head of another created character, Watson, and addressing us, the readers, outside the story, directly. Watson's failure to recognise that the husband described in the letter is Ferguson himself is a case in point. And as he reads through the accounts of past cases in the volume marked V, he reads:

> "Voyage of the *Gloria Scott* … That was a bad business. I have some recollection that you made a record of it, Watson, though I was unable to congratulate you on the result."

Although Watson is the one we are bound to trust for our information, he is not particularly trustworthy! Our minds and imaginations will be delightfully engaged in disentangling the truth and the distortion from the narrator's record as well as from the facts and evidence of other characters.[3]

Character

It is clear from our discussion of Point of View how Holmes and Watson are designed completely as foils for each other. This is a universal throughout the series. If we analyse the problem of *Character* in "The Sussex Vampire,"[4] Ferguson and his wife are also foils for each other: Ferguson is so obvious, so English, so respectable, so recognisable, so easy to identify with, while

62   *Literary Narrative*

his wife (who is the only character in the story who is given no name—'Mrs Ferguson' would hardly do!) is dark, mysterious, passionate, foreign, alien to our (i.e., Holmes' and Watson's) way of life and full of potential threat, until we eventually learn how nobly she has been hiding the truth.

Most of the other characters, as usual in detective stories, simultaneously fulfil their functions as nurses, maids, offspring, pets, etc., and as potential villains. They are part of the pattern of true and false clues that we grope our way through and Conan Doyle is very skilful in making Watson introduce them all equally carefully and dispassionately.

Setting

The *Setting*, too, is full of true and false clues: which are we to look at most closely in the large central room at Ferguson's home—the panelling on the walls, the modern watercolours, or the South American utensils and weapons? It turns out to be the latter, and we would have realised this if we were alert when Holmes' particular interest in them is alluded to. But it could have been the others. And again, what is the relevance of the shuttered window through which Holmes gazes so intently,[5] or is it another false clue like the door leading to Ferguson's wife's room?

> I followed the girl who was quivering with strong emotion, up the staircase and down an ancient corridor. At the end was an iron-clamped and massive door. It struck me as I looked at it that if Ferguson tried to force his way to his wife he would find it no easy matter. The girl drew a key from her pocket, and the heavy oaken planks creaked upon their old hinges.

Apart from clues for the detection plot, the setting is most relevant to the theme. The very title of the story presents the basic opposition: *The Sussex Vampire*—what an oxymoron! The mysterious, threatening, terrifying, bloodthirsty world of vampires, normally restricted to Gothic castles in Hungary, Transylvania and other outlandishly un-English places. But all this in Sussex? In one of the cosiest and most familiar of the 'Home' Counties? In a part of England that is "full of old houses which are named after the men who built them centuries ago. You get Odley's and Harvey's and Carriton's—the folk are forgotten but their names live in their houses"? Admittedly, Ferguson's house, like the man himself, is "large and straggling, very old at the centre. Very new at the wings" and "the floors sagged into sharp curves," but it still has "towering Tudor chimneys and a lichen-spotted, high pitched roof of Horsham slabs," and the ancient tiles which lined the porch still bear the original builder's trademark. A house, in a word, in the best of English traditions, secure in the clay weald between the North and the South Downs, not an hour's journey from safe-old, cosy-old London! Whatever could vampires be doing here?

The setting seen in this light appears to substantiate Scheglov's formulation of the underlying theme of the Sherlock Holmes stories as the opposition

Security/Adventure (here he is referring particularly to the 'outer,' or 'basic' story prior to the appearance of an individual client):

> The theme as a whole could be labelled 'security complex,' and its subthemes respectively—'possession of security' and 'provision of security' . . .

The basic requirement for building the world of Holmes and Watson (in its personal aspect) is that these characters, their activity, way of life, pastimes, interests, the accessories which surround them, etc., should combine the two opposing principles:

1. adventure, dangers, changes of fortune, movement, drama;
2. comfort, safety, domestic convenience, tranquillity, satisfaction;

It is the writer's task to look for conditions which will permit the foreground heroes (i.e., Holmes and Watson) simultaneously to receive a physical and spiritual 'shock' by getting involved in all kinds of dramas and adventures and yet not quit their normal element, not to yield in any way their accustomed comforts, to enjoy full immunity. What is more, taking part in the drama which for the other directly interested characters may mean risking their lives, or at any rate security, family happiness or honour, must be for our heroes just a game, an amusement, a hedonistic pastime. This world, uniting the terrifying and the safe, movement with tranquillity, discomfort with comfort, offers a combination of conditions in which the most sober of citizens would agree, would even volunteer, to have adventures and to come face-to-face with danger and horrors and so on. The ethos of Holmes' and Watson's world is an ethos of 'excitement on the cheap.'

This theme is a sort of utopia created on behalf of the comfortably-off Victorian man-in-the-street the educated middle-class, small shopkeepers, men of property, etc. The theme is a product of the world-view peculiar to this social stratum: on the one hand, an attachment to his calm, enlightened, law-protected life and to the civilisation and progress which guarantee this comfort; on the other hand, a bit of 'romance,' excitement, contact with other, more cruel and sadistic, fiercer modes of conduct, in particular, the crime report provided John Citizen with his most vivid excitement."

Scheglov argues cogently for his 'Adventure/Security' formulation of the theme in terms of character, setting, etc. within the 'outer' story, but does not, perhaps, take fully into account the basic and universal mechanism of the detective genre—the intellectual pleasure the reader has in weighing the evidence in terms of facts and motives as the story proper progresses and in enjoying finally the elegant rationalisation of apparently irrational behaviour. In some sense this opposition of the Irrational versus Reason is at a deeper thematic level than Scheglov's and is just as easy to relate to the unconscious needs of a positivist-minded educated middle-class reading public in Victorian and Edwardian England. If one confines one's analysis

64 *Literary Narrative*

and synthesis to the prologue of the stories as Scheglov does, i.e., to the interplay between Holmes and Watson and the stages in the appearance of the client preceding the exposition and investigation of the case proper, the focus is too strongly on Holmes and Watson and on the emotional content of the notions of Security, Comfort, etc. The fascination of the stories considered as whole units (and is it, in fact, valid to generate only a part, however consistently and predictably it recurs, from a 'theme' which is, by definition, relevant to the whole?) is surely in the mechanism of the deductive process whereby a rational solution is reached from an apparently irreconcilable mass of conflicting evidence.

We will attempt, therefore, to generate elements in the structure and text of "The Sussex Vampire" out of our theme (the Irrational/Reason), seeing Scheglov's 'Security/Adventure' opposition rather as a first-stage realisation of our more abstract formulation. We will follow as far as possible the principles which Zholkovsky and Scheglov have outlined in their papers, while representing the various stages in the generative process more schematically than they have done. This should clarify both the essential nature of the operations involved and the way they function in a particular case. The main operations that the two Russians have distinguished so far are shown in Figure 3.2 in the order: Symbol (our convention)—Name of operation (the translation we have adopted)—Transcription of the original Russian term—Alternative translations (in some cases).

1. (realisation):

   Irrational/Rational → Adventure/Security

2. (multiple realisation):

   Adventure → exotic (A), sick (C)
   Security → maternal love (B), filial love (D)

(We may point out here, in order not to have to make the qualification at every stage in the generation, that the elements resulting from a realisation of a realisation still contain elements crucial to the original theme.

+	Combination	Sovmeschenie	-
→	Realization	Razvyertyvanie	unfolding, elaboration
<	Reinforcement	Usilenie	intensification, strangthening
||	Repetition	Povtorenie	-
/	Juxtaposition	Protivopostavlenie	-
{ }	Multiple Realization	Vypolnenie odnoi I toi zhe funkstii tselym ryadom	Fulfilment of one and the same function by a number of means
⇒	Becomes, is transformed to		

Figure 3.2 Expressiveness Devices

Analytic and Synthetic Approaches 65

This must be true by definition of the relationship between generated element and theme. So 'exotic' in the world of Holmes and Watson subsumes semantic components like 'foreign, alien, un-English, incomprehensible, threatening' and therefore viewed *irrationally*; similarly 'sick' subsumes 'abnormal, alien, contagious, impenetrable, threatening'; whereas 'maternal love' and 'filial love' in their normal, non-pathological manifestations are essentially *'reasonable'* emotions. The letters A, B, C, and D which we use to label the elements are merely a convenient shorthand to save lengthy repetition at later stages.)

3. (combination and realisation)

    A + B → Senora Ferguson
    C + D → Jacky Ferguson

(This stage in the generation provides a starting-point for both characterisation and plot. We may assume that a complex generative process takes place simultaneously on several levels, as in the author's mind, rather than linearly, as here. For convenience we will outline the generation of the plot first and then characterisation, without, however, making any assumptions about the order of these two sets of operations.)

4. (combination) Add the plotting elements of detective fiction as a genre:

    Mystery → Apparent (X)/Real(Y)

(The diagram from Zholkovsky and Scheglov (1967, op. cit.) shown in Figure 3.3, indicates how they conceive the relationship between universal genre elements and elements peculiar to a particular writer's canon)

This combination gives the following range of possibilities:

(a) AY + BX (Senora Ferguson = villain)/AX + BY (Senora Ferguson = innocent)
(b) CY + DX (Jacky = villain)/CX + DY (Jacky = innocent)

5. (combination and juxtaposition):

    Ferguson's hypothesis: (AY+BX) + (CX+DY)/Holmes' explanation: (AX+BY) + (CY+DX)

6. (realisation):

    Replace (/) above by (⇒) and a semantic opposition becomes a syntactic process: the static becomes a dynamic:

    (AY+BX) + (CX+DY) ⇒ (AX+BY) + (CY+DX)

7. (reinforcement):

    AY + BX < vampirism
    AX + BY < warm Latin love
    CY + DX < crippled soul
    CX + DY < dearest, most loving heart

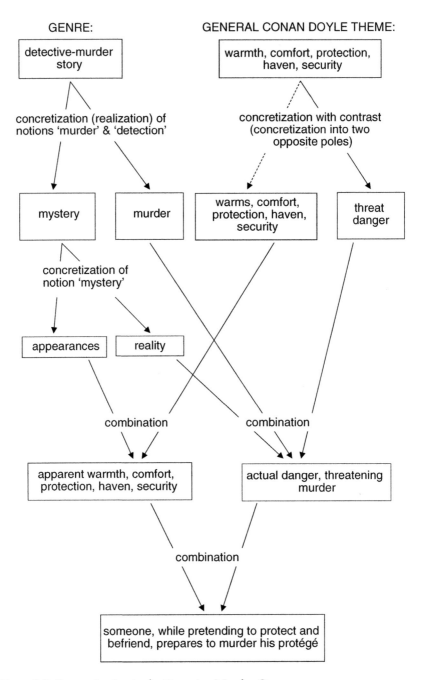

Figure 3.3 Concretisation in the Detective-Murder Genre

Analytic and Synthetic Approaches 67

(It might be argued here that this reinforcement need apply only to one of the elements, i.e., given AY (the reality of the exotic element), do we need BX (apparent maternal love)? We do, because, as the next stage (8) shows, each of these separate elements is elaborated at some point in the plot, characterisation or setting, or through combinations of these, and in the very language of the text.)

8. (realisation of each element through plot, character, setting and language)

AY →

Plot:

£5 for nurse's silence
Vampirism—some wild tale of foreign parts
"As if some frenzy had seized her"
"How do I know what strange impulse might come upon her?"

Character:

Peruvian: foreign birth and alien religion
Sides of her character which F. could never explore or understand
Traits alien to (BY) her ordinarily sweet and gentle disposition
Jealous with all the strength of her fiery tropical love
Frightened but (AX) beautiful eyes … flushed and (AX) handsome face
"She is ill but (AX) she is quite rational" (Watson)
Dolores as extension of Senora F.—A friend rather than a servant ("wife's character would really be better known by D. than you?"), tall, slim, brown-faced girl; indignant eyes; quivering with strong emotion; foreign accent
Dog = 'Carlo'

Setting:

Fine collection of South American utensils and weapons
Curare or some other devilish drug
Vampirism—And yet here in the very heart of English Sussex

BX →

Plot:

Assaulting the poor lad in an unprovoked way
Biting the baby's neck
Mother waiting to get at baby
"Day and night the silent, watchful mother seemed to be lying in wait.…"
Blood all round her lips
Small angry red pucker → (BY) upon the cherub throat
Sucking blood → (BY) sucking wound to draw poison

68   Literary Narrative

Character:

"As a wolf waits for a lamb"
Jealousy of stepmothers
Again and again said she hated Jacky

Setting:

Nursery (scene of vampirism)
Senora F's room as prison/haven

AX →

Character:

Very beautiful
As loving a wife as a man could have
"She is the most loving woman"
Beautiful eyes ... handsome face

BY →

Plot:

"Do I not love him—even to sacrifice myself rather than break his dear heart."
"I want the child. I have a right to my child."
"Cut to the heart."
Assaults take different forms: a real clue (maternal ≠ stepmotherly) upon the cherub throat—(BX) small angry pucker
Sucking wound to draw poison ⇒ (BX) sucking blood

Character:

"If ever a woman loved a man with all her heart and soul, she loves me."
"A loving mother, (BX) save for assaults on stepson."
"(Why wound—BX)—dear little baby?"
"Cut to the heart."

Setting:

Position at cot-side

CX →

Character:

Unhappily injured
Poor inoffensive cripple
Fall in childhood twisted spine
Shambling gait etc.

DY →

Plot:

Flame of emotion and joy on seeing father
Boy cooed and nestled his head on father's breast

Character:

Charming and affectionate
"Dearest, most loving heart"
Affection ... great comrades
Devotion to memory of his mother

Setting:

Comfortable drawing-room over tea

DX →

Plot:

Assaulted twice
Tried poison on dog
Pricked child with poison arrow

Character:

Probably very developed in mind since his body circumscribed action

CY →

Plot:

Penetrating and unfriendly gaze
Hatred and jealousy glimpsed on face in window reflection

Character:

Maniacal, exaggerated love for Ferguson and his dead mother.

It will be clear from many of these elements that the combinations tend to generate pairs of opposing features: "wild tale of foreign parts/and yet here in the very heart of English Sussex"; "frightened/but beautiful"; "flushed/and handsome face"; "a loving mother/save for assaults on her stepson"; "traits alien to/ordinarily sweet and gentle disposition"; "Not very prepossessing externally/but a heart of gold, and devoted to the child," etc. Stylistically, then, many elements of plot, character and setting are presented in oxymoron-type structures reminiscent of the story's title. We will consider the implications of this after completing some further stages in the generative process:

70   *Literary Narrative*

9. (combination of clue elements):
   - (a) Weapons, whereby AY ⇒ AX + DX
   - (b) Dog, whereby CX ⇒ CY + DX
   - (c) Window, whereby DY ⇒ CY + DX
   - (d) Baby's neck, whereby AY ⇒ BY + DX

   All of these now point to the reality of Jacky's sickness (DX_ and the perversion of filial love (CY).

10. (reinforcement) enrich the mixture by strengthening:

    'Security' element in: Ferguson's character and background; London and Sussex setting; Holmes' and Watson's attitude.
    'Adventure' element in: Ferguson's changed persona; Dog; 'Walk-on parts' (nurse, Dolores); Watson's and Ferguson's hypothesis.

11. (realisation) all these elements in a style which is marked by alternations of the dramatic and the reassuring, of doubt or fear (in the speech and thoughts of Ferguson and Watson) and rationality and common sense (with Holmes).

It would be absurd to claim that all the elements of structure, let alone all the elements of style are generated automatically and in a strictly premeditated way as if a computer were programmed to churn out Sherlock Holmes stories. Scheglov appears to be tempted by the mechanistic fallacy when he suggests that:

> a practical extension to descriptions of this kind would be the creation of 'new Sherlock Holmes stories' (attempts of this kind have, of course, often been made, and with some success, although they have not been based on any such clearly formulated rules). To achieve this, however, a great deal of work is needed to formalise the rules (if we have in mind the automatic rather than 'manual' generation of stories).[6]
>
> (1967, p. 80)

—as if every theoretical discovery in science must instantly start spawning a new technology! No, the measure of the generative poetics hypothesis, as both Zholkovsky and Scheglov are normally at pains to make clear, is in its explanatory adequacy and descriptive power. Does it assist in explaining such relationships in a literary work as those between 'theme' and 'text,' between 'form' and 'content,' between the various devices a writer has at his disposal in delineating and mutually reinforcing plot, character, setting and so on? Does it enable us to account more adequately for the way certain underlying—and, at present, hypothetical—authorial skills, whether conscious or unconscious ('competence'), produce particular observable effects, and patterns in a literary text ('performance')? Does it provide systematic concepts and a terminology which help in the description of the work itself, of the process of communication in literature?

Analytic and Synthetic Approaches 71

We have noted that a recurrent feature of the language in which characters are described is a pattern of antithesis. But this pattern is so marked at various linguistic levels throughout the greater part of this story that it becomes a kind of 'dominant.' Some examples at the levels of nominal or adverbial phrase, clause and even paragraph will make clear how dominant is this juxtaposition of opposing notions of the rational and the irrational, of safety and adventure. We will use Scheglov's notation, S (security, safety) and A (adventure) to characterise the halves of the antithesis:

PHRASE:

      S   A
For a mixture of the *modern* / and the *mediaeval*
   S   A
of the *practical* / and of the *wildly fanciful*
      S   A
communication of even date / concerning *vampires*
    A   S
Ferguson's *gaunt* features / *softened*
    A   S
a pair of *frightened* / but *beautiful* eyes
   A   S
her *flushed* / and *handsome* face
        S   A
I could not see *honest Bob Ferguson* / in the character of *fiend or devil*
    S   A
a very *penetrating* / and, as it seemed to me, *unfriendly* gaze
     A   S
small, *angry red pucker* / upon the *cherub* throat
   S   A
on its *chubby* neck / there was this small *puckered mark*
     S   A
Ferguson put *his big hand* / to his *furrowed forehead*
      S   A
a cry in which *joy* / and *surprise* seemed to be blended

CLAUSE:

A	S
It was a ship which was associated with the *giant rat of Sumatra*	/ a story for which the *world* is *not yet prepared*
S	**A**
Anything is better than *stagnation*	/ but really we seem to have been switched on to a *Grimm's fairy tale*

72 Literary Narrative

S The world is *big enough* for us	/	A *No ghosts need apply*
S a smile of *amusement* upon his face which gradually faded away	/	A into an expression of intense *interest and concentration*
A a *Peruvian* lady, the daughter of a Peruvian merchant	/	S whom he had met in connection with the *importation of nitrates*
S The lady was *very beautiful*	/	A but for the fact of her *foreign birth* and of her *alien religion*
A began to show some *curious* traits	/	S quite alien to her ordinarily *sweet and gentle disposition*
S a very *charming and affectionate* youth	/	A though *unhappily injured* through an *accident* in childhood
S Day and night the nurse *covered* the child	/	A and day and night the silent, watchful mother seemed to be *lying in wait as a wolf waits for a lamb*
A We had thought it was some *wild tale of foreign parts*	/	S And yet here in the very heart of *English Sussex*
S His *great frame* His *flaxen hair* his *shoulders*	/	A had *fallen in* was *scanty* were *bowed*
A A fall in childhood and a *twisted spine*	/	S But the *dearest, most loving heart* within
S It may be a *mere intellectual puzzle* to you	/	A but it is *life and death* to me
A 'It is certainly *delicate*,'	/	S said my friend with an *amused* smile, 'but I have *not been struck up to now with its complexity*'
A The idea of a vampire was to S me absurd	/	S Such things do not A happen in criminal practice in England

PARAGRAPH:

at this level we have: Holmes' eyes moving "slowly and lovingly over the record of old cases" (S) juxtaposed with the adventure and terror of the irrational of their titles (A).

A		S
horrified last paragraph of Ferguson's letter	/	the postscript about playing Rugby with Watson
A		**S**
"Is it madness, Mr. Holmes … I am at my wits' end"	/	"Very naturally, Mr. Ferguson. Now sit here and pull yourself together and give me a few clear answers. I can assure you that I am very far from being at my wits' end."
A		**S**
How can I ever forget how she rose from beside it with its blood upon her lips?	/	A smart maid … brought in some tea
A		**S**
"Do you like her, Jack?" … His expressive mobile face shadowed over, and he shook his head	/	The boy cooed and nestled his head upon his father's breast

The Sherlock Holmes addict will recognise these and many similar antitheses as unmistakably typical of Conan Doyle's style, which, as we have seen, is largely the product of the mentality of Watson, his chosen mouthpiece. They occur so frequently in this story that the whole work becomes a sort of extension of the oxymoron of the title, almost a pastiche of his own canon. And yet we can now see this feature of the language not merely as decorative, a kind of embroidery of the surface texture, but as the expression of a crucial thematic opposition. Nor should we claim that the linguistic formulation all happens at our stage 11, as a culmination of the generative process. From experience and common sense we know that quite often linguistic form determines the precise notion being expressed ("How do I know what I mean until I hear what I say?"—W. H. Auden). As we have seen, certain phrases seem to emerge as a product of earlier stages of the synthesis. The sequence as we have expounded it is not conceived as the order of real processes, but as a model of the sequence of relationships from abstract theme to concrete text.

Our synthesis enables us to examine in detail the progression from the static to the dynamic: the way a fundamental semantic opposition is given syntactic form in art. From the title onwards elements at every level of the text, whether of plot, setting, characterisation or language can, in principle, be accounted for as ultimate realisations of the theme.

A generative approach to poetics begins to make it possible to account for 'narrative universals,' to study the interplay of a finite 'set of rules' operating on a finite 'lexicon' of people, actions and objects to produce an infinite variety of possible textual realisations. It provides instruments to help us explore some of the subtle and complex mechanisms of the human mind.

Of course, generative poetics is in its infancy, and (*pace* Zholkovsky and Scheglov) cannot claim to be the only structural poetics any more than generative grammar can claim exclusive validity in the study of language. It does not appear to be able to account adequately for the purely linear or syntagmatic relations in the surface structure of a text (and may, indeed, obscure their significance at times). It is doubtful whether it can tell us anything about complex ironies or shifting and unreliable points of view. Side by side with a synthetic approach we need a 'functional poetics' which through analysis can begin, like functional linguistics, to describe not only the 'ideational,' but the 'interpersonal' and 'textual' functions of elements in a text.

Generative poetics, like other structural-semiotic approaches to the study of literature, offers a theory with considerable potential. Only detailed application of the theory to a large and varied range of texts will refine this, so far, tentative model and show its full potential. Exaggerated claims and bogus scientism must be avoided in the study of such complex organic structures as works of literature. Perhaps the best poetics will combine the virtues of the analytic, functional approach and the synthetic, generative approach. For the time being, both can help thoughtful and sensitive critics to write good literary criticism.

Notes

1. This was expressed more elegantly by Edgar Allen Poe nearly 200 years ago (though Poe probably did not see the scientific implications of his formulation): "A skillful literary artist has constructed a tale. If wise, he has not fashioned his thoughts to accommodate his incidents; but having conceived, with deliberate care, a certain unique or single *effect* to be wrought out, he then invents such incidents—he then combines such events as may aid him in establishing this preconceived effect. If his very initial sentence tends not to the outbringing of this effect, then he has failed in his first step. In the whole composition there should be no word written of which the tendency, direct or indirect, is not to the one pre-established design." From a review (1842) of Hawthorne's, *Twice Told Tales*. E.A. Poe, *Complete Works*, Vol. 13. New York, 1965, 153.
2. A stimulating attempt to explore the problem of point of view systematically is B.A. Uspensky's, *Poetika kompozitsii*. AZBUKA Sankt-Peterburg, 1970; English translation, *The Poetics of Composition*. Berkeley: University of California Press, 1974.
3. A number of commentators have drawn attention to Agatha Christie's achievement in taking this aspect of point of view to its ultimate refinement in *The Murder of Roger Ackroyd*.
4. Of course Point of View and Character are not really separable in this kind of story, since with Ferguson too we have to rely on his narrative for certain evidence from the past. Like all the analytical levels discussed here, these levels interact and reinforce one another: we separate them only as a descriptive and heuristic device.
5. Surely Conan Doyle was not perpetrating an unconscious pun (that Freud himself might have been proud of) on the word *jalousie* (French for *shutter*) thereby anticipating Robbe-Grillet by some thirty years?
6. Yu. K. Scheglov 'Opisaniye struktury detektivnoi novelly', Preprints for the International Symposium on Semiotics, Warsaw, 1968.

4 Dimensions of Semiotic Space in Narrative
"Joseph and His Brethren" and James Joyce's "Eveline"

Introduction

I moved from the University of Essex (founded in 1964) to an even newer university in Perth, Western Australia, Murdoch University (founded in 1975) in mid-1981. Three years before my departure I discovered that a team of mathematicians at Essex led by Ronald Atkin were contributing topological theory and analytical procedures to a whole string of social, administrative and even artistic phenomena (see References and examples in the chapter text).

I tested this analysis of two famous stories on my colleagues in the Neo-Formalist Circle and on an international audience at a symposium held at the Porter Institute for Poetics and Semiotics in Israel under the title "*Synopsis 2:* Narrative Theory and Poetics of Fiction" in June 1979. This paper was published in the first volume of a new series from Tel Aviv: *Poetics Today*. Vol. 1:4 (1980) pp. 135–149.

Analysis

I

The observation and interpretation of spatial relationships in narrative texts is a significant recurrent theme in recent semiotics. Binary oppositions such as high/low, near/far, enclosed/open have been interpreted as systematic textual realisations of fundamental categories of mythic thought by Lévi-Strauss, Toporov and Ivanov, of moral or cultural codes by Toporov and Lotman, and in terms of psycho-analytic oppositions by many post-Freudians. Lotman and Barthes, among others, have attempted to relate spatial oppositions in literary narrative to the dynamics of plot and point of view or the delineation of character. One semiotic system, space relations, has been regarded as a kind of metaphor for other semiotic systems in a text. A purely binary opposition, however, while giving us direct and valuable insights into indicial relations in a narrative, especially in terms of myths, rites and moral values, may blur our perception of other aspects of semiotic space, for example, the extent to which it may have no *spatial* correlates at

76 *Literary Narrative*

all, and the extent to which its dimensions are *measurable*, i.e., perceived in our reading as themselves consisting of graded relationships.

Out title is a pun on both the key words: under "space" we do include *spatial* relations as perhaps one of the most clearly structured and recognisable dimensions of meaning in a text—a semiotic system that models the world of the narrative. But we also use "space" in its more general sense as used by mathematicians (Lotman reminds us in passing of the concepts "chromatic space" in optics and "phase space" as used by electrical engineers, but he does not look more closely at the implications of this analogy (Lotman, 1968, 1970).

Under "dimension" we include both the notion of *cross-section*, assuming that the art work can be "cut" at many different levels and angles and that many of these "cuts" will reveal meaningful and semiotically determined (coded) sets of relations. What is more, these dimensions can be shown to share points and edges and faces with each other (which is a mathematical way of saying that they are related semiotically, as I hope to show). In other words, "dimension" is also used here in its common meaning of *measurable proportions*.

Of all the many influences on contemporary poetics I don't believe any is stronger or more pervasive than Gestalt theory; the notions that "the whole is more than the sum of its parts," of the perceptibility of "good Gestalts," of the opposition of "figure" and "ground," are deeply entrenched in poetic theory and method—and rightly so. But they remain insights of a general kind which are very hard to prove and even harder to be actually specific or precise about when it comes to analysing a work. Most of the attempts to measure the working and effects of these notions have been made by experimental psychologists who are notoriously good at isolating single features for accurate measurement to such a degree that all sense of complex systematic relations—which we must have for poetics—is lost.

The branch of mathematics known as topology may help us in mapping and measuring these complex systematic relations so as to take account of all kinds of semiotic space, to avoid the over-simplification of merely matching binary oppositions, and to give some real meaning to the notion of a work of art as a complex but integral semiotic sign made up of a network of semiotic relations. As I hope to show, the procedures offered to poetic analysis and synthesis by topology are far from "reductionist" in the way so many models imported into linguistics and poetics from the so-called "hard" sciences tend to prove. On the contrary, they are extremely flexible, as delicate and precise as any particular piece of analysis requires, and have an aesthetic elegance which both matches the structure of our own intuitions about the work of art and prompts new and richer intuitions in subsequent readings. Topology may even offer us some interpretation of the role of art, both in society and in our individual lives.

I start from the title of a book by a British mathematician: Ronald Atkin's *Multidimensional Man* (1981, Penguin Books). Atkin argues that, far from our world being bounded by the three-dimensional space of so many of our

Dimensions of Semiotic Space 77

cultural and scientific assumptions which are still tied to a Newtonian paradigm, or even the fourth dimension which is often added through a naïve reading of Einstein, we are actually used to living in a space of many dimensions, whether in our public careers and social relations, our families and friendships, or even within our own conscious and unconscious worlds. His contention is that "every man lives in a multidimensional space and with his fellows helps to create a precise mathematical structure in which they may live together." (It is intriguing to note that Lotman cites the Russian topologist Alexandrov (1956) in at least two contexts where he wants us to read more than mere spatial relations into his use of the word "space," but as he does not appear to investigate this connection further we are left with an analogy rather than a set of procedures.)

Atkin's procedures have been well tested already on a remarkable range of human activities: town planning; university administration; architecture and social life; traffic analysis; chess; the clinical psychology of marital tensions; a painting by Piet Mondrian; and *A Midsummer Night's Dream* as seen by producer, actors and audience (Atkin, 1981). He illustrates his latest book with examples from horticulture, social hierarchies, jokes and comedy in literature, a Shakespeare sonnet, family TV tastes, and the geometry of such disparate phenomena as colours, love, the space-time continuum and the Jungian *anima*. What he is careful to stress at all times is that, while we may allow ourselves—or may not be able to prevent ourselves—being trapped by some social hierarchy, a set of laws or customs, a scientific paradigm or the psychological "games people play," nevertheless a precise mathematical model can offer us a key to our freedom. Far from having to remain trapped in life at some particular dimensional level,

> Each of us, depending on his energies and his imagination, will be able to change the dimensional structure in which he lives ... and this ability to change the multidimensional structure is a fascinating peculiarity of living organisms.

Before we set about trying to analyse the multidimensionality of a short story (which, we normally assume, is also in some sense a living organism), we must sketch the procedures which will help us to perceive the dimensions of its semiotic space:

1. First the data must be sorted into meaningful sets.
2. Then sets may be related to each other in matrix arrays. These show the structural properties of the relationships between set members which may be
3. projected into a multidimensional geometry where the sharing of vertices and faces should clarify the precise nature of these properties.
4. Finally, in order to establish that this is not a static model, "freezing," as in a series of still photographs, the dynamic processes out of which our

narrative text grows (as often seems to happen with those monumental metaphors of "construction" and "composition" we are prone to apply to literary works), we will have to mention the topological notions of "traffic" and "forces which warp the geometry" as essential dynamic features of Atkin's model.

I will outline each of these procedures in turn, illustrating first with one of Atkin's examples and then with an aspect of the stucture of the story of Joseph and his brethren from *Genesis*. After attempting to pull some threads together in a too sketchy synthesis of the dimensions of this story, I will attempt to show how the model may help us account for the dimensions of semiotic space in James Joyce's "Eveline" from *Dubliners*. I hope the resulting commentary will enrich rather than conflict with Seymour Chatman's (1969) application of Roland Barthes' narrative model to that story. I chose "Eveline" mainly because it is so short and relatively easy to grasp and remember as a whole. The fact that it was written while Einstein was working on his First Theory of Relativity is, relatively, coincidental.

In describing the structure of his garden to us Ronald Atkin takes the individual species of plants as his base level, N. Thus the set N contains Yellow Roses, Red Roses, Daffodils, Lilac, Azalea, Oak, Ash and Grasses. But since these form classes, at a more general level ((N + 1), i.e., one stage up in a hierarchy), that set would contain Flower, Shrub, Tree and Lawn. At a higher level still, the "cover set" would contain Garden, Park, Cultivated Square, etc.; and the hierarchy of sets will take the form:

N + 2   {Garden, Park, Cultivated Square ...}
N + 1   {Flower, Shrub, Tree, Lawn ...}
N   {Red Rose, Yellow Rose, Daffodil ... Lilac, Azalea ... Oak, Ash}

Thus (N + 2) would be of more interest to the town planner who would be inclined to relate cultivated spaces to housing, industry, transport areas, etc. at (N + 3), whereas the lanscape gardener would work at (N + 1), and the householders who choose and cultivate the individual plants would view the hierarchy from the level of N. A nurseryman might, of course, be more interested in the many varieties of yellow or red rose at (N − 1) and a botanist, no doubt, would take the set (N − 2) of roots, stems, leaves and flowers, or (N − 3) of petals, stamens and calyx—all the way to the microbiologist slicing away at (N − 5) or so.

In other words, the model leaves us free to choose the point of entry which will suit our analytical needs best.

II

We might start looking at the story of Joseph and his brethren by listing all the characters individually and seeing what cover sets they were grouped

Dimensions of Semiotic Space 79

under, but narrative is about the relations between characters and events (relations we will come to in due course), and since the drama is presented to us in a sequence of scenes, let us take the dyads around whom these scenes revolve as our N-level. Leaving aside for the moment the rather personal matter of Jacob's relations with his wives and concubines, we may focus on the set

$$N \quad \{(J + Jacob), (J = Benjamin), (J + Reuben), (J + Simeon), (J + Judah) \ldots \\ (J + king), (J + Potiphar), (J + Potiphar's wife), \ldots \\ (J + wine steward), (J + baker) \ldots (J + servant)\}$$

The cover sets for these dyads at (N + 1) will be

(N + 1) {Joseph and his eleven brothers), the Egyptian royal family, Potiphar's family, prisoners, servants}
At (N + 2) we need to distinguish {Jacob's clan, the Egyptian court, Goshen}
At (N + 3) simply {Canaan … Egypt}

At this point we recognise the need, mathematically perfectly respectable, for a metahierarchy. God is using Joseph and the rest in his working out of the destiny of the Jewish people, so He and his heavenly host are not simply a cover set at (N + 5) or so. He is outside the hierarchy—"deus ex machina"—and has the power to modify and extend it. And so has the narrator. And so have we, the listeners and readers. So in another semiotic dimension to that of character there is a hierarchical dimension of points of view (analogous to the hierarchy of specialists from town planner to microbiologist scrutinizing Ron Atkin's garden for their own purposes). Let us label this dimension PV:

PV + 3   {God as creator and destinator}
PV + 2   {God as revealer of His purposes (via Holy Writ)}
PV + 1   {God's servant, the faithful narrator (x the number of versions of the story)}
PV   {What Jacob/ Joseph/ the brothers/ the king/ Potiphar's wife/ common rumour said happened}
PV − 1   {What Joseph/ the king/ etc. was thinking}
PV − 2   {Embedded plans, suppositions, speech, etc. within Joseph's thought (conscious)}
PV − 3   (Dreams of Joseph, the king, the wine steward, the baker, Jacob (unconscious)}

Clearly, this metahierarchy of points of view can interact with the character hierarchy in different ways: a single character (at PV) might have simply listed all that each of the other characters did, one by one (producing a

Biblical shaggy dog story not unlike the listing of Jacob's family in Chapter 46 of *Genesis*, or the enumeration of who begat whom which mars for some readers the *Book of Chronicles*). Or an omniscient historian might have simply described the political relations between Canaan and Egypt with scant regard for the key personalities. Two semiotic dimensions, those of character and point of view, are intersecting in this story, and the range of possible modes and scales of narration could be mapped on a matrix in such a way as to highlight the richness of the narrative complexity we actually find in the story.

Apart from Characters and Points of View, what other dimensions of semiotic space can we measure hierarchically in sets? Well, for one thing, the spatial dimension. With L for *locus*, we get:

L + 3   {All Egypt ... Canaan ... Mesopotamia}
L + 2   {Jacob's farm ... wilderness ... road to Canaan ... Goshen}
L + 1   {King's palace ... brothers' camp}
   L   {private quarters of king, Potiphar, Joseph, Jacob}
L − 1   {king's bedroom, Potiphar's bedroom, council chamber, well, cell, J's private room, J's bedroom}
L − 2   {bed × 4, sack for corn}
L − 3   {cup, money bag}

A glance at these sets shows why space is so often treated as a binary opposition by scholars like Lévi-Strauss and Lotman who wish to see it as correlating with a story's underlying myths: God's destiny for the Jewish people (at N + 3)), perceived at (PV + 3), is actually made to depend on what happens at (L − 1) or (L − 2). That is to say the crucial turning points in the life of God's (and our) hero take place in a well, in Potiphar's wife's bedroom, in a prison cell, in the king's bedroom, in the council chamber and in Joseph's private room (all (L − 1)). Moreover, those stages in the story when God appears to be influencing Joseph most directly involve the (L − 2) spaces of Joseph's bed (his prophetic dream), the beds of the wine steward and baker in prison (their dreams), the king's bed (his dream), and the top of the cornsacks in which Joseph has the cup and money bag hidden. In other words, the opposition "enclosed/spacious" is important for conveying the myth of God's *secret* (L − 2) plans for a *whole people* (L + 3).

Unfortunately, too strong a focus on this binary spatial opposition blurs many other important aspects of the story. There is the close bond between Joseph and Benjamin, the only sons of Jacob's—and God's—chosen one Rachel, which invests the story with a further mythic dimension—and much of its poignancy. Apart from this, in terms of the movement of the plot and the authenticity of the setting we need the intermediate points on the spatial dimension such as, at (L + 2), the wilderness, the road to Canaan, and Jacob's farm in Goshen, or, at L, the quarters of the king, Potiphar,

Joseph and Jacob, where, after all, most of the dyadic encounters occur. In other words, the "frames of reference" which Benjamin Hrushovski (1974, 1976) suggests that we construct as we read a narrative text include elements which fall naturally into a pre-existing hierarchy and not a binary opposition.

A set of time coordinates for the Joseph story produces a similar hierarchy which we might present as:

T + 4   {the destiny of the Jews ... Egyptians ...}
T + 3   {the life of Jacob, or Joseph, or Rachel, etc.}
T + 2   {Joseph's time in Canaan, in Egypt, or Jacob and family in Goshen}
T + 1   {7 years of plenty, 7 years of famine, x years of Joseph's governorship}
T   {episode-time for dramatic scenes: the well, Potiphar's household, prison, brothers' first visit, their return to Jacob, their second visit, apprehended on road, recognition and reconciliation}
T − 1   {dialogue time, order time, conspiracy time, warning, dream, interpretation, tears, etc.}
T − 2   {sudden acts: snatches robe, rewards, cuts off head, conceals money, accuses, etc.}

Once again, as with the spatial dimension, we note how crucial the base-line (T) dimension of time is for the drama of the key scenes in the story (what we might call the "syntagmatic" time unit which enables us to piece together the links in the dramatic chain), whereas (T + 4), like (L + 4), depends on the sudden shifts which happen in (T − 2) units (a "paradigmatic" axis to the story).

III

Our first procedure of collecting sets of semiotic data on various obvious dimensions such as characters, locations, time and point of view, and then ordering them in hierarchies may help to clarify certain basic relations in the text and may promote an occasional insight, but there is nothing particularly mathematical about it—and it is the sort of thing that greengrocers and football managers, for example are doing all the time. For that matter, the insights can hardly be said to stem exclusively from this data-sorting process. Let us return to Ronald Atkin's garden for a more sophisticated view of the relations between sets of data.

The garden consists of a set of fairly distinct areas, $A_1 - A_6$ which is related to a set of garden plants: Red roses (RR), Yellow roses (YR), Herbaceous plants (H), Shrubs various (SH), Fruit bushes (F), Conifers various (C), Deciduous trees (D), Lawns (L), Annual bedding plants (AN) and Vegetables various (V). (Note that the classification does not need to be botanically

82 Literary Narrative

precise by species; *for this purpose*, the layout of the garden has more to do with the relation of visual functions (size, texture, colour) to areas.) Atkin constructs a matrix array to represent the relation, λ, between the set of areas, A, and the set of plants, P, where a 1 in row A and in column F means that area A_1 contains Fruit bushes:

λ	RR	YR	H	SH	F	C	D	L	AN	V
A_1	1	2	0	1	1	0	1	0	0	1
A_2	1	0	0	1	1	1	1	1	0	0
A_3	1	1	1	0	0	0	1	1	0	0
A_4	0	1	0	0	1	1	0	1	0	1
A_5	0	0	0	0	0	1	0	1	1	0
A_6	1	0	1	1	1	1	0	1	1	1

This is really a multidimensional diagram of the garden. Seen from one angle, reading along the rows, it shows the dimensions of each area (its q-value) in terms of the set of plants which name the columns. Thus,

$$\dim(A_1) = 5, \dim(A_2) = 5, \dim(A_3) = 5, \dim(A_4) = 4, \dim(A_5) = 2, \dim(A_6) = 7$$

(We should recall that a "dimension" is *1 less* than the number of points which make it up, so a *line* (one-dimensional) joins 2 points, a triangle (two-dimensional) joins three points, etc.) So in Atkin's garden

> The area A_6 has the largest dimension (q + 1 = 8, so q = 7) whilst A_5 has the least. This expresses the fact that A_6 possesses the greatest *variety* of plants, whilst A_5 possesses the least; so A_5 is relatively monotonous. The other areas are roughly equal; so in this case, with respect to the relation between garden areas and garden plant-types, dimension corresponds to one's sense of visual and horticultural variety.
> (Atkin, 1981: 74)

But we can see the matrix array from another angle, reading down the columns, and this gives us the dimensions of the plant-types in terms of their *spread* through the garden. Here the dimensions of Lawn are 4 (i.e., 5 areas minus 1), Red roses, Fruit bushes and Conifers—3, other plants—2, except for Herbaceous plants—1. This is known to mathematicians as the "conjugate" or "inverse relation" of λ and is denoted by $λ^{-1}$.

The question arises, of course, how all these sets of vertices can be said to constitute a "geometry" that we can visualise, since even our attempts to draw the simplest *three*-dimensional figure like a tetrahedron usually risk an optical illusion (Figure 4.1):

Dimensions of Semiotic Space 83

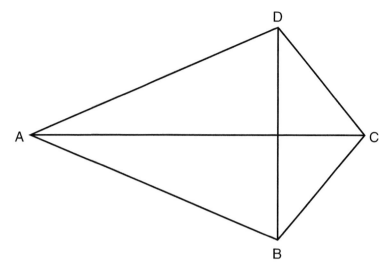

Figure 4.1 Tetrahedron

So how are we to perceive 7 dimensions of garden area, or 10, or 20? The problem is that our visual powers are structured to enable us to move around a physical world which is generally 3-dimensional, but if our visual cortex had the power of our semiotic cortex there would be no problem. As Atkin puts it,

> How are we to experience those relations $\lambda, \mu \ldots$ between sets (like Y and X) which result in a description couched in the language of multidimensions? The short answer is that Life is full of them.
> (Atkin, 1981: 72)

If we return to the story of Joseph we might expect the relationship between him and his brothers to represent an important dimension of the semiotic space of the story. The rows of our matrix array will represent the brothers who are named in some way, either singly or in groups. Roughly in order of their appearance in the story, these are:

Joseph's Brothers

A. Joseph.
B. The group of 4 sons who wanted to kill Joseph.
C. Reuben, Jacob's eldest son, by his first wife Leah.
D. Judah, his fourth son, by Leah.
E. Simeon, his second son, by Leah.
F. Benjamin, his youngest son, by Rachel, full brother to Joseph.

84   *Literary Narrative*

The remaining three sons by Leah are merely extras in the party who go to Egypt to get corn.

The fraternal relationship is expressed by the following features which include the brothers' parentage, their behaviour in the plot, their attitudes to Jacob, Joseph and Benjamin—which are morally, emotionally and narratively pivotal—and their treatment by those in power (Jacob, God and Joseph):

1. Sons of Leah, Jacob's first wife.
2. Sons of Rachel, his second wife.
3. Sons of Bilhar and Zilpah, Jacob's concubines, his wives' slave girls.
4. Hate Joseph (jealous because of Jacob's love, the robe, and Joseph's dreams).
5. Deceive Jacob (send Joseph's robe, daubed with goat's blood).
6. Venial (sell Joseph for 20 pieces of silver).
7. Intercede (Reuben for Joseph and Benjamin; Judah and Simeon for Benjamin; Joseph for family).
8. Take responsibility for others (offer self or sons as hostage).
9. Family favourite (first Joseph, then Benjamin).
10. Marked for special treatment (Joseph's robe, prophetic dreams, ability to interpret dreams, governorship, physical beauty, respect; Benjamin as youngest: silver cup, extra food, clothes and silver).

The matrix array to express the relationship (FRAT) between Joseph and his brothers will appear as follows:

FRAT	1	2	3	4	5	6	7	8	9	10
A	0	1	0	0	0	0	1	1	1	1
B	0	0	1	1	1	1	0	0	0	0
C	1	0	0	0	0	0	1	1	0	0
D	1	0	0	0	0	0	1	1	0	0
E	1	0	0	0	0	0	1	1	0	0
F	0	1	0	0	0	0	0	0	1	1

Thus Joseph is defined fraternally by the simplex of vertices A: 2, 7, 8, 9, 10: his brotherhood is 4-dimensional. The others are:

B: (3, 4, 5, 6); C: (1, 7, 8); D: (1, 7, 8); E: (1, 7, 8), F: (2, 9, 10)

The striking and obvious meanings we can read from this are: (1) that Reuben, Judah and Simeon share the same three faces geometrically; (2) that Joseph and Benjamin share three faces, although even here Joseph has more dimensions; and (3) that the brothers Dan, Naphtali, Gad and Asher share no faces with anyone except each other.

If we read the matrix array in columns, as the inverse relation FRAT^{-1}, we note the *distribution* of the qualities and roles among the brothers. Thus, hatred, deception and veniality are concentrated in those sons born to Jacob by the concubine slave-girls, Bilhar and Zilpah; the urge to intercede is concentrated in Jacob's sons by his first wife Leah, although, on a grander scale, Joseph also intercedes for the whole family and race; while the favouritism and special treatment is reserved for the sons of the wife Jacob sought longest and loved most, Rachel. In other words, the brothers' roles in the story are predetermined by the semiotic space of the myth about Jacob's marital relations with those nice daughters of his uncle Laban (Leah and Rachel) and his extramarital relations with their slave-girls, Bilhar and Zilpah. For the author(s) of *Genesis*—and, presumably, God—breeding is what counts in the end, and blood is thicker than water. Those interminable genealogies do matter after all.

Now part of the argument of this paper is that our perception of and engagement with the narrative is governed by the relationship between this semiotic space (FRAT), with its dimensions of honesty or corruption and matrilinear legitimacy, and other semiotic spaces in the story. We could map more precisely the dynamics of the plot and show how powerful are the three basic "actant" roles of hero-favourite (Joseph and Benjamin), villain (the four "concubine" sons), and intermediary (Reuben, Judah and Simeon). Or we could relate the spatial structure we have already outlined to the "plot space" and "fraternity space" and show that while the heroes and villains operate around the extremes of the space dimension, at (L − 2) or (L + 2) (a *well* in the *wilderness*; from *prison cell* to governorship of *all Egypt*; a cup in the top of a sack brings the family to Goshen), the intermediaries tend to shuttle around the region bounded by (L + 1) and (L − 1). There are clearly more matrix arrays we could construct to express this multidimensional geometry, had we space and patience, but hopefully the point has been made: the structure of the Gestalt represented by a narrative work of art is, in principle, describable.

One further mathematical refinement needs to be added before we move on to another story. Speaking of a more modern family whose relationship is defined partly by their shared and distinct tastes in television programmes, Atkin shows that the mother and daughter are connected by a two-dimensional face (the interest they share in historical drama, children's programmes and old-time music-hall).

> Because it is a 2-dimensional face we call it a *2-connectivity* ... In the total geometry of the relation TV, in that simplicial complex formed by the whole family, this special 2-dimensional space E^2 is where they meet—and they do not meet anywhere else.

(Similarly, Joseph and his half-brothers share an edge of fraternal contact: their willingness to intercede and take responsibility for others.)

> So the general idea of connectivity of that complex, numerically specified as it can be, tells us how the family is joined up to form a whole—and also

how it is not connected. The possibility of meaningful contact between the members of the family is therefore constrained by the connectivities of the geometry which represents their relations ... this new geometry would be a *backcloth* against which their mutual actions would have to take place.... And although this is not the whole story (because there are many more relations which connect the members together), yet it is typical (paradigmatic even) of *how that story can be told*.

(Atkin, 1981: 86)

The notion of a backcloth of relations, either mapped by matrix arrays or in a multidimensional geometry, allows for the idea of *traffic*, that is, some kind of movement around the structure. Where the dimensions are of semiotic space, we might assume this traffic to consist of the reader's creation of further patterns of meaning. Such traffic might be generated by obstacles (known to mathematicians as "q-holes") such as ambiguities, digressions, metaphors, etc. Poetry, according to Shklovsky and the Russian Formalists, is "form made difficult." We might formulate this topologically as "structure generating a lot of traffic around a multiplicity of q-holes."

One form of traffic might be the reader's engagement with our narrative. Christian readers of the *Genesis* story might be predisposed to seek antecedents of the Christian myth in it: the robe taken from Joseph in a well might be matched with the shroud left by Christ in the sepulchre; or the selling of Joseph to the Ishmaelites—with the betrayal of Jesus for thirty pieces of silver. This kind of predisposition would clearly affect the structure of the semiotic space perceived by such a reader. In other words, the topological model does not merely specify static structures; it actually helps to account for the dynamic relationship between the supposedly "fixed" objective text and the "fluid" subjective text that each reader (including each manifestation of you and me as reader on different occasions) recreates.

IV

Table 4.1 Spatial dimensions in "Eveline"

one's own	alien
home	out there
enclosed space	open space
intimate life	public life
selfhood	social role

The spatial dimensions of Eveline's world in James Joyce's story are well defined and relate the basic opposition of which is at the core of many, perhaps most, narratives. At first glance, both Eveline's motivation and the outcome of the story hinge on this opposition: it opens in the security of the parental home and finishes with the threat of embarkation for an unknown city half a world away; nearly every paragraph involves a movement from the homely and familiar to the distant and alien, or vice versa. And yet the intermediate dimensions are significant: the intervening semiotic spaces—and their relation to other dimensions of the story—affect the reader's interpretation more than we at first realise.

The obvious place to take as our L-level is that echoing motif: Home. At the (L − 1) and (L − 2) levels will be the partitions of the home and the household objects. At the (L + 1) to (L + 4) levels will be the concentric circles of Eveline's topographical knowledge and imagination from her gate to Buenos Aires and beyond:

L + 4 {back to England, in Melbourne, in a distant unknown country, distant countries, in Buenos Aires, out to Canada, through the Straits of Magellan, air of Italy}

L + 3 {Belfast, down somewhere in the country, to the old country}

L + 2 {before the new red houses, a field there, bright brick houses, in out of the field, outside the stores, in a house on the main road, out to do her marketing, at business, in the stores, in the theatre, Hill of Howth, in the station at the North Wall, the quay wall}

L + 1 {out of the last house, along the concrete pavement, cinder path, *their* little brown houses, the avenue, at the gate, beyond the barrier}

L {Home 1, "Home 2"}

L − 1 {round the room, in the close dark room at the other side of the hall, at the iron railing}

L − 2 {at the window, against the window curtains, dusty cretonne, all the familiar objects, yellowing photograph, broken harmonium, coloured print, dust, at the fire}

The locations in these sets are perceived in a number of different ways by Eveline: through soliloquy, observation, memory, fears and hopes. Quite a simple matrix array of the relations between these modes of perception and the spatial vertices tells us a certain amount about the story:

PV/L	L − 2	L − 1	L	L + 1	L + 2	L + 3	L + 4
Soliloquy	1	1	0	0	0	1	1
Observation	0	0	1	1	1	0	0
Memory	1	1	1	0	1	0	0
Fears	0	1	0	0	0	0	1
Hopes	0	0	1	0	0	0	1

Reading along the rows, we note that her soliloquy is three-dimensional with regard to place, focussing mainly on the nearest and furthest areas: she is, after all, weighing the security of her present home against her hopes and fears about going to Buenos Aires. This opposition is emphasised by the recurrent set of motifs of {dust, cretonne, yellowing, broken, close, dark} contrasting with {Buenos Aires ("Fresh Airs"), sea, open-hearted sailor, "Bohemian Girl"}. Eveline's memories all revolve around the intimate life of the L down to (L − 2) areas, offset by her childhood memories of playing with her brothers and friends in the field and by her more recent acquaintance with Frank (both at (L + 2)). The intensity of soliloquy and memory is relieved by the middle ground of the heroine's observations, the very neutrality and ordinariness of roads and pavements and houses viewed through a living-room window. Her hopes and fears are projected to the outermost space, her life with Frank in Buenos Aires, although one strand of hope actually transports the "home" scene (L) to Buenos Aires:

> But in her new home, in a distant unknown country, it would not be like that. Then she would be married—she, Eveline. People would treat her with respect then.

The spatial oxymoron seems to be neutralised by marriage—as I suppose it often is in real life!—but the very next sentence in the story hints at that anomalous 1 in the matrix array relating Eveline's fears with (L − 1):

> She would not be treated as her mother had been.

But to understand the force of the traffic in the structure of Eveline's life generated by this q-hole, we need to look at some other dimensions of the story's semiotic space.

An important dimension to the heroine is the scale of intimacy or distance on which she arranges (or, if you prefer, the reader *re*arranges) the people she knows. As with the analysis of the Joseph story, we will take N to be the dyads, etc. she forms with members of her family and intimate friends; after all, she is only named as an individual (Eveline, Miss Hill, Evvy) in the story's title, in one projected hope we have quoted above and in the direct speech of Miss Gavan at the Stores and Frank. At the (N − 1) and (N − 2) levels we can then group the outer parts of her body and the organs which connect her most intimately with the world out there: eyes, nostrils, heart and lips. The (N + 1) level will be more distant people, mostly anonymous and in amorphous groups, at (N + 2)—total strangers, and at (N + 3) figures so alien as to constitute mythic beings: The Blessed Margaret Mary Alacoque, the terrible Patagonians and those damned Italians (so eponymous in her mind that they are inseparable from their Homeric epithets!):

> N + 3 {the Blessed Margaret Mary Alacoque, the terrible Patagonians, damned Italians}
> N + 2 {a man from Belfast, the priest in the yellowing photograph people in a distant unknown country, through the crowds, the swaying crowd at the station}

N + 1   {man out of the last house, the children of the avenue, the Waters,}

> A matrix array relating these levels to the modes of perception (PV/N), similar to our PV/L one above would show Eveline *soliloquizing* about each level except (N − 1), *observing* mainly the intermediate levels (N + 1) and (N + 2), *remembering* N, (N + 1) and (N + 2), and centering her hopes on N and (N + 2), her fears on N and (N + 3). We must return to these hopes and fears which give the story its dynamism (i.e., generate traffic in the structure) after providing one more set analysis.

Observation, memory, hopes and fears betoken a time structure, and a very subjective one. Strictly topologically, we cannot construct a time-scale stretching from past to future in a proper hierarchy of sets and cover sets unless we adopt that absurd fiction around which we pretend to model our lives, whereby the units, second, minute, hour, day, week, etc., represent a rank scale. This would not reveal much in Eveline other than how long she had put up with her father and how suddenly she abandoned her future (relevant information, but trivial). Subjectively, Eveline perceives the dimension of time as a continuum from the remotest past (say, (T − 3)) to the remotest future (T + 3). This is not a series of points on a single line ("Newtonian" time), but rather, as Atkin has shown, a series of simplexes:

> Newton said that time is experienced as events move from one point to another point; Einstein said that time is experienced as events move from one tetrahedron to another; we are saying that time is a multi-dimensional experience as events move from one set of simplexes to another such set, and in that set there will at any one occasion be events at various dimensional levels. We will experience 0-events, 1-events, 2-events, 3-events ... p-events.
>
> (Atkin, 1981: 160)

Eveline's past is a multidimensional space defined by the vertices and faces she shares with her family, while her future space is largely defined by the vertices Frank has persuaded her to share with him. Unfortunately, blood again proves thicker than water. Her relationship with her father is the persistent polyhedron that looms over the past, present and future. Most of his appearances in the story are threatening:

T + 3   {Her father used often to hunt them out of the field with his blackthorn stick}
T + 2   {Her father was not so bad then.}
T   {Even now, though she was over nineteen, she felt herself in danger of her father's violence. She knew that it was that that had given her the palpitations ... he had begun to threaten her ... he was usually fairly bad on Saturday night....}

90   *Literary Narrative*

> T – 1   {Of course, her father had found out the affair and had forbidden her to have anything to say to him.}
> T – 2   {She remembered her father strutting back into the sick-room saying: "Damned Italians! Coming over here!"}

So is Eveline's father the force that warps the geometry of both her former life at home and her future life with Frank? Or is it, rather, her mother: her mother who is mentioned so rarely yet so poignantly?

> T – 2   {That was a long time ago ... her mother was dead.}
> T + 3   {She would not be treated as her mother had been....}
> T – 2   {She remembered the last night of her mother's illness; she was again in the close, dark room at the other side of the hall and outside she heard a melancholy air of Italy ... As she mused the pitiful vision of her mother's life laid its spell on the very quick of her being—that life of commonplace sacrifices closing in final craziness. She trembled as she heard again her mother's voice saying constantly with foolish insistence: "Derevaun Seraun! Derevaun Seraun!"}

The force of Frank's personality and adventurousness had invaded the stable geometry (a complex of relations of kinship, place, time, etc.) of her domesticity and taken her up the hierarchies to high hopes, independence, self-assertion and adventure. Ultimately, though, the pathetic memory of her mother dying, at (L – 1), in the "close, dark room at the other side of the hall," accompanied by the mocking irony of the street organ playing a melancholy air from Italy (L + 4), lays its "spell on the very quick of her being" (N – 3?) and drags her back down the hierarchies to the fear, self-pity and agoraphobia of (L – 1), (N – 1) and (T – 1). The fear of going mad opens up a psychological and semiotic abyss.

Joyce is deliberately ambiguous about whether the "final craziness" was due to a flaw (q-hole) in her mother's personal geometry or one in the geometry of the shared faces of her mother's and father's relationship. Whichever it was, it generated enough traffic around Eveline's structures to reduce her to a "helpless animal," no longer able to relate: "Her eyes gave him no sign of love or farewell or recognition." As always, the flaw may be due to nature or nurture, or both.

"Eveline" ends with an oxymoron which ties together the furthest ends of the story's semiotic space: "All the seas of the world tumbled about her heart": (L + 5) overwhelms but is contained by (N – 2). In this instance the climax represents an opposition whose dimensions we grasp without placing its elements on a scale. I have tried to show, however, that the intermediate dimensions are semiotically significant as we reconstruct the "space" of the narrative in reading; that our sense of the scale of the oppositions depends on their hierarchical relation to some base level, N; and that, perhaps more often than we notice, some crucial peripeteia in the narrative structure, some clue to character, or some point of conflict originates somewhere along a hierarchy, or, rather, at a point of intersection of the vertices of several hierarchies.

One of the functions of art may be to create a suspended self-sufficient and coherent multidimensional world, a good Gestalt. In doing so, it extends our cognitive and perceptual awareness of the reality of semiotic space; it enables us to explore the more precipitous "edges" of this space (e.g., the shared vertices of "risky" personal relationships or of time simplexes, through the warping of memory or science-fictional displacements); and it reassures us by its sense of closure and completeness that we can survive these risks. It reminds us that we are living in a multidimensional world—and that the experience may even be enjoyable.

Part 2
TV Narrative

This chapter provides a link between the four chapters on literary narrative and the three chapters on classics of the Russian cinema by Eisenstein and Pudovkin. It shares with written narrative the linear structure, extended characterisation, intersecting plots and varied settings, while exploiting the visual functions of film style (Representation, Modality and Composition) to satirise and entertain.

Satire is, almost by definition, *dialogic and intertextual*. These terms, developed by Mikhail Bakhtin and his colleagues in the 1920s, closely linked with the Formalist theorists, assume that language and all other codes of human communication combine with the transmission and exchange of facts and experience the exchange of speech roles, degrees of certainty and the speaker's attitude both to his/her interlocutor and to what they are talking about. Thus every interaction is fundamentally dialogic. Hence the centrality of the Interpersonal function at every rank of unit in M.A.K. Halliday's *systemic-functional grammar*.

The only monologic forms of discourse are such phenomena as holy writ (in any religion), proverbs and sayings, and authoritarian rules and conditions. According to Bakhtin, the novel and novella evolved as dialogic because they always allow readers to identify with particular characters and share their triumphs and defeats. They also incorporate a great deal of intertextuality. While every speech event is by definition dialogic, every narrative—whether in spoken or written language, on film, in printed advertisements—may exploit the potential for intertextuality. This imports into the basic story line references, quotations, registers and styles from other kinds of text which illuminate or comment on that story line, its characters, setting, point of view and style. The reference may be limited to the immediate context or it may "infect" a whole episode. As our analysis of an episode from the American TV cartoon series *South Park* illustrates, it may satirise the dependence on coffee of one family (Tweek and his father) or it may pervade the whole culture of film-making, film-showing, film viewing, film criticism and film history, including all the power relations involved.

I chose a *South Park* episode for a plenary paper at a Multimodal conference at the University of Singapore firstly because the hosts of the conference,

Dr Kay O'Halloran and her colleagues, asked me to link my interest in written literary narrative with a growing interest they had in testing the power of systemic-functional categories for the analysis and interpretation of filmed narrative. Secondly, because at the time (in the first decade of the twenty-first century), this famously subversive satirical series was either banned or not networked in Singapore, where rather conservative attitudes to political and commercial (and even family) power were dominant. My audience of young Singaporeans understood the double-think of parents, teachers, cinema managers, TV interviewers and leading Hollywood directors, all motivated by financial and cultural conservatism masquerading as a belief in "Progress."

5 Art versus Computer Animation
Integrity and Technology in *South Park*

Introduction

Animated series such as *The Simpsons* and *South Park* have improved significantly through the use of computerised animation and enhancement. This has been most evident in the speed of production and the realism of the representation of character portrayal and settings, but has also intensified the impact of the modal and compositional functions of meaning-making in TV cartoons.

In the first episode of *South Park*, Trey Parker and Matt Stone used construction paper and stop-motion animation, requiring months to produce a somewhat simple-minded story with schematic characterisation, limited facial movement, no crowd scenes and shadows of crepe paper models frequently obtrusive. The quirky characters, both children and adults, the strong sense of community and the self-referentiality of the narrative, which have become trade-marks of the series, were all there in embryo, however. By the time of the episode "Free Hat" in Season 6 digital techniques had not only speeded up the production process, but had led to richer characterisation, realistic facial expression, authentic speech (except where cartoon schematics were preserved for humour), individuality within crowd scenes and graded colour and shading. Most pointedly, it allowed the realistic depiction of recognisable public figures like the talk-show host Ted Koppel and the film directors George Lucas, Steven Spielberg and Frances Ford Coppola, who are attacked by the children of South Park for digitally remastering their best-known films, thereby losing, purportedly, their artistic integrity.

[Note that for technical reasons it was not possible to print my selected screen shots alongside the analysis. Since the whole series of *South Park* is in the public domain, readers who wish to compare my written analysis of the screen shots with the shots themselves can open Trey Parker's and Matt Stone's brilliant critique of remastered films on the internet for themselves.]

Analysis

Previews

The opening to Episode 609 (July 2002), "Free Hat," of the TV comedy cartoon *South Park* has four South Park kids sitting in the Bijou cinema watching previews for forthcoming films. The booming voice of the announcer proclaims:

> "Coming this summer, it's the classic film that changed America, *E.T.: The Extraterrestrial*, the new, redone version for 2002. All the E.T effects have been digitally upgraded. All the guns have been digitally changed to walkie-talkies. And the word 'TERRORIST' has been changed to 'HIPPIE.'"

Stan asks: "Aw, dude, why would they do that?"
Cartman responds: "Yeah, hippies and terrorists are the same thing."
Kyle explains: "No, dude. They only changed 'terrorist' to 'hippie' to make E.T. more P.C."
Stan, satisfied: "That's gay."
The preview resumes:

> "Coming this summer, it's the motion picture that changed America. *Saving Private Ryan*, the re-re-release, where the word 'NAZI' has been changed to 'PERSONS WITH POLITICAL DIFFERENCES' and all their guns have been replaced by walkie-talkies."

Stan is incensed: "Why the hell do these directors keep updating their movies?"

When an even more extreme—and absurd—digital makeover of *Star Wars: The Empire Strikes Back* is announced, the boys walk out and demand their money back, without success. The following dialogue ensues:

KYLE: Why don't they leave those movies alone? We liked them the way they were!
TWEEK: Don't you see what this means? All our favorite movies are going to be changed, and updated, until we can't even recognise them any more.
STAN: Tweek is right. It isn't fair for those asshole directors to keep changing their movies and making them different. Movies are art, and art shouldn't be modified!
KYLE: Yeah, what if they had modified the Roman Coliseum every year? It would just be another big douchey stadium now.

Stan and Kyle propose that they form a "Save Films From Their Own Directors" club, and they nail a sign on a phone pole outside the South Park Elementary School gymnasium announcing a rally the next day to "Save Our Nation's Films." Cartman adds the words "FREE HAT" at the bottom of the sign on the grounds that "You have to offer fabulous prizes if you want people to show up for your stupid crap." The three regular members of the quartet, Stan, Cartman and Kyle, go off to get the gymnasium ready, while Tweek, the nervy newcomer (replacing Kenny, who is dead again), is ordered to go home and make fifty paper hats.

Art versus Computer Animation 97

When they meet next day to see if anyone has turned up for the rally, they are amazed to find the room full: "Dude, there's like a thousand people in there!" But it turns out that the people have not come to save the nation's films from digital remastering, or to collect a free hat, but to free Hat, i.e., organise the release from prison of Hat McCollough, who had been convicted in 1982 of the serial murder of twenty-three babies.

The shots of the crowd in the gymnasium demanding the release of Hat are a nice example of the richer and more complex animation made possible by CGI (Computer Generated Imagery). Whereas the stop-start animation of earlier technologies involving paper models, including the first episodes of *South Park* in 1996, lacked fluidity and range of variation within the shot, CGI makes it possible for Trey Parker and Matt Stone to have a diversity of signs being waved: "*FREE HAT*," "*FREADOM* [sic] *FOR HAT*NOW! " and "HAT DIDN'T DO IT," a range of movements in the crowd, and even individualised facial expressions:

> Much of the humour in this opening episode is purely visual, depending on the modal functioning of intertextuality (Nudge-nudge, viewer, what does this shot remind you of?):
>
> 1. The opening shot of four little figures in an almost deserted cinema: the many films about film-viewing: *Cinema Paradiso*, Buster Keaton's *Sherlock Jr.*, Woody Allen's *Purple Rose of Cairo*, etc
> 2. The words "Coming this summer," accompanying a pompous announcer's voice, "zoom" towards the viewer.
> 3. Animated versions of well-known shots from *E.T.* (the kids flying across the sky with the moon in the background; the kids taking off from the road; the police moving in to stop the kids—but with walkie-talkies in hand instead of guns); from *Saving Private Ryan* (the landing at Normandy in all its bloody glory, but with ridiculously animated soldier figures holding not guns, but walkie-talkies).
> 4. The roughly scrawled notice pinned to a phone pole ("Wanted" notices in any number of Westerns).
> 5. The "captive audience" in the gymnasium (political protest films), but with the boys' and our gradual discovery that it's the wrong audience.

And then, apart from these generic shots from film history, much of the intertextuality hinges on what we know of the characters and their town from the previous 87 episodes of *South Park*. The four children: Stan and Kyle (who represent Matt Stone and Trey Parker themselves) are good friends and relatively 'normal,' motivators of the plot. They are also foils for the oddities like Cartman, a 'know-it-all' bully with an unsettled family history, and Tweek, a frightened little neurotic, with a protective family who feed him too much coffee. All these four are depicted as circular blobs

98   TV Narrative

in distinctive costumes, though Cartman is too fat to walk, so he waddles; and Tweek is too nervy to take life as it comes, so he reacts to every crisis, small and big, with squeaks and absurdly jerky blinking with his triangles of eyelids. Even Tweek's father and the Bijou's ticket salesman are known to aficionados of *South Park* from their behaviour in earlier episodes.

The Representational function is carried visually by the characters and their actions together with the developing plot lines concerning the boys' opposition to the digital remastering of films and the mounting campaign for the release of Hat McCulloch. Compositionally, Parker and Stone's animation allows for the alternation of symmetry (inside the almost empty cinema; inside the crowded gymnasium) with asymmetry (as the boys meld into a group and split as they disagree; as Tweek, "seeking his centre," dreams a hippie vision of harmony in his bedroom, fortified by yet another cup of coffee).

In the verbal mode, too, the Interpersonal function is realised in the humour:

1. The hyperbolic claims of the film announcements: "the classic film that changed America"; "all the E.T. effects have been digitally upgraded"; "it's the motion picture that changed America"; "the entire cast has been digitally replaced by Ewoks."
2. The "crescendo effect" of the claims: "the new, redone version (of *E.T.*)" < the RE-RE-RELEASE (of *Saving Private Ryan*) < the classic RE-RE-RE-Release of *Star Wars*).
3. The supposed PC (political correctness) of the corporate changes of vocabulary: "TERRORIST" has been changed to "HIPPIE"; the word "NAZI" has been changed to "PERSONS WITH POLITICAL DIFFERENCES"; the word "WOOKIE" has been changed to "HAIR CHALLENGED ANIMAL."
4. The boys' American youth idiom: "Oh, cool.," "Aw, dude," "That's gay," "Goddamnit, that pissed me off!," "You asshole!," "another big douchey stadium," "No, fatass," "stop with these faggotronics," "your stupid crap," "Dude, there's like a thousand people in there," "Then I'mo kick your ass, Tweek!"
5. This contrasts with the register of chairing a public meeting: "Okay, uh, we wanna thank you all for coming. We're really happy to see such enthusiasm for our cause." "Uh, one thing before I continue. Unfortunately, we don't have enough of the … free hats for everyone." "Yes, we apologise, but our friend Tweek here didn't make enough of them."
6. Then there is the contrast with the rowdy chanting of the slogan "Free Hat!"

2. *Nightline*

Later, as the boys count the sign-ups for their campaign (which the signatories assume is to free Hat), Tweek comes in with the news that Ted

Koppel, the TV current affairs commentator, wants them to appear on his programme *Nightline*. The opening shot on air, like the earlier formal situations, is composed symmetrically: Koppel sits at his interview desk with the four boys in an inset over his left shoulder.

His relationship with his guests, however, is anything but symmetrical:

TED KOPPEL: A new movement is sweeping the country, led by four determined boys from South Park, Colorado. The organisation was created to protect Hollywood's classic films from the hands of their directors. And also to free Hat McCullough. So, boys, I ask you the question that's on everyone's minds, why does your organisation want to free Hat McCullough, the convicted, confessed serial murderer of twenty-three babies?

As with most media commentators these days, the secondary—but scandalous—issue takes precedence over the main one. Cartman is stumped by this unexpected line of questioning:

CARTMAN: (*blinks and gazes at camera*) I think that can best be answered by our official spokesman, Tweek. [*the camera moves from Cartman to Tweek*]
TWEEK: Gaaarh!
TED KOPPEL: Well, Hat McCullough admitted he killed those toddlers. Why do you want him free?
TWEEK: (*"TWEEK, ADVOCATE OF TODDLER MURDER" appears at the bottom of the screen*) Oh, Jesus, man! ... N'ahah!
TED KOPPEL: Just answer me this, Tweek: what do you see as "positive" about toddler murder!
TWEEK: (*still with the subtitle*) Ahah. U-uh. It's easy?
TED KOPPEL: Yes ... (*looking sinister*) it is easy ... Alright, then, on to your other cause, saving films from their directors. What got you boys interested in this, especially given your pro-toddler-murder status?

Koppel rounds off by attaching a complex nominalisation "pro-toddler-murder status" (which resists deconstruction) as a permanent label to everything the boys stand for. As his other guests, Steven Spielberg and George Lucas walk in to the studio, they share in this labelling:

TED KOPPEL: Gentlemen, these toddler-murder fans think you're insane and shouldn't be allowed to alter your films. Your response?
SPIELBERG: Well, first of all, both George and I are very firmly against the murdering of toddlers.

Visually, the arrival of Spielberg and Lucas in the studio allows the *South Park* directors some interesting play with computer animation. Previously in the interview the boys were seen in a frame with some brick buildings with arched windows behind them—presumably a location shot from South Park—and the camera cut regularly between speakers, the dominant figure of Koppel in the TV studio, presumably in Hollywood, and the frame of the boys. But Spielberg and Lucas walk straight into the broadcast frame where the boys are, thus increasing their fear and subordinated status, as well as the unlikelihood of the encounter.

The computer generation also allows much more movement and characterisation than was ever possible with manual animation techniques. Throughout the interview Tweek is constantly quivering with fear and anxiety, while his companions only move when they speak. When Koppel, Spielberg and Lucas are speaking their heads and mouths move quite naturally. Although animated figures, they are also clearly recognisable from their common photographic or filmed images.

In the face of the boys' attack Spielberg maintains, "Changing *E.T.* was the best thing I ever did.," to which Kyle responds, "Dude, don't you see that it's not? It'd be like changing *Raiders of the Lost Ark*!" To the film's director, Steven Spielberg and its producer, George Lucas, this idea is a stroke of genius: "Why didn't we think of it before?!" (*a snatch of dramatic music from Raiders*)

3. Capturing the Lost Ark

At a further meeting of their new club, Stan announces:

> Members, this is our darkest hour. We've just learned that George Lucas and Steven Spielberg now intend to update and change *Raiders of the Lost Ark*. There's only one way we can stop this important and historical piece of art from being harmed. Mr. Secretary? (*hands the mic to Cartman, who moves over to an easel*).
>
> CARTMAN: Thank you. (*turns a page on the easel to show a plan of George Lucas's Skywalker Ranch*) Our intelligence tells us that the original negative to *Raiders of the Lost Ark* is currently somewhere in George Lucas's house. We need to find and usurp that negative.
> MAN: And if we get hold of the negative they can't change the movie?
> STAN: That is our understanding.

After this play with the procedures and language of public meetings, the camera moves into the visual register and creepy music of secret nocturnal break-ins, as the boys creep into Lucas's house in California, with a string of dark shots of his study and a torchlight on the videos on his shelves (including not only the updated versions of *Star Wars*, but "digitally enhanced" versions of his *First Day at School, Wedding Day, Kids' First Swimming Lesson* and *Weather*). They have just seized the original 1982 negative of *Raiders*, when Lucas comes in, demands the negative back and phones for the police. Kyle tries to reason with him:

KYLE: It's not too late to do what's right. Give us the print. There's still some good in you, Mr. Lucas, We know there is. You yourself led the campaign against the colorisation of films. You understand why films shouldn't be changed ... When an artist creates, whatever they create belongs to society.
LUCAS: Have I ... become so old that I've forgotten what being an artist is all about?
STAN: Give the print to us so that we can protect it from Spielberg and anyone else who wants to alter it.

Enter Spielberg with three goons armed with walkie-talkies. The previous lyrical piano music reverts to *Raiders* sound track. Spielberg begins to behave like a Nazi (an ironic reference to his film *Schindler's List* and an anticipation of his later role in this story)

SPIELBERG: You haven't let these doe-eyed children affect your judgement, have you, George?! (*voice lowers*) Don't forget: you belong to me. (*snatching the film from Lucas*) Now take the children prisoner! ... You troublemakers shall be my guests of honour at the premiere of the NEW *Raiders of the Lost Ark!* Your gay little club is over!

4. Digital Irony

While Spielberg's goons sieze Kyle, Stan and Cartman, Tweek manages to escape and the film directors exit. At this point the most extended visual joke of the whole episode begins. A blank screen is filled with the zooming words "COMING THIS SUMMER" and the unctuous announcer's voice, as in the opening sequence in the Bijou cinema, proclaiming (over triumphal music

"Coming this summer: (*title*: RE-RELEASE OF EPISODE 1 SOUTH PARK) It's the digitally-re-enhanced re-release of the very first pilot episode of *South Park!* (*scenes from "Cartman Gets an Anal Probe"*) Yes, the classic, rough, hand-made first episode is getting a make-over for 2002. The simple, funny aliens are now super-badass and kewl! Flying saucer? No longer cheap construction paper, but a 4.0 megapixel non-drop digital masterpiece of technology! Yes, everything's new! New is better!

With the critics they had created—Stan, Kyle and Cartman—out of the way under Spielberg's control, the creators of *South Park*, Trey Parker and Matt Stone, turn the critique of digitalisation against themselves:

TREY PARKER: When we first made *South Park*, we didn't *wanna* use construction paper. We just *had* to because it was cheap.
MATT STONE: And now with new technology we can finally remaster *South Park*, make it look sharp, clean and focused.
TREY PARKER: Expensive. (*Both men nod their heads*)

102   TV Narrative

ANNOUNCER: Yes, all the charm of a simple little cartoon will melt before your eyes as it is replaced by newer and more standardised animation!

[A special-edition DVD of "CGAAP": new version for 2002 is shown. "ACT NOW" blinks on the screen over the DVD]
Get this special enhanced version quick, because another enhanced version will likely be coming out for 2003!

This self-reflexive joke about the creators of *South Park* themselves abandoning the "charm" of their original style for the sharpness and standardisation of a remastered digitalised version is not only rhetorical, however. Parker and Stone resist the temptation of doing cartoon versions of themselves and, in contrast to the cartoon figures of the other film directors, Spielberg and Lucas, appear as "real-life" figures filmed in interview mode—something they hardly ever do throughout *South Park's* many episodes. They are "on trial" in the flesh before the jury of film history, guilty of remastering their own historic, and much-loved, creation.

Another ironic intertextual reference to *Raiders of the Lost Ark* enriches this sequence even further, since the archaeologist-hero, Indiana Jones, was motivated to find and protect the Lost Ark of the Covenant by his desire for historic preservation, while his rival, Belloq, is motivated entirely by greed.

5. Improved History

Tweek, who has escaped capture by Spielberg's guards, now tries to enlist the support of the Free Hat Club to release his friends and prevent the premiere of the remastered *Raiders*. But the townsfolk are less interested in artistic integrity than in the release of the notorious serial baby-killer, Hat, so Tweek decides he must act alone. He is perfectly cast to enact that clichéd *topos* of Hollywood action films, the coward turned brave hero.

The episode which follows is an extended parody of the last major sequence in *Raiders*, where Jones follows Belloq and the Ark and threatens to destroy it with an anti-tank missile launcher unless Belloq releases Marion, his heroine. He and Marion get tied up and have to watch the ceremonial opening of the Ark by Belloq and his Nazi helpers. However, Jones is aware of the danger of seeing the spirits released from the Ark and he and Marion shut their eyes. As the lid is removed, the spirits within burst out and attack the Nazis and their heads melt or explode.

As Spielberg, Lucas and their henchmen march through the desert with the new *Raiders* being carried in an Ark and Tweek's three friends as prisoners, Tweek appears on a hill overlooking a ravine, ambushing the procession with a bazooka—another narrative cliché of modern Wild West films. He threatens to blow up the Ark unless his friends are released. Spielberg confronts him:

SPIELBERG: All your life has been the pursuit of seeing a great film! This new version of *Raiders* has digital effects beyond your wildest dreams! You want to see it screened just as much as I.
KYLE: Come on, Tweek! Blow it up!
SPIELBERG: Son, we are simply passing through history. This ... is imPROVED history. Do as you will.

Tweek hesitates and three guards appear over the hill behind him. He lowers the bazooka.

6. Dénouement

The "Free Hat" episode ends as it began—with a scene in a cinema. This time it is a makeshift open-air theatre somewhere in the desert, displaying the sign: "*RAIDERS OF THE LOST ARK. Premiere Tonight*" in flashing lights. In priest's robes and with an air of religious ritual, Spielberg and two assistants open the Ark and withdraw a film reel.

SPIELBERG: This is the birth of the NEW version of *Raiders of the Lost Ark*! We shall screen it here, and then destroy all the old prints in celebration!

As the opening shots of the film run, the boys tightly shut their eyes in protest, but the "celebrity guests and other rich people," all dressed in evening dress, as for an Oscar Awards Night, make appreciative noises.

SPIELBERG: It's beyooootiful! [*A scene of Indiana Jones using a whip to swing across a chasm. Flaming arrows shoot past him. As he lands on the other side, natives approach. They look and chatter like Ewoks.*]
VIEWER 1: Wait a minute. This version is awful!
VIEWER 2: Yeah, they ruined it!
VIEWER 3: Oh my God, it's terrible!
LUCAS: (*suddenly scared stiff*) AaaaAAAAA!!

The three directors (now including Frances Ford Coppola) huddle in terror. On screen, Indiana Jones is reaching for a golden item. Rays of light burst like snakes from the screen and move out over the audience, shooting through the viewers' chests and killing them. Coppola, Lucas and Spielberg are overwhelmed by the energy from the rays. They become disfigured, then their faces melt away. Spielberg's head explodes. The rays diffuse, then gather back into the Ark. The spirits of all killed are gathered into the Ark as well. Finally, with a roll of thunder, the lid lands on the Ark.
The boys open their eyes. The ropes that bound them are gone and they are the only survivors. The next scene is in the daytime in South Park, which is celebrating the release from prison of Hat McCullough (still not cured of his hatred of babies).

The boys walk down the street away from the celebration.

KYLE: Do you think we did a good thing, Stan? I mean, no-one even seemed to notice.
STAN: Yeah well, sometimes the things we do don't matter right now. Sometimes they matter ... later. We have to care more about later sometimes, you know? I think that's what separates us from the Steven Spielbergs and George Lucases of the world.
CARTMAN: That and youth. Those guys are old.

7. Conclusion

In addition to lampooning (verbally, visually and musically) Spielberg and Lucas for succumbing to the "Fascist" efficiency of computer animation, Parker and Stone (by now regularly using advanced computer animation techniques themselves) represent themselves in a live action insert as "humane" in their remastered version of Episode 1 of *South Park*.

As always with this series, intertextuality, parody and self-referentiality serve a modal function, bonding viewers with the absurd but honest politics of the child protagonists. Play with sub-frames and destruction of the space between screen and audience exploits the compositional potential of the digitalised audio-visual medium and enriches with purely visual jokes the humour of the story-line.

I want to claim that the story-line is both the challenge and the problem in writing a paper of this kind. When I was presenting the argument to a live audience at 4ICOM, the story was largely carried by the clips on my Powerpoint and I was able to focus more specifically on the visual, audial and linguistic functions of individual scenes. Much of the multimodal work on cinematic/televisual texts to date has, sensibly, been limited to the analysis of a single significant scene in a classic movie, or a single product being advertised, or a single news item. To begin to do justice to a 25-minute episode from *South Park*, one has to tell enough of the story to clarify what is going on in individual scenes. This is quite laborious in running prose. But one also has to show the narrative or rhetorical functions of particular lines of dialogue or visual devices, and to explain the intertextual nature of the jokes—visual, verbal and audial—in terms of the little world of South Park and its inhabitants and in terms of the larger world being satirised—in this case, the world of Hollywood directors and the fashion for (and economics of) remastering their most successful box-office hits—to say nothing of the intricate parodying of those hits.

We need to develop a narrative theory and a rhetoric as well as a grammar for the complex and moving multimodal texts of the TV and cinema. The work of the Russian Formalist theorists in the 1920s (several of whom laid the foundations for early film theory as well as literary poetics) introduce the important concepts of "the foregrounding of functions" and "the dominant" of a whole artistic work. These can help us to relate the micro-analysis of the grammar of the language, visual images and sound-track of specific scenes to the way they function in the text of the whole work.

To be really multimodal, I would like to finish with music (No, don't worry, not a song!). It was Walter Pater in his *Giorgione* who claimed that "all art constantly aspires towards the condition of music." I believe this to be true, and would like to claim some artistic status for "Free Hat." Not only is there a strong relationship (through a verbal pun and a political movement) between what one might call Theme 1 (the opposition to the digitalisation and re-release of film classics) and Theme 2 (the support for the release of Hat McCullough), but they intersect in the course of the whole episode in a rhythmic way, with particular characters (instruments) dominating one theme or another. What is more, the *rhythm* of the modalities of the cartoon (American spoken dialogue, cartoon layouts, sound effects, music track) is what makes us keep watching and wanting to return. The whole of "Free Hat" charms the viewer with its musical structure and rhythms—and these remain with us after we have laughed at all the jokes.

Acknowledgements

1. The creator/producers of the series are Trey Parker and Matt Stone. The director of this episode was Toni Nugnes.
2. My son, Janek O'Toole has given me invaluable help in selecting the *South Park* episode, in appreciating the characters and humour, and in relating the satire to the work of Steven Spielberg and George Lucas. Janek's knowledge of the world of *South Park* and of recent film history is encyclopaedic and I could not have presented this paper without his constant advice and encouragement.

Bibliography

O'Halloran, Kay L. and Smith, Bradley A. (eds.). 2011. *Multimodal Studies: Exploring Issues and Domains*. New York and London: Routledge.

O'Toole, Michael. 1994/2011. *The Language of Displayed Art*. London: Leicester University Press/ Pinter Publishers; 2nd edition: extended with CD Rom: London & New York, 2011, Routledge.

Taylor, Richard (ed.). 1982. *The Poetics of Cinema*. Russian Poetics in Translation, Vol. 9 (the Russian original edited by Boris Eikhenbaum: *Poetika kino*. Leningrad: Kinopechat,' 1927.

Part 3
Film

My publications up to 1967 had included *A. P. Chekhov: Three Farces*, London: Bradda Books, 1963: a student edition with notes and vocabulary; *The Gateway Russian Song Book*, London: Methuen, 1964: a collection of 41 Russian folk and popular songs, with melody line, guitar chords and glossary; and two audio-visual Russian language courses, *First Year Russian*, London: BBC, 1966, later published as *Passport to Moscow*, Oxford: OUP, 1972, and *Second Year Russian*, London: BBC, 1968 (later *Passport to Odessa*, Oxford: OUP, 1976). Both courses were broadcast twice on BBC Radio 3 in 1966–1967 and 1968–1969.

Thus my commitment to audio-visual media, including stage plays and songs was well established before my work on Chekhov's story,' The Student' (Chapter 1 in this book, (around 1970 and the more "academic" publications that followed.

6   Eisenstein in *October*

Introduction

Eisenstein's famous film about the 1917 uprising in St. Petersburg had been shown and discussed at an Essex University film festival celebrating the 50th anniversary of the Soviet Union. This was also a period when Film Studies were being argued for and introduced as a serious subject in the humanities at Essex and other progressive universities.

My approach in this and the next two chapters was to attempt an "explication de texte" relating the visual sequences to the immediate and overall themes of the film under study. This became the main orientation of my subsequent papers on literary style, narrative structure and the semiotics of the visual arts of painting and sculpture.

2. Eisenstein's *Strike*: a structuralist interpretation
     (Journal, *Essays in Poetics*, 1977)

3. Early Soviet Cinema: Eisenstein vs Pudovkin
     (Journal: *Exeter Film Studies*, 1981)

Analysis

> "You've got to be an awful film snob to like this stuff!"
> "Perhaps if one knew the historical background better...."
> "Yes, but the titles are so naïve. And this montage that everyone makes so much fuss about is pretty obvious really."

This snatch of conversation, overheard in the gents' toilet half-way through the University Film Society's recent showing of *October*, probably sums up the reactions of most of the audience during any of Eisenstein's early films and evokes some response even in those who profess to know and appreciate Eisenstein.

The snobbery question is a real one and I will deal with that last. The historical background one must know, and the Film Society missed an opportunity for educating us all about a significant moment in film history by not providing us with a few essential historical and political facts relating to the subject of the film and the circumstances of its creation, some indication of the film's sociological significance and perhaps the seeds of a discussion of its artistic merits. The three major disciplines of our School of Comparative Studies could have contributed to an interpretation of what may be one of the most important works of art to emerge from the Soviet Union in the 1920s.

At the beginning of 1927 a number of film directors, along with other Soviet creative artists, were called upon to produce a film to celebrate the tenth anniversary of the great October Revolution which had brought Lenin and the Bolsheviks to power. The focus of attention was Leningrad where the tsars had ruled until the first, 'bourgeois,' revolution of March 1917 brought the Provisional Government and Alexander Kerensky to power. The old name of 'St. Petersburg,' which had a Germanic ring, had been changed in 1914 to the more Slavonic 'Petrograd,' which the city remained until Lenin died in 1924, when it was renamed in his honour. Pudovkin set out to direct an epic film spanning two centuries entitled *Petersburg, Petrograd, Leningrad*, but this grandiose project was too ambitious by about 199 years, so, having only some nine months in which to complete the film, he settled for *The End of S. Petersburg*. Eisenstein and Pudovkin had trained together in 1924 under Kuleshov, but by 1927 there was a considerable divergence in their approach to montage and other aspects of film theory and Pudovkin was amused to find that in this anniversary year their rivalry extended to their choice of location: "I bombarded the Winter Palace from the Aurora [a warship anchored in the river], while Eisenstein bombarded it from the Fortress of St. Peter and St. Paul" (Pudovkin, 1928, p. 3). Film enthusiasts often remark on the incredible authenticity of the crowd scenes in *October*. In a period when the theatre as well as the cinema aspired to be a mass spectacle and when the events portrayed through both media were a climactic moment in everyone's personal history as well as that of their country, some thousands of Leningrad citizens must have come to regard the odd 'assault' on their Winter Palace as very much all in a day's work.

Eisenstein had aimed to depict collective action in his first film *Strike* (1925) and the epic *Battleship Potemkin* (1925) and, in these heady days before the 'cult of personality' became instinctive to most Russians, he took it as axiomatic that he should focus on the events of October 1917 as an expression of a spontaneous national anger against the oppression of the tsars and the ineptitude of the Provisional Government rather than on the plotting and demagogy of the Bolshevik leaders. Edward Tisse, the Swedish cameraman with whom Eisenstein began a fruitful and historic partnership in *Strike*, had opened his Soviet career with a film of the first May Day parade in Red Square in 1918 and had since worked at the head of a documentary film unit, so he too was committed to the notion of film as essentially a portrayal of the masses, by the masses and for the masses. The only important individuals in *October* are Kerensky, Lenin and Trotsky.

As we are reminded in several sardonic titles, Kerensky, as both War and Marine Minister while Russia was still at war with Germany, by May 1917 had assumed effective control of the Provisional Government and by July had been made Prime Minister. Kerensky typifies for Eisenstein—as for all the Bolsheviks—the representative of the bourgeois classes who had no contact with the mass of the Russian people whom they had chosen to try and govern. Unaware of how sick they were of the war, he strove to start a new offensive against the Germans. We are shown a vulgar upstart, self-important and tactless, who chose to govern from the Winter Palace among the trappings of autocratic power.

Lenin, as founder of the Bolsheviks, had been living in Switzerland since 1914, but on his arrival in Petrograd in April 1917 proposed a programme which was totally in harmony with the current aspirations of the people: immediate peace, immediate distribution of land to the peasants and the seizure of factories by the workers, and, most essentially, "all power to the soviets" [people's councils]. In *October* he is seen at three stages of the struggle for power: his arrival in the city in April to lead the class war, his clandestine political activity after the disappearance of those Bolshevik leaders who were arrested during the July uprising, and his final triumph in November when he became President of the Council of People's Commissars, the new Bolshevik cabinet.

And Trotsky? He undoubtedly appears in the film a couple of times, although the mane of hair, the glaring pince-nez and black moustache are apt to get confused with those of other revolutionaries. But two brief appearances are hardly the right proportion for the greatest propagandist for the Bolshevik cause, Lenin's Commissar for Foreign Affairs and the chief architect of the new Red Army during the Civil War. So where *was* Trotsky? Was the mysterious and suspicious delay in the appearance of *October* something to do with his portrayal? For while the anniversary films of Pudovkin and several other directors were comfortably completed in time for the celebrations on November 7, Eisenstein's contribution only appeared four months later, in March 1928. And of the 13,000 feet of film that were shot only about 9,000 finally appeared. (This proportion would not seem unusual today, but in those days film editors could not afford to take vast quantities of excess footage for granted.) Only a year after Lenin's death, in January 1925, Trotsky had been relieved of his post as Commissar for War, but for some time quite open and frank discussion continued between the 'Opposition Group,' led by this major contender for the leadership, and the 'Government Group,' led by Stalin as Secretary of the Party. By October 1927, however, Trotsky and his colleagues had sharpened their tactics and organised a demonstration in Leningrad followed by one in Moscow on the very day of the Jubilee.... If Trotsky had won the struggle for power this demonstration would have seemed a characteristically skilful piece of political opportunism. As he lost, it now just looks rather tactless. As Soviet histories still [1967] do not mention the name of Trotsky except as a term of abuse, the question of a Soviet interpretation of the event does not arise. At all events it would appear that this third major figure in the October (1917) struggle had been destined for a role in the film comparable to that of Lenin. We may never know what was on those other 4,000 feet of film.

Now what are we to make of all those naïve titles which punctuate the film: "The Emperor's lackey," "The upstart," "A Bolshevik dies," "Cutting down the standards," "All power to the Soviets," etc.? They seem incredibly childish to a generation that takes for granted fast-moving, naturalistic talkies and the even more glib sophistications of televisual directing. But in the mid-1920s the classics of the silent cinema needed titles to pinpoint the important moments of the story. They had to be brief and simple so as not to hold up the action and were not often ironic in tone: the irony, like other effects, was much more often purely *visual*, for this was the classic age of the cinema.

Beyond these technical considerations, however, we must remember the audiences for whom *October* was made. This was *their* revolution, only ten years after the event; these were the figures they had revered or hated; these the slogans for which men had lived and died. The repetition of these stark phrases was part of a ritual re-enactment. The propaganda for the Bolshevik cause had been strong during these ten years and few Russian film fans were literate even now, let alone educated to resist propaganda, but still they had put their trust in Lenin, who had their interests and those of Russia at heart; and their hatred for Kerensky and the bourgeoisie was not a xenophobia generated in time of war against the foreign enemy—it was a deep pathological hatred of an evil in their own Russia which it had taken the miseries of a civil war to cleanse.

The use of montage in *October* may also seem stilted and naïve at times. Both Eisenstein and Pudovkin had learned the elements of this vital cinematic technique of film-editing by juxtaposing similar or contrasting visual elements or scenes, when they worked together under Kuleshov in 1924. By 1927 their use of this technique was already becoming more refined and here too they diverged. Pudovkin as a rule followed Kuleshov in regarding montage as primarily a linking device: finish one scene looking at a pair of oppressed worker's boots and cut to another pair of boots, worn this time by the policeman who dominates the next sequence. Although it may involve visual shocks, this convention improves continuity and Pudovkin's films normally seem to flow more smoothly.

Eisenstein, on the other hand, sees montage as a collision of two planes of visual reality. It is the shock of one person's view of a statue toppling over being cut with another's, and another's, and another's: it may represent the total process of the statue falling, seen from every point of view, parallel, perhaps, to the (then) recent experiments of Cubist painters, striving to represent in a single dimension the many facets of each object or person portrayed. Eisenstein and Tisse were fascinated by the ritual acts which characterise a man or a social group. Thus the ritual kissing of Orthodox priests and their well-fed congregations is juxtaposed with the rituals of working-class solidarity—the sharing of bread and the fists raised in mass protest. Or, in another scene, the ritual servility of the last Tsar's footmen as they shake hands with the new Prime Minister, Kerensky, is juxtaposed with the servility of Kerensky himself as he stands waiting to enter the royal apartments at the summons of a mechanical peacock. The peacock, of course, is a visual pun, much loved by Eisenstein, symbolizing the vain pride of the shallow Kerensky. Or take the preceding sequence, where Kerensky walks up the palace staircase followed by his aides. As Pudovkin analyses this famous sequence in depth (in Taylor and Christie, 1928), Eisenstein cuts repeatedly between the actual image of them and the mirror-image in which the whole scene spirals in reverse: this represents, perhaps, their duplicity, or their vanity, or their lack of contact with reality. For we may interpret these juxtapositions as we will. A certain consistent thread of message runs through the film, but the separate images are fluid and often ambiguous.

Eisenstein's films are not prose, primarily aiming to convey either information or a series of events in a strongly sequential order, but poetry. The historical element is there and he and his audience can take it for granted. But the language of the film draws attention to itself in a way that only happens in poetry. It is not the fact of the statue falling that is important: it is the series of rhythmic impressions conveyed by the montage which heightens the significance of this event as we relive it in the film. The humour of Kerensky being juxtaposed with a mechanical peacock is banal, but this visual pun is almost a rhyme among the patterns of visual repetition and contrast which are Eisenstein's poetic vocabulary.

Most intriguing and moving of all is the complex metaphor of the horse falling as the bridge is raised, which forms a central image for the whole film. A peaceful Bolshevik demonstration in Petrograd is broken up—one demonstrator with a banner is attacked and killed by a White officer and a horde of bourgeois ladies with umbrellas—a pile of newspapers, the Bolshevik *Pravda* (Truth), floats in the river nearby, now surfacing, now drowning—banners calling for elementary human rights furl and unfurl in the streets and in the water—as the bridges are raised to stop workers crossing into the centre of the city from an industrial suburb—a woman demonstrator with long blonde hair gets killed, her hair flowing across the crack between the two halves of the bridge as we see it widen from alongside, above and below. Finally all these emotive images of hair—paper—flags (free-furling in contrast to savagely tight umbrellas), the symbolic blacks and whites, are brought together in the symbolic image of the white horse which has fallen in the traces in the centre of the bridge, held to one side by the carriage it had been pulling, and gradually slipping off the other side, white mane last, as the halves of the bridge part. Eisenstein firmly fixes these related images in our visual memory in a highly rhythmic sequence of cuts which is repeated several times as the various elements slip and twist, due to the inexorable motion of the bridge and the river current. Finally, all attention focuses on the horse and, as its body and mane slip over the edge of the bridge, as it hangs head downwards over the water, as it slips from the harness and plunges into the river, its carriage careering back down the slope of the bridge, we are seized by the poignancy of the image. This is not just a metaphor for the tragedy of noble lives lost to no purpose in a clash with an evil but all-powerful system. This idea is present, but is too banal to interpret our experience of this sequence. The image has taken over, has assumed a complex existence of its own, as in poetry, has spawned a crowd of new visual and mental images, swirling away from that central comparison like galaxies in an infinitely expanding universe. Eisenstein has created through the complex *moving* medium of the film something like the effect that Leonardo da Vinci achieves in those obsessive drawings of hair and water in the *Notebooks*: a simile, basically, but through the rhythm and flow of its repetition, a private world of images, linked and contrasted.

Now are we snobbish to like this sort of film? To my mind there is a widespread snobbery about Russian films, particularly contemporary ones. A mediocre film like *The Forty-First* and a fussy mannered one like *The Cranes Are Flying* are awarded international prizes at Cannes and other film festivals, in preference to far more exciting and adventurous French, Japanese, Polish or American films, because Russia after Stalin is still rather strange and exotic, and an appreciation of things Russian, just because they are Russian, is supposed to confer some kind of *kudos*. But to approach an acknowledged classic hoping to discover why it is a classic, to persevere in learning the language and conventions of an unfamiliar art form, and only then to attempt reasoned criticism—this is humility, not snobbishness, and far preferable to the attitude of the philistine in the gent's who knows what he likes and refuses to seek further.

7 Structural Interpretation of a Film
Eisenstein's *Strike*

Analysis

> The basis of the formal method is quite simple: a return to craftsmanship. The most remarkable thing about it is that it does not deny the content of ideas in art, but treats the so-called content as one of the aspects of form. Thought is juxtaposed with thought, word is juxtaposed with word, and image is juxtaposed with image.
> —Victor Shklovsky, *O teorii prozy* (On the Theory of Prose), Moscow 1925

> The unanimously warm reception of *Strike* by the press and the way it has been evaluated allow us to view the film not just as a record of a revolutionary victory, but as an ideological victory in formal terms. This is particularly important at the present time when people are so fanatically committed to persecuting all work on form in art, labelling it "formalism" and preferring, apparently, empty formlessness. In *Strike*, however, we have an example of revolutionary art where for the first time the form turned out to be more revolutionary than the content.
> (Eisenstein, 1924, in Il'in, L.A., 1964, p. 109)

Any attempt to analyse and interpret a film by Eisenstein is a rather daunting task, certainly humbling. The more so if the analysis is to be done in terms of a critical theory, since one of the greatest of all film directors also happened to be one of the profoundest and most original theorists of the cinema and an acute critic of his own and other directors' techniques. Still more daunting if a structural analysis and interpretation are to be attempted is the reminder that Eisenstein's own film theory and criticism is highly formal, that he was a friend and close associate of the key figures of the Formalist movement in the 1920s (few of whom neglected to write about film), and that his articles, essays and letters are still proving a source of inspiration to a new generation of Russian structuralist critics and theorists.

It is curious, however, that among the mass of critical essays and books about Eisenstein there is little concern for a close analysis of the film which first brought Eisenstein into the front rank of Soviet film directors. Few critics get beyond the final montage sequence of the bull being slaughtered in an abbatoir intercut with the crowd of striking workers being massacred by the Tsarist mounted police, although reference is made occasionally to other sequences that seem to exemplify Eisenstein's notion (or the critic's notion of Eisenstein's notion) of a "montage of attractions." Even Eisenstein himself quotes only the bull sequence in his important section on montage and conflict in *Film Form*. He does, however, make some general observations about the relationship between revolutionary form and revolutionary content in his article '*Strike* 1924: on the problem of a materialist approach to form.' I will be discussing some of these observations in the course of this paper. I know of no systematic attempt to apply to *Strike* the central and crucial critical procedure of the whole Formalist-Structuralist enterprise: to analyse in turn each level of formal technique proper to the chosen art medium and to relate these levels to the content they are expressing, to each other and to the overall theme and intentions of the work as a whole (a hermeneutic spiral). To do this adequately with a film as rich and complex as *Strike* would require a whole book. Within the scope of a short article I hope to show how we might set about the task.

One of the universal devices of all the arts to which Victor Shklovsky was drawing attention in the early 1920s was that of "ostranenie," or "making strange":

> The purpose of art is to transmit a sense of the object as a seeing, not as a knowing: the device of art is to "make things strange" and to make form difficult, increasing the difficulty and time taken to perceive, since the process of perception in art is an aim in itself and must be prolonged: art is a way of experiencing the making of an object, and what has already been made is of no importance.

We certainly experience this "renewal of vision" as we enjoy the shock of the fairground "attractions" of *Strike*: the photographs in a "rogues' gallery" album of police spies come alive, smile and get dressed and one hangs his bowler hat on the photo-frame; the same spies' faces fade in and out of film images of the animals that have given them their nicknames (Monkey, Fox, Owl, etc.); a crane carrying an enormous metal wheel looms threateningly towards the camera, and we flinch as the factory foreman is knocked down by it; two workers fighting in one of the workshops stand on a board that has fallen across a third man and—straight from the circus—we have a human see-saw; a typewriter that retreats into its desk as soon as the distraught factory director tries to use it is accused of also being "on strike"; a key scene for the plot where a corrupt police-chief, living in luxury, bribes a worker to betray his comrades, while two figures in evening dress dance and quaff champagne—and as the camera retreats, we discover that they are dwarfs dancing on a table laden with luxuries; the "King" of the gang of crooks, whom the police call in to provoke the striking workers, lives in a derelict limousine and is attended by another dwarf, and when he whistles to summon his gang, they pop up, like Ali Baba's forty thieves, out of rows of barrels set in the ground. Finally, in a kind of prologue to the final scene of massacre, a police chief gloatingly points out on a map of the workers' settlement how his cavalry will take over the district and, when the worker who has betrayed the other strike leaders, angrily bangs the table with his fist, the ink bottles fall over and ink gushes over the streets which, with the massacre, will turn to "rivers of blood."

These are perhaps the most vivid shock effects exploited by Eisenstein in *Strike* and are clearly examples of "ostranenie." But to place the device of "making strange" aspects of the world we have come to take for granted at the centre of an aesthetic theory is to put a high premium on innovation for its own sake. It is to conceive the history of art as a series of revolutions against automatised forms, and quite often a revolution in form is automatically assumed to be revolutionary in content. Too often examples of "ostranenie," like fairground and circus "attractions" and the surprise montage effects that Eisenstein built out of them, renew the world in glimpses; they do not create a new vision. Now although the great film theory debate between Eisenstein and Pudovkin—and too much of the discussion since—hinged on their theories of montage, Eisenstein makes clear in the article on *Strike* and at many points in his writings that he was seeking to convey revolutionary themes and ideas through every technique at the film-maker's disposal, and the shock tactics involved in a "montage of attractions" were just one of the formal devices available to him, and a rather superficial one at that.

In *Film Form* Eisenstein insists that montage is far more than the mere juxtaposition of shots or sequences in order to highlight ideas. Within the shot, the smallest unit of film language, great tensions may be generated by the interplay of line, of scale, of volumes, of light, of depth, of movement, and so on, and the dynamics of shots related through montage create further tensions that build up a rhythm. It is the violent, tension-laden rhythms that stand out as the hall-mark of Eisenstein's films and it is the rhythms which convey their revolutionary message in its purest form:

> Montage is conflict.
> … Conflict within the shot is potential montage, in the development of its intensity shattering the quadrilateral cage of the shot and exploding its conflict into montage impulses *between* the montage pieces.
> … If montage is to be compared with something, then a phalanx of montage pieces, of shots, should be compared to the series of explosions of an internal combustion engine, driving forward its automobile or tractor: for, similarly, the dynamics of montage serve as impulses driving forward the total film.
> … The compression of all cinematographic factors and properties within a single dialectical formula of conflict is no empty rhetorical diverson.

... This makes it possible to devise *a dramaturgy of the visual film-form* as regulated and precise as the existing dramaturgy of the film-story.

Thus Eisenstein conceives of film syntax as a complex but highly controlled system of formal conflicts at every level: juxtapositions within the shot of line, scale, light, depth, movement, patterning, which are built up into larger oppositions between close shots and long shots, pieces of graphically varied direction, pieces resolved in volume with pieces resolved in area, pieces of darkness and pieces of lightness, conflicts between an event and its duration. All this creates a 'visual counterpoint' extending through the whole film.

Our analysis of *Strike*, then, must start with a recognition of the conflict of *line* in individual shots: chimneys or a factory hooter cutting obliquely across a square-framed sky; workers clambering to a secret meeting on a tracery of girders in the top-left diagonal with the other half of the frame masked by factory roof, or over a conglomeration of wheels with their own counterpoint of curved rims and straight spokes; crooks framed in a 'checkerboard' pattern of round barrel tops within the squared frame, or a spy glimpsed through a round hoop in a pet shop, or upside-down in the spherical glass of a lamp framed in a square shop-window; or a child framed by shifting patterns of horses' legs—this image later built up into a highly syncopated sequence where the strikers and their wives and children are caught up in a maze of tenement buildings with landings sweeping off at oblique angles from the central squared frames created by bridges and horses' legs. Even the purely technical devices of fade-in and fade-out, vertical or diagonal wipes, round or diamond-shaped iris contribute to the tense rhythms Eisenstein creates in many of these sequences.

Or take the conflict in *depth* between factory managers desperately telephoning (in close-up) from wall-telephones intercut with a long shot of a massive gantry swarming with strikers which appears to be moving down on them, ineluctably, to crush them out of existence; or close-ups of police chiefs phoning, or shareholders gloating, intercut with lyrical long shots of workers running through the woods inspired by the joy of united revolt. Conflicts in *scale* abound: between individual figures of workers and the vast machinery of the factory floor; between a pathetic kitten lying in a doorway and a worker and his wife fighting over their last few possessions to be pawned for food; between the child and the police horses, the workers and the tenements; between bottles of ink flowing across a map and panic-stricken crowds flowing through the streets represented on the map.

Light is appropriately the element Eisenstein most favours for his montage effects, whether within the shot or between shots and over whole sequences. In *Strike*, as in *Battleship Potemkin* or *Alexander Nevsky*, it is second-nature to the graphic artist in Eisentein to cut the frame obliquely with bands of light or shadow against light; to open up a shot with a diagonal wipe or a camera sweep from a dark lower right-hand corner to a bright upper-left, to reflect first workers' legs (an inverted rhyme with factory chimneys), then whole figures in a brilliantly lit puddle; to make swimming workers converge on a suspended anchor in splashes of light; to frame the heads of laughing shareholders in a bright cloud of tobacco smoke; to frame the dark figures of *agents-provocateurs* and police in flames and smoke from the liquor-store fire; to create a double and inverted image of workers' wives running to join their striking menfolk along the banks of a stream, with static verticals of trees and running shapes of legs and bodies reflected in the water; to flood a dark screen with light in the form of water in the fight at night between two police spies and a worker through torrents of rain, or explosions of water from fire-hoses on sections of the crowd or individual workers. Form and content are inextricably linked in this kind of shot. As Eisenstein insists in *Film Form*, these are not mere cameraman's technical tricks:

> Similarly with the theory of lighting. To sense this as a collision between a stream of light and an obstacle, like the impact of a stream from a fire-hose striking a concrete object, or of the wind buffeting a human figure, must result in a usage of light entirely different in comprehension from that employed in playing with various combinations of 'gauzes' and 'spots.'

We might note how many of the most dramatic instances of montage with light in *Strike* exploit the dynamics of a highly mobile medium for reflected light (water and smoke in particular) in preference to direct sources of light such as lamps, searchlight beams or fire: light is already transposed metaphorically out of some other substance before it begins to create images of conflict with the surrounding darkness.

The implicit montage creating a conflict between objects and their dimensions or between events and their duration is used much less boldly in *Strike* than in Eisenstein's later films. The former device is used with rather obvious propagandistic intent in the shareholders' meeting sequence when we have a close-up of the new-fangled lemon-squeezer crushing the juice out of a lemon (intercut with rearing horses' hooves threatening strikers, but with well-judged dramatic tension when a close-up of the child under the horses makes them seem gigantically dangerous); otherwise this device is confined, interestingly, to close-ups of laughing, yawning, snarling, smirking mouths—breaking the 'sound barrier' of the silent film, as it were—and eyes staring or blinking for the police spies, gloating or winking for the shareholders and crooks, and finally rolling in anguish for the bull as its throat is cut and the blood gushes.

Nor is there any play with the temporal dimension to match the Odessa Steps sequence in *Potemkin* or the toppled Tsar's statue, Kerensky's climb up the palace stairs or the raising of the Neva bridges in *October*. The three scenes in *Strike* where the technique is clearly in evidence are, however, key ones: the final intercut sequences of the bull being slaughtered and the strikers being driven into the river and massacred; the brief scene that prefigures this of the factory manager and foreman being rolled into the river by the workers when they first go on strike; and that characteristic Eisensteinian centerpiece to the film, the shareholders' meeting, where every instantaneous verbal or emotional reaction, every act of smoking, laughing, drinking, every grimace and gesture is tracked by camera and subtitle in turn around the four fat capitalists. This virtuoso sequence is rounded off and given its full narrative impact by one of Eisenstein's stairway set-pieces: a lackey is summoned to remove the paper which has been used to wipe a piece of lemon off the shoe of one of the capitalists, a paper which—inevitably—turns out to have been the very reasonable demands of the strikers for a wage rise and shorter working hours. He slowly descends an interminable grandiose stairway, picks up the precious paper and lemon and interminably mounts the stairway again before taking a smirking glance at the writing on the paper. Each shot is slowed down by being intercut with angry or grinning capitalists' faces and by the alternation of close-ups and long-shots of the stairway. The formal restructuring of time here perfectly restructures the content of this crucial scene in the film: it juxtaposes the value of the workers' demands formulated at the risk of deprivation, loss of work, imprisonment or death with the value placed on these demands—as on human life and welfare—by the shareholders, isolated by capital, comfort and cocktails from anything resembling the real world.

The deliberate slowing down of "real" story-time in this sequence serves to highlight it as a crucial moment of conflict in the film's narrative structure, the peripeteia which reverses any hope of a peaceful settlement of the strike or a *modus vivendi* between capital and the proletariat. It also serves to interrupt the momentum of rhythms that have been built up in the early part of the film and which have to be generated once more in the sequences which follow. More than this, it is a beautifully judged formal mimesis for the production rhythms of the factory which have been brought to a standstill by the strike. Thematically, too, the scene argues the crisis of pre-Revolutionary capitalism: in the context of the film the directors and shareholders have the whip-hand and their refusal to bargain can only lead to the scenes which follow of workers suffering poverty and conflict among themselves, betraying each other and finally succumbing to police suppression. But this is only within the story-line, the *histoire*. The *discours*, the way Eisenstein conveys the story is quite different at this point: the capitalists, for all their wealth and power and self-satisfaction, form a tiny besieged square in a vast empty hall and every shot of them underlines their isolation, the artificiality of their way of life and the bankruptcy of their policies. This scene lends ample support to Eisenstein's assertion that the film's newness was nothing to do with its revolutionary theme, its lack of an individual hero, the mass action and absence of a unified plot line. No, "for the first time the subject matter—the mode of production of the past of our revolutionary present—was perceived from the correct angle of vision."

The purpose of "ostranenie," of the fairground "attractions," of the montage of conflict within frames and between shots and sequences, and the tense rhythms which relate shot sequence and episode is, then, genuinely dialectical. The formal devices serve in authentically cinematic terms to create an angle of vision, or point of view on the events depicted, analogous to, but quite distinct from the way a novelist refracts his narrative through his choice of language.

Eisenstein is overstating his case in claiming that there is no unified plot line. Certainly there is no individual hero or family with whom the audience can cosily identify as in conventional "bourgeois" drama; the Proletkult Collective (Pletniev, Eisenstein, Kravchinovskii, et al, 1927) conceived the scenario in terms of "a formal visual play on a chronicle of events." The events are in clear chronological order and there is a six-act structure to the chronicle (almost certainly reflecting the single-reel projection which was the norm in 1924), so that each of the six reels would be designed to end on a moment of crisis or tension like the chapters in a serialised novel: the first "act" ends with strike notices all over the factory and the foreman being knocked down by the mobile crane; the second opens with the theft of the micrometer which leads the worker responsible to commit suicide, thus precipitating the strike, and ends with the Foreman and Factory Manager being dumped in the slimy river; the third opens with happy family scenes during the first euphoric days of the strike and ends with the departure of the shareholders after their late night meeting, "Having carefully studied the welfare of the workers" (title). Up to this point the montage rhythms, like the events themselves, have been running in the workers' favour. But the shareholders' meeting and their summary dismissal of the strikers' claims is the critical turning point dramatically as well as ideologically and the final three "acts" are almost a mirror image of the first three with the tide turning against the workers: "Act Four" opens with scenes of domestic misery and strife and closes with one of the strike leaders being tricked into betraying his comrades; in the fifth the gang of crooks are called in by the police, they set fire to the liquor store and the act closes with the hoses being turned on the workers, while the final act moves from the "chapter heading" title of a press cutting announcing that the cavalry have been called in and the scene of the child wandering among the horses' legs to the final slaughter of strikers and the bull.

Each "act" has a very marked unity of tone and a clear progression of rhythms, and the underlying sense of structure is unmistakable. However, in a sense Eisenstein is right in claiming that plot has been demoted, since there are no temporal shifts such as flashbacks and the causal links between events are self-evident and do not require highlighting. To use another key pair of concepts enunciated by the Russian Formalists and the Prague

School Structuralists, plot is an "automatized" element and "foregrounded" elements are to be sought elsewhere in the film. Each of Eisenstein's films is basically the story of a conflict, yet the causal-sequential relationship between events is left to emerge of its own accord from the chain of apparently unrelated montage sequences. Unlike Pudovkin who spells out every link in the plot (built around individual figures with whom we clearly identify), Eisenstein challenges his audience to reconstruct the deep logic by which the often quite disparate events in each montage are related. He is the poet of the cinema, building visual metaphors, rhymes, rhythms, puns, hyperbole and litotes out of the paradigmatic relations between sets of objects or people; whereas Pudovkin, like most film makers, relies on the links in a syntagmatic chain, on metonymic relations, to involve his audience and convey his message.

Where an artist consistently "foregrounds" certain devices and elements in the structure of a work at the expense of other "automatized" elements, we may note the significance of what the Formalists and their successors termed a "dominant." Eikhenbaum, writing on the special colloquial style of Leskov's narrative prose, was one of the first to develop this concept:

> Any element in the material may become prominent as a formative dominant and by the same token as a basis of plot or construction. The plot is merely the commonest type of construction. *Skaz* (characterised oral narration) projects to the forefront those elements of language which naturally fade into the background in genres which are strong in action or description—such elements as intonation, semantics ("folk etymology," puns), lexical choice and so on. This accounts for the development of highly coloured narrative (*skaz*) forms at precisely those periods when the great forms of the novel are for some reason stagnating.
>
> (1927)

If writers like Leskov and Gogol and Zoschenko project to the forefront elements of colloquial language, what are the elements of film language that Eisenstein "foregrounds" at the expense of the standard "automatized" ingredients of plot and characterisation? We have noted the juxtapositions of line, scale, light, depth, movement, shot-length, direction, dimension and duration out of which the rich fabric of *Strike* is woven, and we have cautiously admired the bravura set-piece shock sequences with which he has ornamented the film. Are we conscious of any component of the work which can be said, in Mukarovsky's definition of the "dominant" to "set in motion and determine the relations between all other components?" I believe we are. In *Strike* Eisenstein is fascinated by circles. And circles have both formal and mythical/ideological properties of peculiar importance to this film. Time and again we are

Structural Interpretation of a Film 123

reminded of the formal tension created by a circle within the square frame of the film shot: the title "BUT ..." has the letters rearranged in a circle which begins to spin, we cut to factory wheels spinning, plotting workers reflected in a round puddle, then a wheel spins and comes to a stop in front of the severe vertical figures of three strike leaders; the spy "Monkey" is discovered in a pet shop framed in the circular hoop on which a real monkey sits; strikers converge on a pile of wagon wheels to hold their secret meetings; a crane looms towards us carrying a massive wheel; in the famous shot of the accordion bellows superimposed on the festive workers walking through the woods, the director not only "breaks the sound barrier" of the silent film with juxtaposed rhythms, but deliberately juxtaposes the curving bellows with the straight lines of trees and the frames; in one of the other few superimposed shots, a round micrometer on a square desk is combined with the figure of the thief fleeing along the factory floor; we are given in close-up the round eye of the spy "Owl," then cut to an oval window through which he is glimpsed in the street, then to a rectangular doorway which widens as the camera approaches, then to a lamp globe which inverts the image of the spy's head; or, again, the owl's eye and "Owl's" eye and the pocket watch (a secret camera—with an iris—) in close-up; and, of course, the rich pattern of smaller circles, shifting in scale and arrangement as the camera moves around the thieves' hideout.

The possibilities for formal interplay between circular forms and square frames or objects leads Eisenstein to film whole sequences within a round iris enclosed by the shot frame, But the iris, like all the other circular framing devices, contributes to the "correct angle of vision" the director was aiming to create, and the angle of vision, created through formal means, is part of the ideological content of the film. This ideological element comes over most strongly when circles are created on the screen: the spinning title "BUT ...": swimming workers converging on a hanging anchor and forming a circle of splashed light on the water as they hold a secret strike meeting; men converge from all sides on the factory floor to form a circle of sympathy and solidarity around their comrade who has hanged himself—until the circle is broken up by the Foreman; most vivid of all (and exploiting most richly the potential for visual ambiguity in the film) are the moving circles of splashing light as the hoses are played on the figures of the strikers.

The dominant motif of circularity in conflict with the constricting square frame thus builds a bridge between the ideological conflicts of *Strike* (circles of workers vs four capitalists sitting round a square table in a square hall) and the formal conflicts created by montage on every level:

> Only the naïve will talk of "contradictions between the film's ideological demands and the director's formal digressions" ... It is time some

people realised that form has to be defined in a much deeper way than as some more or less clever superficial "trick."

For Eisenstein, as for the Russian Formalist critics, content becomes an aspect of form, just as the formal devices on every level of "film grammar" contribute to the creation of a "correct angle of vision" which, if one is depicting revolution, is incontrovertibly part of the content of the work of art.

8 The Revolution in Techniques and Human Values
Early Soviet Cinema

Introduction

Early in the 1970s I was invited by the Media Unit at Exeter University to contribute an audiotape feature for private study by students on early Soviet Cinema. This seemed an ideal opportunity to expand some work I had been doing on the distinctive theories and use of montage by two of the Russian directors, Eisenstein and Pudovkin and also to provide some of the social and political background which made their work both possible and necessary.

Russia in 1917

Looking back nearly a century, now, as we take for granted an almost non-stop flow of visual imagery on television, film, instant cameras, colour supplements and coffee-table picture books, it is hard for us to imagine the impact of film on Russians in the years following the Bolshevik Revolution in 1917. But we can't begin to account for the significance of that momentous decade in the history of the cinema and the history of a great nation unless we can project ourselves back to that time.

If we put ourselves in the politician's place, we find that the Bolshevik leaders had more to contend with in promoting the cinema than the recalcitrance of the audience. There was a desperate shortage of film-stock and too few roubles to buy adequate supplies from abroad, and the list of priorities was enormous. First, the War had to be ended, the Civil War won, and a vast and multiracial country unified. In order to guarantee the population at least enough bread, the peasant had to be shown his role in the economy and given a sense of his own significance. The proletarian work-force had to be promoted as the vanguard of the Revolution who were going to make the Russian economy viable and usher in a new era of socialist ownership of the means of production. There were the practical tasks of improving health, hygiene and education and eradicating corruption, alcoholism and religious superstition. But this was not only Russia's revolution: it was seen as the first step in a chain-reaction of revolutions all over the world that would sweep away capitalism and make the new socialist order universal. Intellectuals and artists, then, had to be made politically aware, excited to contribute to the revolutionary cause and committed to the idea of art in the service of the state. It was a bold and impressive step to appoint a Commissar for Enlightenment with responsibility for the arts as a central member of government, and the Soviet Union was fortunate in having two outstanding intellectuals, Lunacharsky and Nadezhda Krupskaya, Lenin's wife, working in that area. Their boldest step was to found in 1919, in the middle of the Civil War, the world's first film institute, VGIK (which stands for the All-Union State Institute of Cinematography) where virtually every great Soviet director, cameraman, actor, editor and make-up artist has either taught or studied.

Many of the cream of Russia's intellectuals had emigrated during the Revolution and Civil War. Hundreds of writers, artists and film-makers had retreated southwards with the White armies and embarked at Odessa and other southern ports as the Reds finally gained control. But the previous two decades had seen an explosion of experimental energy in all the arts. In many respects the experiments with form were even more radical in St. Petersburg than they were in the Paris of Paul Valéry, Pablo Picasso and the Lumière brothers, so that many of the most far-reaching ideas of that time are only just being explored today, nearly a century later. Russia and the Bolsheviks were fortunate in the fact that many of the most exciting experimenters in all the arts remained. How did all these artists feel about their future in the new Socialist Russia?

In many cases the Revolution and its optimistic ideologies and urgent practical problems seemed to offer the perfect opportunity for evolving new meanings through new artistic forms. The poet Mayakovsky with his astounding experiments with rhyme and rhythm and imagery; Zamyatin, who wrote a major anti-utopian novel entitled *We*, a decade before Aldous Huxley's *Brave New World*; Tatlin, who designed outrageous structures to house the outrageous new political organisations of the Bolsheviks; Prokofiev, who explored the limits of musical expression as daringly as any of his German contemporaries. And above all, the young film-makers like Lev Kuleshov, who was only eighteen at the time of the Revolution, but who rapidly became one of the pioneers of montage, a radical film theorist and one of the great professors of film at the Cinematographic Institute.

What were the aesthetic and social ideas that inspired all these great artists? The aesthetic ideas were not a product of the Revolution as such; rather, like the political upheaval, they were "something in the air" at the time, a product of the impatient optimism that seems to come with the turn of a century and a social, political, economic and spiritual crisis that was both a culmination of trends that had been developing in the late nineteenth century and a reaction against them. A dominant aesthetic idea was of art as "a device for renewing man's vision of the world": a *device*, because it was the laws of artistic form itself that make art powerful and every art form is by definition a coherent patterning of devices. One thing that devices like vivid metaphors in poetry or new tonal harmonies in music or shocking montage effects in film achieve is to renew our vision of the world, to shock us out of our complacent acceptance of objects and people and emotions and ideas in their normal context and to make them strange and perceptible once more. Art, therefore, involves a certain degree of psychological manipulation of the audience at some conscious or unconscious level. For the Bolsheviks it was quite in order that art should be recruited to change man's ideas and emotions at a quite conscious level. And if that involved some rather new and recherché artistic forms and devices that they didn't altogether understand, then so be it: artistic creation was as specialised a job as the forging of high-grade steel or the propagation of new strains of wheat.

For the first artists and theorists of the Soviet cinema—Kuleshov, Pudovkin, Eisenstein, Dziga Vertov—films exemplified these aesthetic impulses. What other art was more obviously dependent on devices and techniques? What other art could more directly renew people's vision of the world? But it had other special revolutionary qualities. It was a mechanical art, reproducing through the camera and projector the rhythms of industrial processes. It was a socially aware art, because it had to engage with social reality whether it depicted that reality or distorted it. It was a mass art, produced not by an individual tortured soul, but by a collective of equal and collaborating colleagues, and not for an individual reader or viewer or listener, but for audiences in their hundreds who would respond collectively, and ultimately for audiences of millions who might join and extend the Revolution. Nor was the film limited by language or national style like poetry and the novel, or music and painting. It could make its instant appeal directly to people of any language or culture, or educational level.

I don't want to suggest that these factors made the early evolution of Soviet cinema easy, or reduced the conflict between the film directors and the political committees and individuals who had to provide funds for this expensive art form. What I do believe, and want to stress, is that the 1920s in Russia provided a unique crucible for the melting together of an urgent set of political messages and a no less urgent set of aesthetic and technical possibilities. And by one of those coincidences of history these two forces reached white-heat simultaneously. What this meant in terms of actual shots and sequences I will try to illustrate through a comparison of two of the greatest Russian film directors of the 1920s, Pudovkin and Eisenstein.

Pudovkin and Eisenstein: Contrasting Techniques and the Grammar of Montage

One of the amazing things about Russia in the 1920s is the vigour and intelligence of the theoretical debates about all the arts. It was as if the Revolution and Civil War—not just replacing one regime with another, but replacing a whole concept of man with another—had made every artist go back to first principles. All that the more comfortable and stable societies of Britain, Western Europe and the United States went on taking for granted had to be called into question in the Soviet Union in the most radical terms. And this was as true of film as of painting, sculpture, poetry and music.

Take the themes chosen by the film-makers. Where Russian cinema audiences before 1917 were used to a conventional diet of Western-style comedies, romances, filmed versions of novels, Biblical epics and horror films, in the 1920s Eisenstein and Pudovkin—to mention only the best known examples—confronted them with the politics of industrial confrontation (in Eisenstein's *Strike*) and the stirrings of revolution (in *The Battleship Potemkin*), while *The Mother* by Pudovkin traced the first stirrings of political awareness in an individual caught up in industrial ferment. Both directors made epics of the Revolution itself in *October* and *The End of St. Petersburg*—and we will be focusing on contrasting the techniques of the two directors in a moment. Then Eisenstein went on to depict the changes the Revolution had brought to the countryside in *The Old and the New* (as did Dovzhenko in his film *Earth*), while Pudovkin focused on the impact it was having on some of the non-Russian peoples of the Soviet Union in his film *The Heir to Genghis Khan*. As we have seen, these were precisely the themes which the Bolsheviks wanted—and needed—to exploit their "art for the millions." They were the themes to which they believed the benighted peasants and toiling proletariat ought to respond best. Most importantly, these were the themes which inspired the great pioneering directors to revolutionise the language of film.

The language of film, of course, is highly complex both technically and semiotically. The spectator responds to a moving sequence of illuminated pictures within a rectangular frame which accumulate to form actions and episodes and stories involving people (either acting or in real life), animals, objects, buildings and landscapes. Even on the most basic level of lighting the cameraman and director have a choice of degrees of light and shade, types of patterning and texture, lighting angles, sudden changes in illumination, direct or reflected light, harsh or soft light. The camera involves a further set of choices involving the length, angle and composition of the shot, depth of shot and perspective to be projected onto the two-dimensional surface of a screen, the framing of the image to isolate it or focus attention on it, the movement of the eye and the object, changes of speed, distance, direction and all the special effects a camera can achieve. The scenario will involve variations in scale and in choice of settings, will turn words into images, will relate silent images to titles on the screen, may try to appeal through the visual to all the other senses—sound, touch and even taste and smell (take, for example, the maggoty meat scene in *The Battleship Potemkin*). Then there are all the dimensions of acting by individuals and groups, characterisation through both casting and direction, various acting styles from the most natural to the most stylised, and all the resources of facial and bodily movement. The film as a whole has to be structured in terms of time and place, the psychology of the characters and the narrative structure of the story line. Cutting and editing can change scenes or create imaginary scenes, build up a composite picture from several angles, or eliminate unwanted space. Emphasis can be achieved through focus, prominence and repetition, and all kinds of devices can be used to "make strange" to us the reality being depicted. And all the literary devices of symbol and metaphor and leitmotif and parallelism can be used in a visual dimension.

For the revolutionary Russian directors, however, a conscious adoption of literary conventions, whether from the theatre or from narrative forms, was not the right way to evolve a proper language for film. For them the essential unit in film was *the shot*, and all other dimensions of the medium—whether lighting, camerawork, acting or dramatic composition—stemmed from the nature of the shot (not the individual frame, we should note, for twenty-four of those whizz through the projector every second, but *the shot* (the length of time that the camera focuses on a particular object or scene). As Kuleshov put it: "The frame should act as a sign, as a letter of the alphabet, so that it can be read immediately and so that the viewer should be clear immediately and comprehensively about what is being said in the given shot" (1918, p. 12). But if the frame is like the letter of the alphabet, the unit of *perception*, the shot is like the word, the unit of *meaning*, and all the theories at that time talked about film being built out of shots just as sentences are built out of words. But this was a naïve comparison, since cinematographic meaning results from shots interacting with each other, just as real meaning in language results from the interactions between words: shots might be joined together, or juxtaposed, or in conflict with each other, and each of these possibilities would be created by montage. Montage, Kuleshov maintained, was the essential grammatical mechanism of film.

In a sense, all the arguments that went on about montage were about its grammatical functions and were purely formal. But the language of film was being explored to see how it might best project new images, new ideas and new ideologies, so the disputes were simultaneously formal and political, and a revolution in politics would require a revolution in form. As early as 1918 Kuleshov proclaimed:

> In the cinema the means of expression of artistic thought is the rhythmic alternation between separate immobile frames or short sequences expressing movement, that is, what is technically known as montage. Montage in the cinema is the same as the composition of the colours in painting or a harmonic sequence of notes in music.

As he began to experiment with making films with the Workshop which he founded, Kuleshov soon discovered that montage could achieve effects that were peculiar to film and not available to painting and music. He wanted a shot of the actors looking at some poles carrying electric cables, but there weren't any such poles in the part of Moscow where he was shooting, so why not intercut shots of the actors looking away from the camera with some shots of electricity poles in another part of the city? This "creative geography," as he called it, could be taken further: different parts of Moscow could be brought together to look as if they were in close proximity. For that matter, so could different parts of the world: he combined shots of the White House with shots of the steps of a well-known Moscow building which his actors had to climb. And if you could synthesise landscapes through montage, why not people? So he synthesised an imaginary woman by combining separate shots of different women's bodies. A century later we have come to take for granted this kind of "cheating" by the cameraman and director. A whole profession of film stunt-men and doubles has grown out of this possibility of several actors contributing to a single role requiring both glamour and daring. And Alfred Hitchcock made a point of showing off his montage tricks to the audience of *Rear Window* or *Psycho*, rather as Pope or Pushkin would suddenly incorporate into their poetry a commentary on their own rhymes or imagery.

Montage was not a Russian invention, of course. Even while working with a well-known pre-Revolutionary director named Bauer in 1916, Kuleshov learned about the techniques used by the American director D. W. Griffith in *Birth of a Nation* and *Intolerance*. His rapid cutting, switches from long-shots to close-ups, and parallel lines of action had already enriched the language of film and, indeed, it was probably the political themes which Griffith was expressing through these revolutionary techniques that aroused the interest of the Russians. But they did not merely emulate; they theorised and argued and evolved whole new sets of possibilities all of which had a place in the overall system of film language. What is more, they made a virtue out of the practical problems that faced them. There was a chronic shortage of film-stock, therefore editing must be as economical as possible. The *agitki* educational and propaganda films had to convey their message by simple visual means, and the direct juxtaposition of the old and the new, of the bad and the good, the capitalists and the workers, backwardness and progress, capitalism and socialism, would make the most immediate and powerful impact. In other words, montage would work like a fairground attraction: it would attract the audience's attention and direct it to specific images; it would concentrete their imagination on the essentials; and it would retain their attention through the rhythm and dynamism of what one theorist called "optical bombardment."

But when we look at the films of the period, especially the great masterpieces of Pudovkin and Eisenstein, we see that these aspects of montage were only a primitive beginning. Montage could be used to create mood, to produce a dramatic sequence, to create visual metaphors, puns and jokes, rhymes and rhythms. If we take our examples from two of their best-known films, Pudovkin's *The End of St. Petersburg* and Eisenstein's *October*, there is a good chance that you will already have seen them or will have an opportunity to do so. Since these films have the same basic theme and were made to celebrate the same occasion, the tenth anniversary in 1927 of the October Revolution, they also offer an interesting opportunity to compare the techniques of the two directors in detail.

Pudovkin uses montage to create mood, to convey the causal and temporal sequences that produce a narrative line or plot and to highlight and explain the underlying economic and social contradictions in Russia that made the October Revolution necessary. Eisenstein, too, dramatises the contradictions, but tends to present them in actual confrontations between social groups. The sequential logic of the historical events leading up to the Revolution is not carried by a narrative sequence, and still less epitomised in the lives of individual Russians. The titles on the screen give us a bare framework for the sequence of events between February and October 1917, but Eisenstein's montage of conflict—the direct juxtaposition of contrasting images—makes us work quite hard to reconstruct a logical narrative. Both directors create mood with montage, but whereas Pudovkin tends to use landscape to engage our sympathy with the plight of his heroes, Eisenstein's is more abstract and intellectual, confronting us more directly with the causes and results of the social conflicts.

I will attempt to sketch the scenario for the first few minutes of each of these films in order to illustrate the differences between Pudovkin and Eisenstein in their theory and practice of montage. There are two problems: firstly, it can only be a broad shot-by-shot sketch, with only an occasional hint about lighting and framing, shot length and depth and angle—and much of the effect of montage depends on these quite abstract and formal aspects of film language; secondly, there is no substitute for seeing the films. All I can hope to do here is to describe each shot in note form and suggest some of its implications, so that you can take the analysis and interpretation much further when you have a chance to view and study the films. The shots are numbered for ease of reference.

As the opening titles for *The End of St. Petersburg* come up we get a glimpse in the background of a bronze statue of a tsar on horseback in a St. Petersburg square, but for the opening sequence Pudovkin takes us straight to the countryside:

Shot

1. Broad expanse of sunlit river, from above [= the calm permanence of nature]
2. Windmills turning, level view, then from below sails [= productivity of the land, man and nature in harmony, timelessness]
3. **Title:** "Peasants from Tver'—Novgorod—Penza" [= the scope of a great agrarian land, implying, perhaps, a question about what is to be said, or shown, about these peasants]
4. Elderly peasant, well-fed, chews grainy bread with pleasure [= man lives on the produce of his labour from the rich soil]

5. The sunlit river again
6. Working peasants share a meagre crust [= the problem hinted at]
7. Poor peasant huts
8. Mother-to-be struggles up steps into hut and collapses [= the problem intensified]
9. Close-up of her face, labour pains
10. Clouds in sky [= threat? /Nature involved in human predicament? Or separate from it?/Happiness possible?]
11. Boy sent to fetch peasant workers from field [= story-line montage: he leaves—runs through grass—appears in view]
12. Title: "Mother is dying"
13. Clouds
14. Older peasant follows boy—intercut with younger resuming ploughing [= problems, but life goes on, toil without a break]
15. Mother looks up smiling [= joy at birth]
16. Mother looks up, anxious [= but new child a problem]
17. Baby admired, sex checked
18. Title: "A daughter—one more mouth to feed" [= problem explained]
19. Grim-faced granny
20. Title: "There's no way out!"
21. Granny
22. Title: "And so one more proletarian has to go to the city to earn." [= opening problem fully explicit: contradiction of city attracting best peasants from the land]
22. Windmill turning—peasant ploughing—farewells [= recapitulation of familiar images summarises problem visually]
23. Clouds
24. 4 windmills turning on horizon, while in foreground telegraph poles pass camera rhythmically as peasants walk to city [= time passing: moving camera produces parallax effect between permanence of rural symbol (windmills) and mobility of urban symbol (telegraph poles): conflict within a single shot]
25. Statue of Tsar on horse [= St. Petersburg motif made explicit]
26. St. Isaac's Cathedral [later to be developed as symbol of state and church power]
27. Sunlit River Neva [= contrast with country river]
28. Imperial griffons, statues of tsars seen from below [= the might of those in power: dominating, alien, unapproachable]
29. Title: "Workers from the Putilov—Obukhov—Lebedev Factories" [the three-fold list rhymes visually with the rural list in Shot 3, but the scale is compressed from all Russia to an industrial suburb of the capital, and the names are not ancient beloved regions which command loyalty, belonging and patriotism, but the names of capitalist factory owners who exploit the workers, grow rich on armaments and earn only hatred].

Revolution in Techniques 133

This is all we'll analyse in detail from this film. The next episode is broadly parallel in structure but rural sunlight is replaced by the glare of iron furnaces, turning windmills by turning machinery wheels, and calm peasants by sweating factory hands. The new crisis is that the Lebedev factory gets a big government order for arms, so that the owner can hire more labour to create more profit for himself and the shareholders. The problem is explained through a montage of images juxtaposing the Stock Exchange—a mass of bowler hats and umbrellas—and the factory floor. The story line continues with the old woman and young man from the country coming to stay with their urban relatives in a tenement block, causing resentment and more feeding problems for the townswoman. Her husband is a Bolshevik who holds meetings in their room with other men from the factory, but is watched by the secret police. And so the seeds of the proletarian revolution are sown, and the national crisis is expounded mainly through its effect on the lives of individuals and their families. Montage is used to highlight the larger issues and conflicts, but Pudovkin favours a conventional linear narrative, and the audience is made to identify closely with the crises and moods of the central characters as in a traditional folk tale or novel or play.

Eisenstein, on the other hand, appears to scorn mere linear narrative. While, like Pudovkin, he can depict villains whom we can *hate*, like Kerensky, the Prime Minister of the Provisional Government, or the gloating bourgeois gents and their wives, he rarely offers us heroes whom we can *love* or identify with. It's true that our sympathies are engaged with Vakulinchuk, the sailor who dies in the "Potemkin" uprising, or, ten years later, with the heroic saviour of Old Russia, Prince Alexander Nevsky, but these figures have mainly symbolic value: they embody abstractions like "the solidarity of the workers," or "patriotism," rather than existing in their own right as lovable human beings. In general, Eisenstein's art, and in particular his approach to montage, is much more abstract and intellectual than Pudovkin's, where it is the content of shots that is being juxtaposed, as with the comparison of Kerensky pompously entering the palace with the mechanical peacock over the door to the royal apartments, or with a brooding statuette of Napoleon. Eisenstein uses montage to create *metaphors*. As so often with metaphors in poetry, the immediate comparison seems to produce other ripples of meaning, other potential comparisons, so that the significance is always extendable, never fully exhausted. Just as often, however, Eisenstein's "montage of conflict" involves purely formal conflicts of light, composition, texture and rhythm which may have no immediately obvious meaning, but which, like the visual metaphors, leave open to the viewer whole areas of potential meaning. Take the contrast between the white sunshades of the bourgeois ladies in the boats on the river which turn into weapons with which to stab the fallen demonstrators, whose red banners and white copies of *Pravda* (*The Truth*) are hurled into the river, creating further patterns of furling, drifting fabric; or the contrasting angles and elevations of the bridge as it is raised to cut off the workers' quarter of St. Petersburg from the centre of the capital: here the interplay of angles, light and rhythm (both of the bridge's movement and the cutting speed) creates something more like visual music. Even the machine-gunning of a peaceful crowd of demonstrators in the July uprisings turns into a rhythmic pattern as the montage of crowds swirling along the street and of a chattering machine-gun is speeded up until the two images merge into a single superimposed shot. For Eisenstein, montage seems to exist primarily to create rhythms and to drain sequences of precise narrative meaning.

October opens right in the middle of St. Petersburg:

Shot

1. Head of statue of Alexander III, the father of the last Tsar, Nicholas II [= the trappings of kingly power (crown, sceptre and orb); the name Alexander is going to be used often later in the film to mock the ambitions of Alexander Kerensky]
2. Title: "Alexander III, Emperor of all the Russias"
3. Crowds rush up the steps towards the statue [= flow of human movement round hard, angular steps and plinth]
4. Ladders leaned against statue [= abstract patterns against sky; lèse-majesté]
5. Ropes are fastened around head and legs of statue by busy demonstrators [= immovable (trapped) stasis vs hectic movement]
6. A forest of rifles held aloft; cheering
7. A forest of scythes held aloft, cheering [= the urban masses and the peasantry united in their hatred of the regime]
8. Title: "February 1917" [= the February Uprising]
9. Head of statue rocks [= symbolic shaking of authority in first "bourgeois" revolution]
10. Rapid intercutting of disintegrating parts of statue [= rhythmic montage, same movements filmed several times (NB the later "rhyme" with this when stability is restored under Kerensky and this sequence is filmed backwards: an even more abstract technical device, with the parts of the statue flying back together to symbolise reconstituted autocracy]
11. Church bells swinging—priest swinging a censer—rich folk nodding and smiling [= the rhythmic rituals of the status quo unshaken]
12. Priest blesses the Provisional Government
13. Title: "Long live ..."
14. Title: "Everybody, everybody, everybody" [= words join in rhythm]
15. Title: "Everybody ?" [= the rhythm cut off by a crucial question]
16. Soldiers in trenches at the front [= how long will they have to live?]
17. Russian and German soldiers meet at the front, joking and swapping hats [= an extended sequence of cuts, with a different kind of celebration: a new international solidarity of the working classes
18. Sharing bread and drink together [= simple folk rituals vs elaborate church rituals]

Revolution in Techniques 135

19. Laughing men [= happiness at end of war]
20. Protest meetings at the front [= but serious revolutionary task ahead]
21. The Winter Palace—marble floor with circular angel motif
22. Kerensky and his aides receive appointment [= divine sanction? A circle of conspiracy? The continuity unbroken despite the February Revolution]
23. Title: "The Provisional Government will honour its undertakings [= the message spelled out]
24. Violent cut to explosions at the front, panic and death in the trenches
25. Wheels and factory machinery [= industry and the war effort. Patterns and angles]
26. Queues in the snow for bread [= a recurrent motif]
27. Title: "A pound of bread'
28. Queues in the snow
29. Title: "Half a pound"
30. Queues getting thinner and more weary
31. Title: "A quarter ..."
32. Queue mostly dead.
33. Title: An eighth
34. Title: "The same old story: hunger and war"
35. Title: "But ..." (in Russian, **HO** ...)
36. Ranks of soldiers
37. Ranks of workers
38. Title: "At the Finland Station—3rd April 1917"
39. Cheering crowds
40. Title: "He ..." (in Russian, **OH** ... i.e., the previous letters in reverse)
41. Cheering crowds
42. Title: "Ulyanov!" [= Ulyanov was Lenin's real surname and its introduction here indicates affection.]

And with the arrival of Lenin from exile in the West, the events leading up to the Great October Revolution get under way. But we should note, even from this brief scenario, that the sequence of events and the essential argument are carried by the titles intercut with images, not by the shots alone. And even the titles are used as part of an abstract *visual* composition—a sort of concrete poetry—as when the Russian **HO** of Title 35 ("But") is reversed in Title 40 to **OH** ("He"). Eisenstein had exploited the same word to even more dramatic visual effect three years earlier in *Strike*, where it is made to revolve like the spokes of a factory wheel with which it is intercut.

In just a short extract from their films we have seen some of the major artistic differences between Pudovkin and Eisenstein. To what extent can we see these great directors as representative of the revolution in human values and techniques of Soviet cinema in the 1920s? Both fully sympathised with the aims of the Revolution in its early phase, with the needs of the population and the problems facing the new Bolshevik government.

Pudovkin responded by experimenting with the cinematic equivalents of conventional prose narrative. His films achieved immediate popularity, but today look quite dated.

Eisenstein responded by stretching the cinematic equivalents of experimental poetry. His films achieved a less broad appeal in Russia at the time, but have continued to challenge—and be quoted by—avant-garde directors all over the world.

Part 4
Painting

By 1986 I was convinced that Halliday's systemic-functional grammar was valid, with modifications, for any semiotic system, including visual ones. I tested this on colleagues in a joint seminar of the Linguistics and Art History Departments at Sydney University and explored it in a number of international conference papers and journal articles. At this time the important work of Kress and van Leeuwen, Hodge and others was being developed for the systemic analysis of other visual and mixed modes such as diagrams, cartoons, advertisements, etc. My development of a systemic semiotics of the visual arts, leading to my book *The Language of Displayed Art*, Leicester UP and Pinter Publishers, 1994; (2nd extended edition, with accompanying CD Rom, London: Routledge, 2010), was the main related work focussed on art. Unfortunately, the published version of this first very comprehensive paper did not appear until 1995. It has been widely used in linguistics and art courses in Australia, the UK, Singapore, Canada and Sweden.

9 Towards a Systemic-Functional Semiotics of Painting
Frank Hinder's *The Flight into Egypt*

Introduction

My thesis is quite simple: Michael Halliday's Systemic-Functional linguistics offers a powerful and flexible model for the study of other semiotic codes besides natural language, and its universality may be of particular value in evolving new discourses about art.

I believe the adaptation of Halliday's model I am presenting here can significantly improve how we perceive art, how we talk about it, and how we teach it. This will have both theoretical and practical implications for epistemological, psychological, social, art-historical, aesthetic and pedagogical theories of art which I can only point to in this chapter. This model is at a provisional and exploratory stage (despite the grandeur of the claims just made!), and readers are invited to share their responses and ideas. A proper semiotics of art will only grow out of a large body of analysis, description, interpretation and theory by people with a range of orientations. I hope that this adaptation of Systemic-Functional grammar will offer at least some shared (or sharable) terminology and assumptions.

I am grateful to the Association of Gallery Guides of the Art Gallery of Western Australia for their challenge to formulate a semiotics of art and for providing a forum for its early discussion. My colleagues and students at Murdoch then sharpened my resolve with their informed and attentive skepticism. I owe a particular debt to the Sydney systemicists—Michael Halliday himself, Jim Martin, Terry Threadgold, Theo van Leeuwin, David Butt and Cate Poynton for extensive and supportive debate. Terry Smith and Richard Reid have made many valuable points from an art-historical perspective, and Nigel Helyer and Geoff Warn, rare practising artists who really care about the quality of art teaching and debate, have always helped with advice.

Analysis

As a grounding for the later theoretical discussion I will show how the model works in the analysis of a single painting, though with reference to

140 *Painting*

other well-known paintings, to illustrate the range of systemic choices available at each rank and function. The painting (refer to colour plate section) is *Flight into Egypt* (1952) by Frank Hinder, a Sydney artist, born in 1906.

The painting hangs in the Art Gallery of Western Australia. Apart from these basic facts, I will not comment at this stage on its history, which is well

Plate 1 Frank Hinder: *Flight into Egypt* (1952). Oil and tempera on hardboard

State Art Collection, Art Gallery of Western Australia
Gift of the Friends of the Art Gallery, 1953
Photographer: Bo Wong

documented in Gooding (1985); nor will I discuss its strengths and weaknesses. Art history and evaluative criticism are dominant cultural practices to which the mode of analysis I am proposing offers a skeptical alternative. I believe a further advantage of this model is that it can situate those practices in a general semiotic theory. Of which more later.

Chart 1: Language (refer to charts) is Michael Halliday's (1973) chart of ranks and functions in Systemic-Functional grammar. For Halliday the *ideational function* incorporates referential meanings (about the real world, 'out there,' or in our minds) into language forms; the *interpersonal function* incorporates meanings about the interaction between speaker and hearer, including the orientation to that real world, into language forms; and the *textual function* structures the ideational and interpersonal meanings into coherent and situationally appropriate texts. The major strength of the model is that meaning making is involved every time we choose an option from the available systems. Semantics is not some separate level of abstract interpretation beyond syntax and phonology. The key word here is *realisation:* social meanings to do with our categorisation of objects and events in the real world, and of the relationships between speaker and hearer, are realised through the systems of transitivity, mood, theme, etc., and these are realised as particular syntactic forms, which are themselves realised as phonologically appropriate strings of sound or graphologically as strings of letters.

Realisation is an equally powerful mechanism for describing how meanings are made in other semiotic systems, including the visual arts. For instance, in Botticelli's *Primavera* (1478). certain neo-Platonist concepts of 'humanitas' are realised in the figures of Venus and Mercury and in the metamorphoses of Earth into Flowers and Love into Beauty.[1] But these are only realised in a particular manner of representation, with a particular modality of address to the viewer and involving a complex of compositional relationships. These in turn are realised in particular lines and planes on the painted surface involving chromatically appropriate colours, rhythms and degrees of illumination. The scale of realisation from semiotic systems to graphological form and substance in painting is analogous to that for language. Hence the universal power of the systemic model.

I will return to the mechanism of realisation when I come to discuss the concepts of register and the social semiotic. For the moment we will concentrate on the 'grammar' of painting represented by the chart (Chart 2 in the Charts section). A first step in the analysis of any semiotic system is to isolate a hierarchy of comparable units of structure. For Halliday the grammatical **rank scale** consists of the hierarchy of units: Sentence, Clause, Group, Word and Morpheme. I am proposing for the grammar of painting: Picture, Episode, Figure, Member, Element (see the headings down the left hand margin of Chart 2).

Early semiotic analyses of film were confused, I believe, by too great an insistence on a 1:1 match between linguistic units and units of a visual code,

142 *Painting*

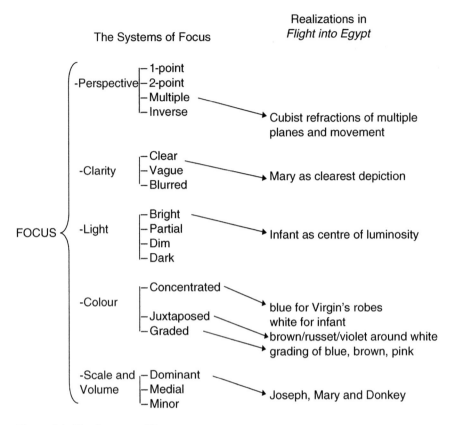

Figure 9.1 The Systems of Focus

and some well-founded opposition has developed to the construction of hierarchies of units for the study of art (see Baxendall, 1972). However, no less an authority than Alberti established in 1435 a hierarchy of four levels appropriate to the analysis of *composition* in painting: Picture, Body, Member and Plane, whereby "Pictures are composed of Bodies, which are composed of Parts, which are composed of Plane surfaces." I find the term Figure more appropriate than Body (which does not seem to allow for inanimate objects), and I would interpose a further rank of Episode, since many pictures like Botticelli's *Primavera* are made up of several distinct episodes (just as sentences are composed of clauses), and a distinct set of systemic options appear to be available at this rank, if my chart is correct. Naturally, a picture may consist of a single episode (Cézanne's *Card Players*), or a single figure (most portraits), or a single member (an arm or a nose by Leonardo), or even a single element (Malevich's *White Square*), just as a sentence may consist of a single clause/group/word/morpheme ('Stop!').

To semioticians or art students of a less linguistic bent, my insistence on a rank scale of units may seem over-schematic: surely a reading of a painting involves a rapid and largely untraceable shuttling between larger and smaller units, and the semantic interest—the 'real meaning'—is in the boundaries themselves, or indeed in the very movement across the hierarchy. Yes, and the same will be true of our comprehension of meanings in sentences of verbal language. But the semiotician, like the linguist, can map the mechanisms of selection and combination that operate at each rank as a first step in observing the interactions between ranks in any one 'text' (painting) (see Figure 9.1).

The Representational Function

For example, in the *representational function* (see the first column on Chart 2), Hinder has chosen the Flight into Egypt as his theme: an episode for the whole picture. This might have been an episode in a larger canvas depicting various stages in the life of Christ or in Herod's oppression of the Jews. Alternatively, he might have chosen a single figure—say, Mary or the donkey—or even a single member—a fleeing foot or garment—to represent this subject. In each case the paradigm of choice would be different: in the first case the system would include the 'transitivity' of Agents (Joseph, Mary, shepherds, wise men, or Roman soldiers and governors) acting on (nurturing, following, bearing gifts to, persecuting) other people, or Patients (the infant, the parents, the firstborn) or Goals (a star, a manger, frankincense, swords). If the picture had consisted solely of a Figure, then the focus of representation would have been on Character (sanctity, piety, patience) or Stance (stepping in flight) or Gesture (gaze of fear, hand raised in horror). Representation of the Flight by a single member would have to concentrate all the Character, Gesture and Transitivity into a single part of the body (a foot, a hand, an eye) or object (a flying robe, a milestone, an arrow). In scanning the picture, i.e., in remaking its meaning, the viewer has all these options in suspension and reads the represented Episode in relation to them. We unconsciously negotiate with the painter, via the same semiotic systems, the rank at which the main depiction is taking place.

This raises the question of whether rank shift occurs in painting as in language. Because it is a general semiotic—and psychological—phenomenon, the answer must be that it does. A painting of 'the artist in his studio' frequently contains an easel bearing a complete painting or drawing with its own distinct subject of representation, modality and composition; or a mirror—as in the *Arnolfini Wedding* by Van Eyck or *Las Meninas* by Velázquez—may represent in concentrated form the same Scene or another one outside the painting. Some Italian and Dutch paintings contain several distinct paintings, like sequences of rank-shifted Relative Clauses qualifying a Nominal Group ('the famous artist who....') in sentence structure. Magritte played with the potential of rankshift, as with most of the logical conventions of painting. An extreme case, as W. H. Auden (1950: 19) so elegantly demonstrated in his poem "Musée des Beaux Arts," is Bruegel's *The Fall of Icarus*, where the central event of the title, the main clause, as it were, is swamped by a series of rank-shifted representations: a peasant ploughing, a ship sailing, birds flying, etc.

Most paintings represent some recognisable and describable subject: an action or event (a crucifixion, an annunciation, a battle, a horse race), or some state of the world (a landscape at a particular season or time of day, a still life in a particular light or setting, a person in a particular condition or mood). These all involve specific participants ('subjects' or objects of processes or states) and specific circumstances of time and place. Our need to know what is represented impels us to seek the title of even quite abstract works. Hinder's painting clearly (well, more or less; see later section under Modality) depicts Mary, holding the infant Jesus, and Joseph, both in somewhat biblical looking robes and head-dresses and with a halo (clearer in the case of Mary than with Joseph). Their pose suggests movement, or readiness for flight. Standing in patient attendance is the donkey. The essentials of St. Matthew's account are all there.[2] Some viewers have also discovered the shadow of an Egyptian pyramid in the rhomboid shaft of light that seems to fall across the upper part of the figures from the left.

The Cubist manner (some might think 'mannerism') chosen by the artist makes possible the simultaneous representation of several moments of action and angles on the subject. This is a point where the boundaries between the functional systems become highly permeable, and we will need to discuss this aspect of the depiction—highly germane, I think, to our interpretation of the painting—in terms of the Modal and Compositional functions as well.

In general it should be stressed that the rather rigid-looking grid of Chart 2 is not designed to constrain or over-determine our interpretation of a painting's meaning. Rather, I would propose it as a map (therefore a schematic model) of the semiotic space created by the work within which our perceptions and conceptions are negotiated. I will return to the question of the viewer's 'negotiation' with the painting later in relation to the social semiotic and the position of the subject. The semiotic space, meanwhile, involves all three functional dimensions of meaning: representational, modal and compositional. It is a crucial advantage for linguistics that Halliday's model does not give special weight to the referential, 'ideational' function of language. It often seems obvious to start with this, but it should have no priority over the interpersonal and textual functions. Similarly, in the analysis of a painting our craven need to recognise what is being represented tends to push us into discussing options in the representational function, as I have done here. I believe, however, that there are considerable advantages to be gained in approaching the modal systems first: hermeneutically, they probably determine our first immediate engagement with the work; heuristically, their adequate description should counteract the form/content dichotomy to which critics and art historians are prone; and pedagogically, recognizing them and having words to describe them may well offer learners and lovers of painting a more direct access to what we actually see, as opposed to what art historians think we ought to know before we start looking. I would argue that a firmer recognition of, and a clearer language for describing the modal function in art would do more to change the quality (and the politics) of art appreciation and education than any other single change. It would give people the words to describe how and why they engage with a painting, and begin to release them from their abject bondage to art historians and teachers of composition. To put it bluntly, the main function of our functional semiotics may be to clarify and share around the discourse.

The Modal Function

The Modal Function is realised by a number of systems of options that determine both how the artist views the reality represented in the painting and how he or she seeks to engage our involvement with the subject matter through various formal devices. It is analogous to Halliday's Interpersonal Function in lexicogrammar in comprising both systems of Modality and of Mood. Just as no verbal message is entirely neutral with respect to either the speaker's view of the experiential world or the relations its enunciation enacts between speaker and hearer, so no work of art is neutral in its representation of 'the real world' or its way of involving the viewer. Art is display: the artist seeks to express some attitude or mood, some 'slant' upon his or her subject, and to draw us into the world of the painting. Modality is an essential dimension of the semiotic space of the painting.

It is also one of the best channels for communication about painting. Rather than talking about how *Flight into Egypt* came to be painted, or about the place of Frank Hinder in the pantheon of Australian painters, or about his debt to Cubism—all of which involve a great deal of extraneous knowledge—I would propose that newcomers try to explain what draws them into the painting and makes them want to recognise and live in its world, however briefly. Some will note the multiple Perspective that gives the moment of flight a dynamism impossible with one-point perspective. Others may find that clarity of Form makes them focus on the figure of Mary, while others are drawn by the intensity of the Light to focus on the much less clear figure of the infant Jesus in her arms. Others may find their religious sense heightened by the discreteness of the coloured shapes that remind them of stained glass. Others may be overwhelmed by the dominant Scale and Volume of the two central figures. All of these would be valid reasons for getting involved because they are all options that the painter has chosen from the systems of Focus available in the Modal Function (see the top central box of Chart 2). A more detailed systemic network for this function at the rank of Picture might have the form described in Chart 2.

Here we have a partial grammar of the systems of the modal function in painting and the options from the available systems that Hinder has chosen to engage our attention. Let me insist at once that these 'choices' need not be rational and deliberate: we are not reviving any intentional fallacy. Both painter and viewer share a 'language' of potentials for meaning that can be described and discussed systemically, like the systems of Mood in the interpersonal function of verbal language; we do not have to stop and choose what to say or what to understand while talking, but, to describe how we talk and are understood, the linguist may use a systemic framework as Halliday does. The semiotician of painting (and the teacher or gallery guide) may find a systemic network equally useful as a starting point for discussion.

Many painters use less abstract modalities for drawing the viewer's attention to their subject, and these may be the ones noted by some discoverers of the painting. They may engage the viewer's eye with the direct Gaze of one or more figures in the painting (the Venus in Botticelli's *Primavera*, and the figures in many of Rembrandt's portraits and self-portraits, are obvious examples). The very absence of eyes in the faces of Mary and Joseph 'looking out at us' is a very powerful example of negative 'eyework.' Sometimes minor figures like servants or children of the main subject, or animal pets, act as Intermediaries engaging our gaze, or simply by their presence admit us to the world of the painting (the patrons in front of Masaccio's *Trinity*, dogs in Jan Steen's *Celebration in a Tavern*, servants and the dwarf in Velázquez's *Las Meninas*).[3] For many viewers the patient donkey, even though also eyeless and seen in profile, plays just the kind of Intermediary role into the world of Hinder's Holy Family: insofar as its head, at the top, and its haunches on either side, seem to frame and enclose the Holy Family, it mediates for us in an original and unique way. Sometimes, as in many landscapes, with and without human subjects the line or curve of a path or stream or a ray of sunshine may lead the eye into the painting. It is arguable that the rhomboid shaft of light (or shadow?) falling from the left across the upper halves of the central figures, mentioned earlier, helps to engage our gaze. The point is that the systems of Gaze (in the same square on the chart) provide another set of modal options, distinct from but combinable with the Focus options we discussed earlier.

Also operating at the level of the whole work (and therefore listed in the same square of the Chart) are the systems of Modality, expressing the artist's slant towards the scene represented in the painting. This is also a set of systemic choices whose recognition should help to train closer observations of a painting. The system termed Frame has to do with how much of the represented subject has been included within the frame, and how much left out, and also the degree to which it is contained by the frame. Hinder's Holy Family is well contained within the frame, whereas many paintings have elements of the subject cut off by the frame (continuing, as it were, in the limbo beyond the frame) or, with more and more modern paintings, cutting across the frame, or altering it, or protruding beyond it in either two dimensions or three (outwards towards the viewer). Just as modernist literature has turned the modalities of writing into a major theme, foregrounding the tacit rules of generic forms, of grammar, of the very act of enunciation, modern painting plays with the modalities of frame, testing its reality, its permeability, and its vulnerability. Even in *Flight into Egypt*, where the subject seems so firmly framed, there are shapes at either side (trees? Moorish arches? Further refractions of the donkey's hump?) hint at the world beyond the frame. And what are we to say of the very pronounced internal framing, in colours and shapes, of the Holy Family by the donkey? Is it protecting them? defining their scope? determining their motion? Many questions of interpretation arise when we study the Modal Function, and they deserve discussion. This, moreover, is where the boundary (on the Chart) between representational, modal and compositional functions becomes permeable, since what has been painted is inseparable from how it is seen and shaped. There is no form/ content dichotomy, because the options from the systems in all three functions are mutually determining.

What I am calling Weight has to do with the scale given to the subject in relation to the world presumed to surround it. This is mainly a matter of internal dimensions, though the actual size of the painting will be part of this modality. I have used Modality as a cover term within this function for the type of slant the artist has chosen to express. Just as modality in language realises degrees of possibility, probability and certainty, modality in the language of painting realises degrees of Fantasy, Irony, and Authenticity. Hinder has not chosen to portray his subject realistically; there is an element of fantasy in the Cubist projection of mobility onto a static group; some viewers have seen irony in the degree of abstraction used ("Jesus may be 'The Light of the World,' but he didn't have to look like an electric light bulb!"), while others consider that the abstraction generalises this particular flight and increases our respect for its representativeness. In other words, the flight into Egypt symbolises other, more recent, acts of persecution and flight.[5] So symbolism is another important aspect of modality, an extension of the system of Authenticity/Fantasy. A further aspect of symbolism is Intertextuality, the deliberate or unconscious references a painting makes to other 'texts,' painted, sculpted, drawn or written. The painting's debt to Cubism obviously prompts connection with other Cubist paintings, but the mysteriously protective and vigilant donkey evokes Chagall and a whole intertextual world of that religious and fugitive painter. One cannot ignore, of course, the intertextuality between the painting and its literary source, St. Matthew's rather sparse account in his Gospel.

Up to now I have concentrated on the systems that seem to operate at the rank of Picture, the whole work. There are, however, other systems operating at lower ranks for each of the three functions. In the Modal function at the rank of Episode (in other paintings that contain several episodes) the scale and centrality of the episode to the whole and its relative prominence of focus may carry a great deal of meaning (Bruegel's distant *Crucifixion* or diminutive *Fall of Icarus* are cases in point). There may be an interplay of

148 *Painting*

modalities between separate Episodes (as in most of Hieronymous Bosch's paintings, Hogarth's satirical drawings, or Tenniel's illustrations to *Alice in Wonderland*). At he rank of Figure, specifics of Characterisation, Gesture, Gaze and relation to the Viewer are comparable to linguistic systems of attitudinal modification in the nominal group. At the rank of Member, degrees of Stylisation (in Mary's and Joseph's heads), of Attenuation (of shoulders, arms, donkey's legs), and Synecdoche (parts of the donkey for the whole, shadow of a pyramid for all Egypt) carry the Modal function at the lowest meaning-bearing rank. Here too, Chiaroscuro—the play of light and dark planes (between the infant, a dazzling source of light at the centre of the painting, and the dark shawl partly enclosing it; or between the halos and the heads of the parents) carries the Focus system at the lowest rank.

One of the major strengths of Halliday's model is the integration of intonation and stress in the lexicogrammar: they are not somehow divorced from meaning or treated as unrelated to the syntax as 'paralanguage' or 'suprasegmentals.' Choice of tone is an essential aspect of the interpersonal function, expressing the speaker's stance vis-à-vis both his or her interlocutor and (ideational) subject matter; and stress has partially a textual function, realizing the Given/ New structure of the utterance. I believe that 'Illumination' in a painting has much the same function. I have discussed Chiaroscuro as a specific aspect of the modal function in relating members and planes, but it clearly has a major role in the whole work in foregrounding what is to be emphasised and in expressing the tone of the painter's, and our, involvement with various areas of depiction. The explosion of light standing for the infant Jesus is contained and modified (modalised) by a complex pattern of dark shapes: the reposed tilt of his head, the protective enclosure of Mary's arm, the tender tilt of her head and the protective support of Joseph's robe and the donkey's rump(s).

Another theoretical issue requiring much fuller discussion (and more expertise than I can offer here) is the place in the model of Colour. There seem to me to be at least three distinct discourses about Colour in the art world. One discusses and analyses colour scientifically in terms of instrumentally measurable and comparable 'hue,' 'value' and 'chroma'. This seems to be equivalent to the study of phonetics in linguistics: it starts from the material base (the 'substance' of pigments, like the substance of sounds), it can be measured on scales of wavelengths (of light, like those of sound), and it is reassuringly precise. Another discourse concerns itself with the symbolic significance of colours in particular genres of painting and particular cultures, This relates more to stylistics and comparative symbolism in literary studies than to the basic semiotic codes of language. It clearly has a role—already well established—in art history and analysis. Thirdly, there is a kind of tacit and—at least verbally—unarticulated discourse about colour that seems to be carried on by painters in paint. As with poets' experiments with assonance, alliteration and rhyme, the theory evolves mainly through practice, through influence and imitation, through deviation and opposition. Thus at the level of substance we have a 'chromatics,' like phonetics, and at the level of genre we have a stylistics of colour. What we need, if this linguistic analogy is valid, is a level for discussing colour as meaningful form, a 'chromatology,' like phonology. Such an approach would focus here on parallelism, juxtaposition and contrast of colour in Hinder's painting like the study of assonance, rhyme, and other sound patterning in poetry.

The Compositional Function

Colour Cohesion (in the top right-hand box of Chart 2) is an aspect of chromatology that has a Compositional function, like phonological patterning in poetry. We have already noted the enclosing ('Framing') character of the dark browns representing the donkey's head and hindquarters. The adult human robes are predominantly shades of blue, while patches of pink prevail in the emotionally tender area around the infant Jesus. Much of the fascination of this painting is in these abstract relations of colour, shape and emotion where the three functions interact.

Whereas Colour Cohesion operates across the whole painting, as phonological parallelisms do across a whole poem, there is also cohesive patterning at the rank of Member (see the bottom right-hand box of Chart 2). The somewhat dispersed parts of the donkey (in my reading of the painting) illustrate this. The curved shape on the left-hand edge of the painting seems to refer to the donkey's rump which we have discerned elsewhere in the painting. If Egypt is to the left (West, whence the pyramidal shadow falls), then this manifestation of the donkey has already started *The Flight*. We could gloss the central image as 'the donkey stood patiently protecting Mary and Joseph,' and this left-hand element would add: 'It started its journey' (where the rump-motif works like the pronominal reference in language). I must hasten to reiterate, however, that I wish to avoid too close a homology between the semiotic systems of language and of painting: one involves sequential syntagmatic relations, the other simultaneous syntagms. This is clear when we consider parallelism, contrast and rhythm as aspects of the cohesion of Members in the painting. It is meaningful pictorially to establish a parallel between the curve of a shoulder and the curve of a rump, or to contrast left and right profiles of the rump 'enclosing' Mary and Joseph, or to set up a purely rhythmic cohesion between the arc of the smaller curve within the left-hand rump and the parallel curves of the circle forming the donkey's jaw. These seem to be essential mechanisms of cohesion in a painting, perhaps more akin to the cohesiveness of an extended metaphor in language than to the devices of substitution, ellipsis or lexical reference that realise linguistic cohesion.

Another crucial area of analysis for painting is in the structure of the Gestalt of the whole work. The interplay of horizontals, verticals and diagonals within the rectangular frame requires close analysis, which we cannot

150 *Painting*

attempt here. Broadly speaking, the relative stability of the vertical figures (however multiply refracted) on a stable horizontal ground is enhanced by the dark line of the human shoulders and animal rump along the line of the 'golden section' of this rectangle. The compositional harmony created by these devices, however, is destabilised by that enigmatic diagonal of light/shadow from the left, which divides the upper background (including the donkey's face, ears and neck) into congruent triangles (probably another golden section), but at the bottom is neither parallel nor complete. The tension between stability plus geometrical regularity, on the one hand, and instability plus irregularity, is a productive dynamic force that keeps our eye scanning the whole composition, yet with enough harmony of proportion, line and rhythm within the Gestalt to please and satisfy.

As the other boxes in the right-hand column show, the compositional function is realized in specific systemic options at each rank in the work. At the rank of Figure the centrality of the infant and proximity to the centre of Mary intensify the decentering (biological as well as ideological!) of Joseph. Parallels and oppositions between curved elbows and the donkey's rump, or between the female and male head-dress of Mary and Joseph, create their own compositional tensions—as well, of course, as providing the vehicle for the representational and modal functions.

Individual Readings and the Social Semiotic

So far I have used the Systemic-Functional chart to explore a single painting and have used the painting to explore the chart. A model of the systems which I believe are universal in the language of painting has revealed how the systemic options are drawn upon and combined—*realised*—in a single text. This is clearly a textual semiotics, an analytical method, which needs to be situated in, and related to, other discourses about painting and art in general. However, we have already needed to refer to aspects of art history (Cubism and other influences; the reception of the painting) and art education (the Modal function as a way into and a way of talking about a work) so that the method can hardly be seen as confined to the purely immanent study of an isolated text. Even if that were the case, I would want to stress the implications for art history, criticism and evaluation of a method of textual analysis that is both coherent and explicit. Too much that purports to be art history, criticism and evaluation lacks a consistent descriptive base and involves—even when there is good will between the participants—incompatible discourses, discourses that share neither theoretical grounds nor a common vocabulary.

If people (i.e., art historians and their peers, critics and their readers, art teachers and their students) could start from the same detailed but coherent description of a given painting, the areas of individual and divergent interpretations and evaluations would be easier to pinpoint and discuss. For instance, a provocative colleague of mine aroused a storm of disapproval when he suggested in a seminar I was conducting about Hinder's painting that the figure of the donkey encapsulating the Holy Family had resonances of the Trojan Horse, with its secret and fateful burden about to destroy one civilisation and create another. Well, he had a right to his opinion and was drawing on a more extensive intertextuality than most of us, but discussions about the realisations of this image within the representation, modality and composition of *Flight into Egypt* provided very little supporting evidence for such an eccentric reading. (Of course, the trouble with eccentric readings is that they are very hard to forget and generate their own momentum—as you will find, dear reader, having read this paragraph.)

The same colleague then proposed that the brownish-black shapes on either side of Mary and Joseph were not only extensions of their shoulders and robes, not only the haunches of the salvatory donkey, but the hands of God cradling and protecting the human vehicles He had chosen to work His will. In representational terms, this was congruent with the recurrent role of the donkey at the beginning and end of Jesus' life (a temporal as well as teleological frame); modally, people found that it intensified the focus on the three central figures in terms of light, colour and shapes; and compositionally, the play of scale and colour between protective hands and the animal and human figures added an interesting further dimension to the painting. After some detailed discussion, using the resources of the model, there were no serious objections to this interpretation.

We were confronted with two readings, a marked and an unmarked one and for most viewers the marked one was too eccentric to be acceptable. But the descriptive framework did enable us to compare our interpretations coherently and courteously. I suppose we were representing our own dominant social semiotic in this discussion. A culture that knows the story of Jesus and has some sense—with or without belief—of how the Flight into Egypt fits into Christian narrative and Christian destiny; a culture that takes for granted certain modes of representation as part of an approved and socially ratified post-Renaissance tradition; a culture that knows how to read certain compositional relationships and responds positively to a certain Gestalt— this white Anglo-Saxon Protestant (and Catholic) culture uses and responds to texts that reflect and perpetuate that social semiotic. A Jewish or Buddhist viewer with a knowledge of *The Iliad* (if one could be found uninfluenced by the dominant Renaissance tradition in art) might indeed have found the 'Trojan Horse' interpretation more acceptable; a Muslim viewer might have rebelled against the modality of representing human figures at all and might enjoy what he thought was a pattern of arch forms and stylised plant forms in the painting; an Australian Aborigine might wonder how a bark painting so lacking in the sacred animals, cross-hatching and earthy ochres of his tribe could possibly represent anyone's 'Dreamtime.' All these viewers would be prisoners of their own social semiotic, as we ourselves are.

An individual text is both a realisation of the social semiotic out of which it has grown (and which invests it with its meanings) and a contribution to that social semiotic. It may be so conventional, so governed by the prevailing rules and typical meanings, as to consolidate the social semiotic (verbally, most newspaper articles and in the visual code most religious or patriotic images do this). On the other hand, the individual text may question, destabilise or subvert the social semiotic. This is one of the tasks modern post-industrialist societies have entrusted to the verbal and visual arts: if a novel or painting does not offer radically new representation, modality, or composition, then it is not art. This notion of the necessity for constant radical change has itself become part of the social semiotic of the arts in our day, ratified by a whole economy of critics, art historians, public galleries, publishers and teachers. At the same time, there is an alternative social semiotic in the world of art that finds radicalism acceptable as long as it has happened 50 to 100 years ago. Collectors, consultants, private galleries, popular publishers, television producers, and the middle-class public at large are charmed by Monet's, Van Gogh's or Seurat's representations, by Chagall's or Picasso's modalities, by Cézanne's or Braque's composition, but feel threatened by a Klee, a Malevich or a John Olsen.

Frank Hinder's *Flight into Egypt* provides a nice case study of conflict in the social semiotic, because it was the subject of considerable controversy when it was first exhibited. (here, at last, we come to one of the areas where semiotic analysis and art history meet. It will be evident that for me the semiotic analysis comes first—in both senses.) There is a good account of the circumstances of the painting's genesis and exhibition in Gooding (1985):

> The 1952 Blake Prize for Religious Art was officially opened to the public on 12 March at Mark Foy's Exhibition Gallery, Sydney. It was the second in the history of the award, the first being won by Justin O'Brien's painting *The Virgin Enthroned*. The annual prize sought to strengthen traditional ties between Church and artist, and in fact stimulated a minor revival of religious art. Another equal aim was to reintroduce original art into homes and churches "to replace the cheap prints and the sentimental shams of mass produced 'sacred art' that so frequently disfigure them."
>
> (p. 3)

Here already we have two social semiotics at work—or at any rate two value systems within the 1952 Australian bourgeois social semiotic: an impulse from the established church to use innovative art to attract a wider congregation (including the artistically sophisticated but agnostic intelligentsia), and an impulse from the art world to use the religious sensibilities of the less sophisticated to improve aesthetic standards of home decoration. Of course, these two impulses may be simultaneously present in one committee, or even in one individual: we all embody and enact many dimensions of the social semiotic.

When Frank Hinder entered his painting *Flight into Egypt* he had little idea of the controversy which would follow its being awarded first prize ... In declaring the winner the judging panel decided not to give reasons for their selection.

> The announcement of the winning entry prompted some critics to question the composition of the judging panel and their subsequent decision. Others condemned the modernist influence apparent in many of the works, with one critic labelling the exhibition "a distinguished collection of assorted artistic idiocies" and stating that the judges might have been better advised to retain the prize money.
>
> (Gooding, 1985: 4)

For Halliday the systems in the functional components are potentials for the realisation of three broad areas of meaning in given registers of the social semiotic. Register is defined by Field (realised by ideational lexicogrammatical systems), Tenor (realised by interpersonal systems) and Mode (realised by textual systems). Register is then a kind of interface between the social context (the sociologically describable) and the semiotic text (generically and linguistically describable). The critics cited above had a different view of the relationship between Field and Mode than the judges and Hinder. For the Field of 'Gospel narrative' a 'modernist' Mode was unthinkable—so the Tenor of their remarks became quite aggressive (they questioned, condemned and labelled as 'assorted artistic idiocies'). In fact, such critics were realizing in their remarks a social semiotic closer to that of the clerics and home-owners who were filling their churches and homes with "cheap prints and the sentimental shams of mass-produced 'sacred art,'" and they clearly felt threatened by the innovative zeal of the judging panel.

The split is epitomised by the comment of James Gleason, a leading art critic (hence representing the innovative trend), that "it has high artistic value but does not fulfil the requirements of truly religious painting" (here representing the reactionary trend).

The role of the economic motive in this debate is revealing. Paul Haefliger's review reveals a nice conflict between Field, Tenor and Mode:

> The winning painting, *Flight into Egypt* by Frank Hinder, cannot be seriously considered. It is a highly efficient work, reasonably well balanced, beautifully executed, but more at home in the field of commercial art than that of art.
>
> (Gooding, 1985: 4)

For this critic the Mode is no problem: he knows good composition when he sees it and gives Hinder due credit. Presumably, he accepts the Field of religious subject matter as valid: the Representation is no problem for what he considers 'art.' However, for him the Tenor is wrong: 'Commercial art' engages the viewer and realises the stance of the artist quite differently from 'real art,' so the wrong options have been chosen in the systems of the Modal function.[5] Economically, the social semiotic of the Sydney art world in 1952 is rather confused about the role of money in relation to art: it is reasonable to award 200 guineas to an artist and promote the patronage of individual art to get rid of 'cheap prints' and 'mass-produced sentimental shams' (shams because they are cheap and mass-produced), but not to admit the validity of the techniques of commercial art. Since then, of course, Andy Warhol and Roy Lichtenstein and others have readjusted the social semiotic of the art establishment.

A new text, an enunciation in paint, involves some kind of negotiation with the social semiotic. Contemporary criticism often reveals whether the conflict with prevailing norms is primarily in the Representational, the Modal, or the Compositional function, and it is often instructive to see which. But the viewer is also involved with the social semiotic, is equipped with a certain range of skills (Compositional) and expectations (Representational and Modal) that are brought to bear in reading, analysing and evaluating the painting. At the same time, we are not just social ciphers, not merely chips off the social semiotic block, and art is one of the prime areas where we negotiate and renegotiate our sense of ourselves. The individual subject is challenged by an art work that upsets one's sense of equilibrium in some way (Representational, Modal, or Compositional) and works through the picture to re-establish equilibrium (see Kreitler and Kreitler (1972) for an excellent discussion of this 'homeostatic' function of art). One reason we look at art, study it, analyse particular paintings and discuss them with other people is as a way of discovering and renegotiating our own subjectivity. I believe that our functional model offers a consistent method of analysis and a coherent language for comparing analyses and interpretations and evaluations that will enrich the individual as well as the public discourse about art.

The Imaginative Function

Lest I seem to have tied up too glibly the epistemological, psychological, social, art-historical, aesthetic and pedagogical aspects of art that I believe can be illuminated by a systemic-functional semiotics, I will mention a crucial function of art that I do not think the model outlined here can account for. A semiotic model presumes that art is primarily communication; not necessarily deliberate, indeed, often unconscious communication; and not necessarily communication with another, but by the artist with himself or herself, by the viewer with himself or herself. But art is also exploration. It is a way of discovering the representable world, a way of exploring different modalities upon that world and with the viewer, a way of juggling with compositional forms for their own sake. Art in this light is more akin to play, a modelling of the world according to the Imaginative function. And this is one of the seven functions of a child's protolanguage, as outlined by Halliday (1975) that has been least explored.

If we accept Michael Halliday's challenge and attempt to explore the Imaginative function, we may simultaneously discover a great deal more about the workings of the other functions when they are highlighted by the specificity of the artistic text.

Secondary Modelling Systems

This brings me to another important *lacuna* in this chapter: I have all the time concentrated on developing the analogies between Halliday's model of the functions of natural language and this model for the language of visual art. A proper analogy (to which this book on "The Hermeneutic Spiral" is devoted) would be between painting and a secondary modelling system built out of language, such as poetry or literary narrative. Occasionally I have compared such aesthetic devices as compositional parallelism or juxtaposition of colours in painting with rhyme, and so on, in poetry, but I hope to develop in future work a proper comparison of systems and texts on related semiotic levels. Another strategy would be to offer a functional description of the systems of visual language in general. This would involve describing modes of representation, modality and composition in texts as diverse as graphs, diagrams, shop-window displays, table settings, flower arrangements, museums, domestic and public décor and room arrangement, and requires a deeper and broader range of competences than I can offer. I do believe, however, that this language of visual arrays is susceptible to a close functional description of the kind I have attempted in this chapter.

A possible short-cut, pending the development of a visual poetics and a general grammar of visual texts, would be to borrow from Formalist and Structuralist poetics the concepts of 'foregrounding' and 'dominant,'[6] and see if they throw light on the meaning of the painting and on the process of interpreting it. One of the earliest literary theorists to develop these concepts was the Russian, Yurii Tynyanov. In 1927 he wrote:

> The work is a system of correlated factors. Correlation of each factor with the others is its *function* in relation to the whole system. It is quite clear that every literary system is formed not by the peaceful interaction of all the factors, but by the supremacy, the *foregrounding of one factor* or group that functionally subjugates and colours the rest. This factor is known among the Russian literary scholars as the *dominant*. (emphasis in original)
> (In O'Toole and Shukman, 1978, p. 35)

If we applied this concept through our functional model to different schools of painting, we would note some fairly clear tendencies. While nineteenth-century 'academic' and 'realist' painting foregrounds the Representational function, Impressionism and Expressionism foreground different aspects of the Modal function (Focus and Modality respectively), and Futurist and Constructivist schools foreground the Compositional function. This is not an occasion to attempt it, but in principle this approach would be useful in developing a functional classification of schools of painting and other arts.

In the more specific context of Hinder's *Flight into Egypt* let me use this principle from Russian Formalist poetics as a way of pulling some threads together. Representationally, Hinder has foregrounded the generalisability of his central figures: the maternity of Mary, the protectiveness of Joseph, the patience of the donkey. They thus become representatives—as he intended—for 'displaced persons' everywhere. These characteristics are further foregrounded by various options that have been chosen in the Modal function: to present them multiply, in the Cubist manner, to deprive them of individual 'gaze,' and to use intertextual references. Compositionally, the harmonious placing and linking of the central figures and the framing role of the donkey (with or without the hands of God) heighten still further their iconic status as universal refugees.

If I have analysed and interpreted these foregrounded elements correctly, then we have here on quite an abstract level a congruence of foregrounded options from each of the three functions. Perhaps we could call this congruence the 'dominant' of the work, the aesthetic unity that stimulates both recognition and empathy in the viewer: in Gregory Bateson's formulation, 'the pattern that connects.'

Notes

1. The iconographic analysis of this painting is fully expounded in well-known articles by Edgar Wind (1958) and Ernst Gombrich (1972), The *relationship* between Panofsky's "iconography" and more recent semiotic approaches to art is well discussed by Christine Hasenmueller. While I feel that a dialogue between iconography and the semiotic model presented here would be most productive, I believe that iconography has failed to come to terms explicitly enough with problems of modality in the work of art which this functional semiotic model can incorporate fully.
2. Matthew, 2: 13–15: "And when they were departed [into their own country], behold, the angel of the Lord appeareth to Joseph in a dream, saying, Arise and take the young child and his mother and flee into Egypt, and be thou there until I bring thee word; for Herod will seek the young child to destroy him. (14) When he arose, he took the young child and his mother by night, and departed into Egypt." [Authorised Version]
3. Boris Uspensky (1970: Chap. 7) has a useful discussion of these devices, although he does not use a functional semiotic framework.
4. As Hinder (1952) says, "The figures are featureless—I wanted them to remain as impersonal as possible, hoping to suggest the general idea of 'flight' and experience of the people of the world throughout history; in many cases, of course, flight from religious persecution as well as from human would-be gods and other unpleasant people."

5. Haefliger may well have been influenced in this judgement by Hinder's very successful design of 1936 for P & O Royal Mail liners, which incorporated some representational and compositional features of this painting. This is no excuse for his sweeping assertion.
6. Relevant quotations by other Russian formalists and by Jan Mukarovsky, one of the literary scholars among the Prague School Structuralists, are to be found in L. Michael O'Toole and Ann Shukman, *Russian Poetics in Translation*, University of Essex, Vol. 4, 1977, 13–48. Among contemporary linguists and literary scholars, Geoffrey Leech (1983) has done most to develop and exemplify these concepts.

10 Captain Banning Cocq's Three Left Hands

A Semiotic Interpretation of Rembrandt's *The Night Watch*

Introduction

A paper dedicated to the memory of Jan van der Eng should, I believe, try to emulate the distinctive standards of aesthetic analysis that he established in his many papers on the classic texts of Russian literature.

First and foremost, he focussed on the text itself, rather than the biographical, historical or sociological information which still—ninety years after the challenges of the Russian Formalists—constitute the bulk of literary scholarship and teaching.

As a teacher, like many of us, of Russian literature abroad, he was not afraid to confront again the major classics, always making new discoveries about texts which might, for Russian critics, have seemed stale and overworked.

Although drawing on and refining tools of literary analysis proposed by Russian Formalists and Western European Structuralists, his analyses were rigorous, but never rigid. He would explore the dynamics of a narrative with the close attention normally reserved for the study of poetry, relating the syntagmatic flow of the 'functions' of a plot-line to the paradigmatic 'indices' of character, setting, symbol, thematic parallel, etc. His ability to relate the closely observed detail to the overall picture of theme, plot and narrative structure make his best work more akin to the analysis of a visual text or a piece of music than most structural analyses of literary narrative ever aspire to or achieve.

Above all, Jan's papers radiate the sheer enjoyment he took in the close reading of Pushkin, Gogol, Dostoevsky, Chekhov and others: *on chital so smakom*, as the Russians would say, and his enthusiasm is infectious.

My own analyses of Russian and English narrative texts attempted, like Jan van der Eng's, to synthesise the most productive theories and methods of the Russian Formalists and the Prague and Paris Structuralists. In the analysis of poetry however, I drew heavily on the Systemic-Functional linguistic model of M.A.K. Halliday (1971, 1985). Unlike many current theories of language, Halliday's starts from the semantics and assumes a meaningful context. Whenever we make an utterance, whether in speech or writing, whether informal or formal, we make three kinds of meaning: through the *Ideational* function we encode entities, states, relationships and acts from the material and social world in which we live; through the *Interpersonal* function we encode our relationship with our interlocutor(s) and audience; through the *Textual* function we construct coherent and generically appropriate texts. The functional choices we make along these three parameters of meaning are then realised through choices we make from the systems available in the lexico-grammar. For instance, the utterance "Was it really Rembrandt who painted that scene?" contains Ideational lexical items like *Rembrandt, paint* and *scene* and encodes them in a transitivity relationship of "A (agent) did X (material action) to B (goal)," but it simultaneously enacts an Interpersonal function by asking a question (Interrogative Mood), rather than making a statement, and by expressing the speaker's incredulity in the Modal *really*. The sentence seems to presuppose a larger text (the Textual function) by referring to "*that* scene" (i.e., which we are looking at, or talking about) and by giving thematic focus to Rembrandt within this text by the use of what Halliday calls "predicated theme": *Was it Rembrandt ... who....*

Analysis

It did not take a great leap of the imagination to see this systemic-functional model of language involving three types of meaning as a prototype for any act of communication, whether through gestures, facework, drawings and paintings, sculptures, buildings or films: i.e., it is a general semiotic model. My own adaptation of Halliday's model for the art of painting was described and tested in O'Toole (2011). As my systemic-functional chart (Chart 2, p. xiii) shows, the three functions and the systems that realise them have to be made code-specific for painting. Thus, actions, states and portrayals of the real world are encoded through the Representational function. Relations between the painting and the viewer are encoded through the Modal function, while the geometric and colour relations between elements and the whole work are encoded through the Compositional function.

To give a simple example, *The Night Watch* (refer to colour plates section) portrays, in its Representational function, Captain Banning Cocq. As we know from other portrayals, his features and build are quite authentic and his costume reflects his rank and social aspirations as well as belonging to the period and circumstances of the group scene. Modally, he engages our attention through his height, his movement and gesture out of the painting towards us, his gaze (looking past our right ear) and the way he is framed by other figures, notably the light (and well-lit) clothing of the lieutenant on his left and the woman on his right. Compositionally, he dominates the centre-foreground of the painting; the white of his collar and the red of his

160 *Painting*

Plate 2 Rembrandt: *Night Watch* (1642).
Oil on canvas Rijksmuseum, Amsterdam

sash stand out from the other hues in the painting, as well as from the black of his costume; and various parallel lines in the whole painting (the company's standard and the musket being cleaned to his right, and the long pike, the musket being blown and the lieutenant's partisan to his left) all seem to highlight his presence in a web of intersecting lines. In other words, even when we examine only a single figure in this complex painting we need to account for three distinct types of meaning: Representation, Modality and Composition.

Naturally, an adequate and convincing interpretation of *The Night Watch* will have to relate these meanings to each other and to what we know, or infer, about the overall purposes of the painting, but it is a valuable technique (and intellectual discipline) to analyse them separately in terms of the systems which comprise the 'language' of all painters before we synthesise our findings in an overall interpretation. I have always felt that Erwin Panofsky (1939) would have fulfilled the promise of his theory of aesthetic interpretation if he and his many followers had got past the 'Iconographic' stage of recognising *what* is depicted in a painting (Representation) and had developed a genuine 'Iconology' by devoting as much attention *to how* it is portrayed, both in relation to the Gestalt and substructures of the whole work (Composition) and in the way it engages the eye of the viewer (Engagement/ Modality), rather than limiting themselves to pre-iconographic 'expressive' meaning.

The Representational Function

In terms of its Representational function *The Night Watch* does, of course, offer a wealth of iconographic information—as attested by the long and still growing 'Rembrandt industry' of writers, curators, restorers and publicists dedicated to discovering and authenticating the historical content of the painting, and, indeed, by the very structure of that part of the Rijksmuseum where the painting hangs. In a small gallery to one side of the painting we can see a silhouette view of *The Night Watch* with the names of the known sitters indicated, together with the sums each paid for the commission. Dutch scholars have not only fitted *The Night Watch* into the tradition of group portraiture which dominated the Northern Netherlands between 1529 and 1650—and this, too, is reflected in the painting's neighbours in its gallery room—but also the social background and traditions of the militia companies, the original commission and hanging and subsequent rehangings of the painting, as well as the two acts of vandalism which robbed viewers forever of the chance to see the painting as Rembrandt painted it. I refer, of course, not only to the knife attack on the canvas by a deranged individual on Sunday 14 September 1975, but to the officially sanctioned 'pruning' of the painting in 1715 when it was moved from the Kloveniersdoelen to the Amsterdam Town Hall, losing about 600 cm from the left edge and about 300 cm from the top edge so that it would fit through a doorway! All of this historical information should not, however, distract us from what we can see represented in the painting, for, as many commentators have pointed out, it is not just a group portrait, but a dramatic scene: it represents not just Portrayal (top left-hand box of Chart 2), but Action. Captain Banning Cocq is stepping forward and gesturing with authority; Lieutenant Van Ruytenburgh is listening intently, looking at his captain and mirroring his stance; a drummer is drumming and a dog is barking, so the action is accompanied by virtual sound effects; banners and pikes are being waved or held aloft, sergeants are pointing and pairs of people at either side of the painting are conversing. More dramatically still, the three key phases of using a musket are depicted in a central left-to-right sequence: the musketeer in red in a cockaded hat is cleaning the barrel of a musket (whose presence is highlighted—Modally—by the gold dress of the girl); to *her* left, a boy with oak leaves on his helmet (but no face portrayed: an anti-portrayal!) is firing the musket, whose barrel we can see between Captain Cocq's left shoulder and the brim of the lieutenant's hat (around which the smoke from the shots is floating), right under the chin of the man between and behind the central officers, whose hand is deflecting the shot; meanwhile, to the lieutenant's left an older man in a shiny helmet is blowing the used powder from the pan of a discharged musket. Rembrandt has not merely portrayed his civic dignitaries—he has realised in a dramatic, yet deliberately half-masked, sequence their very raison d'être for coming together.

By enumerating these various sequences of action in the Representational function, of course, we have moved down a rank on Chart 2 from the Picture as a whole to the Episodes that comprise it. To complete the list we should add the standard-bearer and the young man in a helmet to his left; to the left of them, the man with a moustache in a tall hat and ruff collar and the indistinct figure who appears to be struggling to look over his right shoulder (who several commentators have taken to be a self-portrait of Rembrandt); the helmeted man whose long pike links him with various background figures with pikes to his left; the dark archway spanning the area from the colour division on the flag to the shiny column above Lieutenant Van Ruytenburgh's hat, with the heraldic shield of the company dimly visible above that; the powder-boy in the foreground who is running off (off-stage, as it were,) to the right of the man cleaning his musket; and, of course, the pike-bearer who now appears to frame the left-hand edge of the painting, but who was accompanied by two or three other figures before the painting was 'pruned.'

In the process of isolating these Episodes, we have given many details of the representation of individual Figures and occasionally have mentioned Members (parts of the body, pieces of uniform or equipment, etc.) of which the figures are composed. The point is, as Chart 2 attempts to show, that particular systems of representation operate for each of these ranks and that there is a real hermeneutic value in considering them separately, even if we are aiming in the long run for an overall reading of the painting as a whole.

The Compositional Function

What is more, these different 'grammars'—or modes of making meaning for each rank—also operate in the Compositional and Modal functions and, we want to stress, the differences in their functioning may be significant. For instance, if we scan *The Night Watch* as a purely visual experience, without concern for the actions and portrayals it represents (try half-closing your eyes as you look at it!), we will observe that Compositionally it divides up into rather different episodes. In the foreground there are three main visual episodes: the group on our left (to the right of the standard-bearer's hand); the central cluster of the Captain and Lieutenant, the head of the parrying figure between them, and the man blowing the musket pan; and the drummer and pointing figure and his interlocutor on the extreme right of the canvas. These three foreground episodes are separated from each other by almost equal spaces in which lively but somewhat indistinct action is taking place: the girls and the shooting musketeer to left of centre; and the barking dog and some pieces of weaponry to right of centre. A second tier of episodes is dominated by the five or six figures in the centre between the standard bearer's arm and the column to the left of the helmeted pike-bearer. The upper tier, mostly very dark, has the standard and pike-blade on our left and a maze of pikes, swords, the columns, capitals and ridges of the architecture on the right framing the enormous curve of the arch. Now, whereas our Representational review showed the action episodes intersecting, interacting and interrupting each other in a kind of deliberately staged chaos, our Compositional review has revealed an extremely stable structure of a pyramid, with its base along the central section of the bottom edge, sloping upwards through the hats of the musket-cleaner and standard-bearer on our left and Van Ruytenburgh and the top-hatted man on our right, to a point at the centre of the arch above. This structure is made even more stable by the X formation, one of whose arms runs from the powder-boy, bottom left. through the faces of the girl, Banning Cocq and the helmeted pike-bearer to the points of the pikes, top right, while the other runs from the tapping foot of the drummer through the hats of Van Ruytenburgh, Banning Cocq and the standard-bearer to the top of the standard. The centre of this X is the face of Captain Banning Cocq, the leader of the company and the dominant figure in the painting. In our earlier analysis of the way the three functions interact in the figure of Banning Cocq, we noted how many parallel lines in the painting seem to construct a virtual Compositional net around him. To his right, the standard, the musket being cleaned, a sword held upwards behind the standard bearer's arm and the Captain's own sword are precisely parallel, while even the sole of his left foot seems to initiate the line of the sword. To his far left, the sides of the drum and even the drumstick in the drummer's left hand follow the same line. Almost precisely perpendicular to these lines are the parallels created by the longest pike, the musket being fired, the musket being blown, the lieutenant's partisan and even the lines of the eyes of many of the key figures. These lines are mimicked on the left of the canvas by the Captain's right arm, the dagger on the back of the firing musketeer, the folds in the woman's dress and the powder-horn held by the running powder-boy.

Particle—Field—Wave

In considering the way that the three (meta-)functions of his grammar relate to each other in extended texts, Michael Halliday develops an interesting idea that was first proposed by the American linguist Kenneth Pike. Pike sees pieces of discourse as combining elements of particle, field and wave. Halliday sees what he calls the Ideational function in language as being realised in *particles* of discourse; the Interpersonal function as being realised as a *field*; and the Textual function being realised as a *wave*. Thus,

164 *Painting*

if our language example earlier: "Was it really Rembrandt who painted that scene?" was reconstituted in a longer conversation, we would find the lexical particles like *Rembrandt paint* and *scene* being matched by other particles like *artist, gallery, depict* and *subject*, while even the action sequences would be scattered like particles through the text. The Interpersonal elements of Interrogative Mood and Modality would be realised as a kind of field, spreading its tone of inquiry or assertion, uncertainty or certainty, over the whole text (because this would reflect the Interpersonal roles adopted by the speakers in the conversation). The recurrence of Theme elements at the beginning of clauses creates a wave-like formation in the interchange of information.

I believe this analogy may help us to understand how the three functions relate in my pictorial version of Halliday's model. Representationally, the various action sequences of people talking, gesturing and stepping forward, holding banners or pikes, firing or cleaning muskets, running, drumming, etc. are scattered like particles across the text, as are the figures and members of those being portrayed and the architectural fixtures of the scene. This would be equally true of a less dynamic scene such as a landscape or a static portrait of one sitter, although we have to admit that Rembrandt has gone to extremes in activating his represented elements and even setting them at odds with each other (e.g., the young musketeer running *behind* the officers to fire his musket). Compositionally, because we are not dealing with a sequential code like language, but a static visual array, I would propose the analogy of a *grid* in place of Halliday's wave. Thus, the imaginary lines of the pyramid and **X** structures we discovered and the real parallel lines of pikes, muskets, swords, drums, etc. form a kind of grid which holds the particles of action and representation still for us. Now we need to consider the Modal function, which we have so far only touched upon in our brief discussion of the figure of Banning Cocq.

The Modal Function

The Modal function involves the ways in which the painter engages the eye and interest of the viewer. As the central column of the Chart indicates, this often requires choices from several systems and ranks simultaneously. If we take the general system that I have called Focus, we will note that Perspective—which even in traditional art criticism primarily concerns the way a picture engages the eye of the viewer—has Banning Cocq and Van Ruytenburgh in the foreground with the rest of the company receding backwards and outwards behind them in a kind of pyramid tipped over with its apex towards our eye. At the rank of Member we might note how the foreshortening of Van Ruytenburgh'a partisan—a technical achievement which caused considerable wonderment among Rembrandt's contemporaries—provides an apex and direction to this pyramid. The Perspective system is naturally supported by the Scale whereby the two officers in the foreground are by far the largest figures.

On the other hand, the systems of Light, Gaze and Frame all tend to focus our attention on the female figure to the Captain's right: her face, hair and clothing shine as brightly as Van Ruytenburgh's; of all the figures in the painting she seems to be gazing most directly at us; and she is framed as elaborately as Banning Cocq between the darker figures of the musket-cleaner and the musket-firer and the pool of darkness above her head, with the oblique parallels of the Captain's sword and the musket being cleaned and the leg of the running musketeer forming a rhomboid frame for her.

Now, the art historical literature on *The Night Watch* offers many iconographic (i.e., Representational) reasons for the inclusion of the female figure near the Captain's right arm (actually, two female figures, though the second is only a blurred and largely obscured head to the left of the first one's shoulder), particularly since most of the military and other group portrayals of the period only depict men. One theory is that they are 'sutlers,' i.e., women accompanying the military troop with provisions to feed the men. This would explain the chicken hanging by its feet from her belt, the drinking-horn which she is carrying and, possibly, the purse hanging near her ankles. On the other hand,—and this is a Modal rather than a Representational issue—it has also been suggested that the chicken is a visual pun on the surname of Captain *Cocq* and/or that the very visible chicken's claws are a visual pun on the claw of a bird of prey that was the emblem of the *Kloveniers* company. This kind of punning Symbolism may be supported by some Intertextual considerations, which also belong in the Modal function of painting. The presence of girls and boys, such as the powder-boy and the young musket-firer—particularly when they are dressed in rich and rather antiquated (for the time) finery—suggests a reference to a quite different form of group portrayal and public ritual that had become popular in Amsterdam at this time: the greeting of royalty and other important visitors by companies of rhetoricians. In other words, Rembrandt is not merely subverting the tradition of male military group portrayals by including women, boys and a barking dog, but he is merging two distinct genres—and, hence, types of event. More hypothetically still, many viewers have noted a resemblance between the girl in gold and Rembrandt's wife, Saskia, whom he depicted as 'Flora' seven years earlier, in 1635, and who had died only a year before he painted *The Night Watch*. My main point is not to try and adjudicate between the degrees of likelihood of one iconographic explanation or another, but rather to point out that our trifunctional model enables us to distinguish between 'pure' Representation and the Modalities whereby the painter engages us with his subject matter.

This brings us—at last—to Captain Banning Cocq's three left hands. My reading of the literature on *The Night Watch* (and an informal personal poll of visitors to the Rijksmuseum and even the gallery guards on duty in the room where it hangs) suggests that no-one has previously noticed that, apart from the *shadow* of the hand which falls across the highly lit coat of Van Ruytenburgh, the *glove* in the Captain's right hand is another version of the left hand silhouetted against the highly lit dress of the girl. This may have a perfectly innocent 'pre-iconographic' explanation whereby the painter realised that Cocq's gesture was simply not going to be visible against his red sash if he kept his dark brown glove on. But who would remove their glove and then hold it suspended by the index finger rather than clenching it to the hilt of their sword? And when did Rembrandt, with his sense of drama and his sense of humour ever do anything so innocent? Iconographically, it has been suggested (Haverkamp: 74) that the glove is a gauntlet about to be thrown down as a challenge to whatever enemy his company may be marching forward to confront, and this ties in with the rather hectic activity going on with muskets all around him.

If we consider the three left hands in terms of our three functions, I believe a more complex set of possibilities emerges. Representationally, the painter may be saying "Here is a hand. Now you see it, now you don't. Yes, it is a gesturing hand, but it's also a shadow of itself, and it's also the glove (carefully—and rather artificially—suspended to show its left-handedness) which contained that left hand. Which is the reality: my representation of a hand, or of its shadow, or of the glove that it wore?" Modally, the shadow and the glove draw attention to themselves as dark silhouettes against the lightest areas of the painting, the costumes of Lieutenant Van Ruytenburgh and of the young woman. The shadow, gesturing with the fingers pointing *downwards* towards Van Ruytenburgh's pubic area could be implying one of those broad Dutch (well, O.K., universal!) male jokes about the relative sizes of the interlocutors' sexual members, or it may be drawing attention to the Lieutenant's partisan, or it may be linking both items—the possibilities are infinite once one recognises Rembrandt's capacity for visual jokes (like visual puns, sound effects, conflicting action sequences, etc.). Meanwhile, the glove itself, besides being a gauntlet (and a discarded glove!), is a receptacle pointing *upwards* in the vicinity of the young woman's vagina. The three hands may also be carrying meaning Compositionally: if we join them with imaginary lines, we get a flattened and slightly tilted isosceles triangle which points upwards to the right at about the same angle as the overall pyramid of the groups points upwards to the left. Is this a deliberate skewing akin to the *contrapposto* of figures in Italian Renaissance paintings? At the same time, the series of "left hands" revolves through 180 degrees both laterally and frontally, a three-stage movement which might echo the three stages of firing a musket which are dramatised in *The Night Watch*.

My detailed discussion of Captain Banning Cocq's three left hands has been an attempt to demonstrate the close interplay between the three functions in any text analysed with our systemic-functional semiotic model, while insisting on the heuristic value of analysing one function at a time—if only to make us use our own eyes to engage with a painting rather than depending solely on the extra-textual information retailed by art historians. When the three functions are working together intensively—as with the three hands, or the figure of the young woman or the figure of Banning Cocq—we have what I have called elsewhere "semiotic hot-spots" where meanings are more intense, but also more ambiguous, where there is no "final" interpretation, and where, perhaps, debate should be focussed, both in our own minds and with others.

It might be appropriate to connect this argument with a quotation from one of Jan van der Eng's (and my) Russian Formalist mentors. Seventy-five years ago Jurii Tynyanov wrote:

> The work is a system of correlated factors. Correlation of each factor with the others is its *function* in relation to the whole system. It is quite clear that every literary system is formed not by the peaceful interaction of all the factors, but by the supremacy, *the foregrounding of one factor* (or group) that functionally subjugates and colours the rest. This factor is known among the Russian literary scholars as *the dominant*.
> (Tynyanov, 1927/1977 20)

I would take it for granted (as did Tynyanov in writing about the cinema) that this theory is as relevant to other arts as to literature. If my readers are not already exhausted by studying the functions of the many factors in Rembrandt's painting, they might like to take the further theoretical step of proposing a *dominant* for *The Night Watch*. The data is all there.

11 Word Pictures and Painted Narrative. Longstaff's *Breaking the News*

The Systemic-Functional Model Relating the Analysis of Pictorial Discourse, Verbal Discourse and Narrative Form

Introduction and Acknowledgements

Breaking the News by **John Longstaff**, 1887, oil on canvas (Plate 3 in the Colour Plate section) is published with the permission of the Art Gallery of Western Australia.

I presented an earlier, shorter version of this chapter, entitled "Multimodality and Isomorphism: The Systemic-Functional Model Relating the Analysis of Pictorial Discourse, Verbal Discourse and Narrative Form" at a conference on Multimodality in the Graduate School of Letters at Nagoya University, Japan in October 2005 and it was published in the Proceedings of the Sixth International Conference of the 21st Century COE Program, (Masa-chiyo Amano ed.) Nagoya, 2006. It has been rewritten for this book with the permission of the 21st Century COE Program and Brill, Publishers, Leiden, the publishers of Arlene Archer and Esther Breuer (eds.) 2015. *Multimodality in Writing: The State of the Art in Theory, Methodology and Pedagogy.*

A thorough, consistent and replicable approach to the analysis and interpretation of art works requires an analytical model which can be applied across genres of verbal discourse and modes of visual communication.

The plan here is to compare the analysis of *Breaking the News* (1887), a famous Australian painting, with three narratives about the Bulli mine disaster in New South Wales: a historian's account, a journalist's on-the-spot report and a literary-style narrative from the point of view of the figures in the painting.

A great deal of written and spoken discourse is in the form of stories, or word pictures. Newspaper reports, historical records, speeches, jokes and even a conversation between two people create a reality that can be grasped as a whole and recreated in our minds like a scene from a film. Language operates through three distinct functions:

- the Ideational function (the referential content of the message),
- the Interpersonal function (the expression of relations between producer and receiver) and

Word Pictures and Painted Narrative   169

Plate 3 John Longstaff: *Breaking the News* (1887). Oil on canvas

State Art Collection, Art Gallery of Western Australia
Purchased with funds from the Hackett Bequest Fund, 1933
Photographer: Bo Wong

Published with permission of the Art Gallery of Western Australia.

- the Textual function (those elements that make each sample of discourse a well-formed and appropriate "text").

As M.A.K. Halliday's chart reveals, each of these functions is realised through distinct grammatical systems (see Chart 1)

To take a simple example, the conversational exchange:

A: "Did you read about that disaster at the Bulli colliery?"
B: Yes, I did. Wasn't it a really terrible tragedy? "

Like all verbal texts, this paints a picture using all three functions. If we write the utterances again, using a different typeface for each metafunction (a convention I will adopt throughout this chapter), the distinct realisations of each metafunction will be clear:

A: *Did **you** read* about that *disaster* at the **Bulli colliery**?
B: Yes, *I* did. *Wasn't* it a *really **terrible tragedy**?*

170   *Painting*

In this version the bold font shows up the Ideational elements of Mental Process ('read'), the Circumstance: Location ('the Bulli colliery') and the Participant in that process ('you'/ 'I'): the Processor.

The italic font shows up the Interpersonal elements of Interrogative Mood ('Did you ... ?' 'Wasn't it ... ?'), so called 'polar questions,' expecting the answer 'Yes' or 'No') and the Modal intensifying adverb 'really.' The plain font shows up the purely Textual features (deictics like 'you,' 'the,' 'that,' 'it') which contribute to making this a text in a possible context (e.g., friends discussing the news in the daily paper). We should note that 'you ' and 'I ' are both in bold font (as participants) and italics (as Interpersonal labels), while 'disaster' and 'terrible tragedy' pertain to all three functions: they describe a real-life event (Ideational), but with heightened emotion (Interpersonal: evaluative), but are semantically related lexis in the structure of this text.

Now it is easy to make up a brief conversational exchange like this to illustrate how the three functions relate to the 'facts,' the interaction of speaker and hearer, and the need to make these work as a coherent 'text.' As it happens, there are historical accounts and newspaper reports of the Bulli mine disaster in New South Wales in 1887, and these involve varying degrees and types of Interpersonal features such as the emotional engagement of the writer and his awareness of his readership (in italic font) and the Textual features which make it a coherent text appropriate to its genre.

Historical Account: March 1887, THE BULLI *CATASTROPHE*

A *terrific* gas explosion occurred in the **Bulli colliery** early on **Wednesday afternoon, 23 March 1887,** and everyone in the **mine** was **killed: eighty-three miners died,** some from the **explosion,** others from **suffocation** behind a *large* **fall of rock** from the **roof** of the **workings.** When an **inquiry** was **held** into the **cause** of the *catastrophe, it became apparent* that **safety precautions** had *often* been **ignored** by the **miners,** *despite* the *frequent* **detection of gas** near the **coal face.** *Unlocked* **safety lamps** were **used, the men smoked** *underground,* **and explosive shots to dislodge coal** were *often* **lit** *with matches.* The *immediate* **cause of the explosion** was *probably* the **firing of a shot** in the **coal face.** As the *disaster* had occurred *only a short time* after an *unsuccessful* **strike,** there was *a good deal* of **animosity** among **unionists,** who **blamed** *'blacklegs'* for *not taking proper* **safety precautions.** A **reporter** gave this **account** of the **scene** after the **bodies** had been **recovered** *from deep* **inside the mine.**
(Frank Crowley, *A Documentary History of Australia*, 3: *Colonial Australia 1875–1900*, London & Melbourne, 1980)

Newspaper Report

We *had just* **turned up the hill** out of the *bustle* of the **main street** when *suddenly there was presented to me* the *full force* of *the catastrophe,* in a way that was *as pointed as a stab*. There before us, on a *little* **green plateau, adjoining an artificer's shop,** *was a* **gang of men** *industriously sawing, planing and hammering at dozens* of **coffins, which were** in all stages of manufacture ... Each coffin was of *plain* black, bearing on its side a chalked inscription of the name of the deceased. Some of the *simple* hearses were *quite* **unattended,** *except by* the driver, who sat on the *topmost* **coffin** and **sought** the *smoothest* road. *Perhaps* the tenants of these *unregarded* **coffins** were *so-called blacklegs,* who **being** *new* **arrivals** had *no* **friends** in the **district to follow** them to *their last resting-place. At almost every step* we **meet** others who **give us news** from the **mine, who tell us, when my companion inquires,** that they *have found* their **relative—brother, son, father, or uncle**—whom they *had been seeking* after the explosion, and that the funeral *will*take place at *such a*time and **place.** There is *an effort at stoical calmness or fortitude,* and the voice *tries to be firm* as these **words** are **spoken.** But a **hand** is *often*raised to **brush away**a *starting tear,* which would *betray the* **sufferings** which *it seems to be thought unworthy* of a *sturdy* **miner** to **exhibit.** And so the *fatal* **news accumulates** and *comes* more thickly the *nearer we get to those two black cavernous mouths* on the **hill,** which are *still belching out such ghastly prey.*

(*Illawara Mercury*, Wollongong, 9 April 1887)

Comparing the Records

In comparison to the historian, painting an objective, almost forensic, picture from nearly one hundred years away, the local reporter is an eyewitness to the results of the tragedy only two weeks after it happened. He and his companion are a constant point of reference and the tenses of the verbs bring the detailed scene alive as it unfolds ('We *had just turned,*' '*suddenly there was presented to me,*' 'At almost every step we *meet* others *who give us news,*' '*who tell us, when my companion inquires,*' 'that they *have found* their relative ... whom they *had been seeking* ... and that the funeral *will take place* at such a time and place,' '*There is an effort* ... and the voice *tries to be firm,*' 'But a hand *is often raised* to brush away *a starting tear,* which *would betray* ... which *it seems to be thought,*' 'And so the fatal news *accumulates* ... the nearer we get to *those* two black *cavernous* mouths ... which *are still belching out*'). As the phrases which are both in bold and in italics show here, the journalist's account very skilfully paints his evolving picture—drawing us, the readers, in with purely grammatical variation of tenses and personal pronouns—in addition to the more obviously emotive Interpersonal choice of nouns, verbs and adjectives: *bustle ... full force ... catastrophe ... as pointed as a stab ... industriously ... plain ... simple ... topmost ... smoothest ... unregarded ... so-called blacklegs ... their last resting place ... an effort at stoical calmness or fortitude ... a starting tear ... a sturdy miner ... fatal ... those two black cavernous mouths ... still belching out such ghastly prey.*

Both of these narratives have their share of the three semantic functions: Ideational for the facts, Interpersonal for the relation between writer/narrator and readers, and Textual for the connecting and textualising features, but my strategy of indicating each of these with contrasting fonts shows at a glance that the historical account is dense with factual information in "bold," while the newspaper report has a preponderance of linguistic items in "italics" making contact with the reader and dramatising the facts. This is a typical contrast for the genres of history and journalism.

Fictional Narrative: The Inside Story

Compared with the 'public' written discourses of history and journalism, a fictional account of the Bulli mine disaster from the point of view of someone intimately involved and at risk has a greater Interpersonal intensity. The tone is less melodramatic than the journalist's account, but the (usually solitary) reader is drawn into a deep sympathy with the experience of the heroine through shifts in verb tense and mood and the Textual cohesion of pronouns:

Breaking the News

Sarah awoke with a start. She had been sitting in the rocking-chair by the fire with baby Emma in her arms and had nodded off. The late afternoon sun was slanting through the window and the last flames of the fire were flickering in the fireplace. The little living-room was simply furnished, but pride of place on the table was taken by the dainty china milk jug and sugar bowl that she had been left by her mother and, on the wall, the picture of a fine French lady in a fancy hat.

She heard the emergency hooter up at the pit and knew that Frank would be delayed because, even if it was a small accident, he had to be there as the pit safety officer. She needn't rush to heat up yesterday's stew for his tea, though it wouldn't do any harm to make up the fire, as they got the coal free anyway. She might boil the kettle and make herself a cup of tea to wake herself up. Still holding Emma wrapped in a shawl, she filled the kettle and roused the glowing embers to a flame with the new bellows Frank had bought her at the market.

Suddenly she heard a knock on the door and George, Frank's dad, rushed in. Dropping his hat down on the chair by the door, he strode up to Sarah and gently put his hands on her shoulders. She always felt reassured by the kind eyes and big white beard of this gentle giant, but his massive frame was blocking her view of the doorway where three of Frank's mates were gently easing through a stretcher with Frank's limp body on it.

George didn't know how to break it to her that Frank had gone down the shaft to check a minor accident and had been hit by a falling rock. "He's taken bad, love. We'll just edge him into the bedroom and lay him on the bed. Then you can wash him and tend to that gash in his head. Charlie has gone runnin' for the doctor."

(A member of the author's audience in Nagoya sensed a similarity in tone and point of view in this piece of fiction of mine to the opening of James Joyce's story from *Dubliners*, "Eveline." I was not deliberately imitating Joyce—although I know "Eveline" well (see Chapter 4 in this volume); in fact I thought I was nearer the style of D. H. Lawrence, who wrote several accounts of mine disasters around Nottingham, where I was brought up. So much for authors' opinions about their own texts!)

Narrative Structure

Theories of genre within SF Linguistics have shown the importance of distinguishing the contextual categories which predetermine the lexico-grammatical choices made through each of the semantic metafunctions.

These link up with earlier theories of narrative structure (O'Toole, 1982 and the first three chapters of this book) which analyse the separate levels of Narrative Structure, Point of View, Fable, Plot, Character and Setting in a story (of any length or degree of complexity). While Narrative Structure, Fable and Plot tend to be realised by choices in Transitivity (types of process, actors and goals) and Character and Setting by qualifiers in the nominal group and circumstances of time and place (all Ideational systems), Point of View is realised by choices of Mood, Modality, Verbal aspect, Comment adjuncts, Attitudinal modifiers and expressive or register-specific Lexical choices (which involve choices within systems of the Interpersonal function). The resulting content (the "Fable," or string of events in their original sequence) and stance is then woven together into a coherent narrative (Plot, which may adjust the temporal sequence yet retain causality) by Thematic sequence, conjunctions and cohesive lexical patterns (which are all aspects of the Textual function). This will be explained further in the section on "Narrative Structure" later in this chapter

A Picture Is Worth a Thousand Words: Systemic Functional Pictorial Analysis

As the above famous American advertising slogan (1911) says, a visual display—whether a painting, a drawing, a cartoon, a photograph or a website image—conveys more information at a single glance than the linear narrative of a written or spoken story, however long.

The extension of SF discourse analysis over the past 20 years to other modalities of meaning-making such as paintings, buildings, sculptures, diagrams, graphs, typography, graphic layout, urban design and even complex and kinetic texts such as film, television and website design offers a set of

174   *Painting*

descriptive tools and consistent terminology not only for analysing discrete texts in these various modalities, but for making meaningful comparisons between texts in different modalities and even complex multimodal texts (O'Toole, 1994/2011; Kress & Van Leeuwin, 1996; O'Halloran, 2004; O'Halloran & Smith, 2011).

In Chapter 1 of my book *The Language of Displayed Art* (O'Toole, 1994/2011), I make the case for labelling Halliday's linguistic metafunctions differently for visual modalities. Thus, the **Representational Function** is equivalent to the **Ideational Function** in language—and they are both represented here in bold typeface; the *Modal Function* is equivalent to the *Interpersonal Function* in language—represented here in italics; while the Compositional Function is equivalent to the Textual Function in language (plain typeface).

My chart of the functions and systems in the language of painting is shown as Chart 2 in the Charts section.

In my S-F analysis of this painting which follows I adhere to the font conventions adopted for the S-F analysis of verbal texts earlier: i.e., **bold for the Representational (Cf Ideational) function**, *italic for the Modal (Cf Interpersonal) function*, and plain font for the Compositional (Cf Textual) function.

Representational Function

Work: Scene

A young woman and elderly man stand in a humbly furnished room. with rough wooden floor, worn rug and unpainted walls. It is late afternoon (lighting).
Period: late nineteenth century (clothes, furnishings).
At the open doorway (right) stand three working men (clothing, facial hair) holding something we can't see. Behind them, the chimney and pithead machinery of a coal mine.

Episode 1 (Reading Left to Right): Scene

A fireplace (fire hidden, probably out); a wooden rocking chair with clothing; a kettle and 2 plates (drying) on shelf above fire; hanging on mantle a bellows and hand brush; on mantelpiece an ornate pendulum clock, small oil lamp, jars and tea-caddy.

Episode 2: Character + Action

The young woman holds a sleeping baby, wrapped in an old woollen shawl; she gazes up at the man in alarm; the man, dressed in working clothes and

with a bushy white beard, looks down into her eyes and holds her shoulders reassuringly.

Episode 3: Scene

Beyond the man—a table covered with off-white tablecloth. On it a floral china milk jug and sugar bowl, a sugar-shaker, a cruet, a bottle and a loaf of bread. Behind the table, against the wall, a tall two-door panelled cupboard bearing several bottles (beer, wine, brandy?), a cup, a large earthenware jar and a newspaper Above it on the wall a cheap print of a painting depicting a young woman in a large hat.

To the right of the table—a late-Victorian upright chair with turned legs. On its seat—a working man's hat.

Episode 4: Scene + Action

In the lit space of the doorway two men in working clothes hold something we can't see covered with a sheet. Above and beyond them—a rough hillside with smoking chimneystack and pithead machinery.

Holding the door open, hat in hand, a third bearded man stands half lit and half in shadow.

Figure

The young woman appears to have jumped up, startled, from the chair by the fire and is gazing anxiously up into the old man's face.

The man stands solidly and looks down at her reassuringly.

The man to the left outside the door appears to be exchanging glances with the man inside, while the other one looks down at their burden.

Most of the furnishings and utensils are standard working-class style for the period. Only the pendulum clock on the mantelpiece and the china jug and sugar bowl on the table suggest feminine domestic pride or higher class pretensions. Perhaps the Renoir-type print on the wall also suggests escape from domestic drudgery.

The men's leather trousers and rough shirts with knotted scarves at the neck are typical for miners of that period. Their hats are battered Australian leather slouch hats. Beards and moustaches were standard in the 1880s. The bushy beard of the old man suggests wisdom and reliability (the family patriarch).

Member

The most significant members are the arms and hands. The woman's hand clutches the baby on her arm, but the pointing forefinger betrays her alarm.

The old man's hand is strong, calm and reassuring. The right hand of the man outside the door (holding the injured man) and the left hand of the man inside, holding his hat, meet in a joint gesture of respect and sympathy.

Modal Function

WORK: *Light + Rhythm: Sunlight slanting into the room from windows off-left divides the space into four roughly equal alternating patches of dark and light. The woman, though well-lit as a central participant, is "still in the dark," while the dominant male elder is fully illuminated, his kindly face framed by his bright silver hair and beard.*

The main features of the setting, around the fireplace and on the table and cupboard are in the brightest patches of the picture, emphasizing their authenticity as signs of period and class and their value as tokens of a way of life about to be disrupted.

Frame: The rhomboid formed by the parallel arms of the young woman and old man frames the sleeping baby who is the unsuspecting victim of the tragedy being unfolded.

The frame of the door, set midway in the darkest area of the interior, engages us with the sunlit scene outside and the nature of the tragedy. The top of the doorway and the sloping hillside frame the patch of smoky sky where the pithead gear—the source of the tragedy—stands, distant but dominant.

EPISODE: *Relative prominence: In scale, centrality and lighting the girl-man dyad is most prominent. It is, after all, the realisation of the painting's title* Breaking the News. *On the other hand, the exact nature of the news to be broken is hidden, from the viewer as from the young wife, outside the doorway.*

Gaze: The mutual gaze of the central figures and of the two workers outside and inside the doorway involves us through a dramatic association more subtle than a direct gaze to the viewer would have afforded.

Interplay of modalities: An important tension is set up by the oppositions between the worlds of domesticity and work, between simplicity and pretensions, between faceless industry and humanity in faces, between the fancy lady in the print and the "real" lady with the child. There is a preponderance of curved forms (clock, lamp, kettle, plates, rocking chair, bellows in the "feminine" left-hand side of the painting, while the rectilinear forms of table, cupboard, print and doorway dominate the "male" right-hand side.

Compositional Function

WORK: The composition is dominated by the four alternating vertical light/dark bands, with the rectangle of the doorway centred within the right-hand dark band and the hidden figure of the injured man ("the news") just visible at the centre of that rectangle. The back of the old man ("breaker of the news") is almost exactly at the centre line of the painting, while his elbow is at the centre vertically. Virtually all the human action and domestic paraphernalia is concentrated in a wide strip occupying three quarters of the space between the upper walls and floor. The oval shapes of the plates, the bellows, the woman's face and the old man's face form a diagonal line in parallel (but in contrast) with the rectangular forms of the fireplace, the arms framing the baby and the picture on the wall.

EPISODE: The episodes are linked compositionally by the vertical lines of the fireplace, the folds in the baby's shawl, the cupboard and table, the corner of the wall and the doorway and by the horizontal alignment of mantleshelf, cupboard top and the shoulders of the men outside. The Renaissance tradition of 'isocephaly' is followed in the approximate horizontal alignment of the human faces—and even the clock face!

MEMBER: Within the doorway episode a series of V-shapes links the men's arms with the shirt and coat collar above and the corner of the sheet below. It is echoed, but inverted, in the triangle of the pithead gear on the hill.

Light and Shade

Some general observations about *Breaking the News* will be appropriate here. The painting is read from the viewer's left to right with the main action (breaking news) in the centre and the news being broken (the dying man on the stretcher) and the cause of his injury (the mine) framed as a separate episode in the doorway, but concealed from us by the doorframe and the man standing in it and from the young woman by the bulky figure of the old man. The darkness surrounding these episodes and throwing them into relief alternates with bands of light shining from the left revealing the poor but proud domestic setting ("stage props," as it were). The painting is "meaningful" to a large number of people—the reproductions of *Breaking the News* are by far the most popular of those sold in the shop of the Art Gallery of Western Australia—and I want to claim that this meaning resides not just in the rather obvious emotional message about family tragedy and the drama of a key moment in a narrative, but also in the Compositional construction of the whole canvas and its component details and in the way it engages the viewer, Modally, through the play of light, framing, facial expression, gesture, stance and the contrasting worlds of work and domesticity, reality and aspiration.

There is a real value in analysing not just the whole painting, but the lower ranks of Episode, Figure and Member, since if we allow ourselves to look at a painting for any length of time we take in the anxiety of a finger of the hand holding the baby, or the exchange of glances of the workmates in the doorway, or the gleam of light on a bottle or lamp as well as getting an overall grasp of the whole scene. This analysis of different systems operating at different ranks of unit is entirely comparable to the analysis of the

178 *Painting*

lower ranks of linguistic unit—Clause, Group, Word and Morpheme—in a verbal text—except that the visual units are all simultaneously present ('a simultaneous syntagm,' as it were), while in any form of verbal discourse the units are strung out in a linear syntagm and we make the relationships and contrasts in function mentally, because of our normally automatic and spontaneous use of our main mode of discourse, language. This is clarified in the section following my detailed analysis.

Breaking the News: SF Linguistic Analysis

1. Sarah awoke with a start. She had been sitting in the rocking-chair by the fire

      Behav.   **Behav.**   circ:loc   circ:loc
            Colloq.   *Aspect*
S.Th   Ref:anaphoric exophoric exoph.

with baby Emma in her arms and had nodded off. The late afternoon sun was

circ:accomp circ:loc   **Behav.**
    Colloq.   *Aspect Colloq.*   *Aspect*
              Conj   S.Th. homophoric

slanting through the window and the last flames of the fire were flickering in the

Behav. Circ:loc.   **Behav.**   **Circ:loc**
Reg:lit   *attitude*   *Reg:lit*
      Exoph. Conj. cataphoric anaph.   anaph.

fireplace. The little living-room was simply furnished, but pride of place on the

             Goal   **Mat:passive**   **Goal**   circ:loc
      attitude attitude   *Reg:lit+attitude*
Colloc. Anaph.   Conj.   Comp.Th.   exoph.

table was taken by the dainty china milk jug and sugar bowl that she had been

Mat:passive   **Actor**   **Benef. Mat:pass**
  Attitude   *Aspect*
     Exoph. Colloc: Conj. anaph.

left by her mother and, on the wall, the picture of a fine French lady in a fancy hat

Word Pictures and Painted Narrative 179

  Actor   Circ:loc   Actor   Qualifier
                 attitude   *attitude*
anaph. Conj *Adj.Th.* *cataph.*   *Colloc.: fine*

2. She heard the emergency hooter up at the pit and knew that Frank would be

Mental:perc. Phenom.   **Circ:loc.** **Mental:cogn Projection**
           Reg:work *attitude:intimate* Modal
S.Th.   *cataph.* Colloc.   homoph.   S.Th.

 delayed because, even if it was a small accident, he had to be there as the pit

Mat:passive Cause Concessive   **Rel: exist Circ:loc Role**
  Comment adjunct attitude   Modal   *Reg:work*
 Conj Concessive Th. Colloc: emergency anaph. anaph. homoph.

 safety officer. She needn't rush to heat up yesterday's stew for his tea, though it

  Actor   Mat.   Goal   Purpose Concessive
Reg:work Modal Colloq Colloq Temp PV *colloq* *colloq*
Colloc.S.Th. Colloc:delay cataph. anaph. colloc: heat, stew Conj.

 wouldn't do any harm to make up the fire, as they got the coal free anyway. She

 Mat=> Rel:attrib Mat. Goal Cause Rel:poss Circ:manner Actor
Modal+neg *colloq colloq* *colloq.* *Comment adjunct*
Colloc:fire. coal anaph.   colloc.:no harm anaph.

 might boil the kettle and make herself a cup of tea to wake herself up. Still

  Mat. Goal Mat. Benef. Goal Purpose Mat. Goal:refl. Circ:temp
Modal   *Marked person*   *Temp PVS.Th*
Colloc: fire, coal Colloc:kettle   Adjunct Th.

 holding Emma wrapped in a shawl, she filled the kettle and roused the glowing

Mat. Goal Mat:passive circ:means Mat. Goal Mat. Goal
Attitude *Reg:lit. metaphor*   Anaph.
Colloc:hold S.Th. anaph.   exoph. Colloc:

 embers to a flame with the new bellows Frank had bought her at the market.

Painting

Circ:result	circ:means	Actor	Mat.	Benef.	Circ:loc
	Attitude	*Attitude*			
Colloc:fire, flame	Colloc: fire anaph,				homoph.

3. Suddenly she heard a knock on the door and George, Frank's dad, rushed in.

Circ:manner Mental:sensation Phenom. Actor Apposition Mat.
Temp PV   attitude   attitude colloq
Adjunct Th. anaph.   exoph.   anaph.   anaph.

Dropping his hat down on the chair by the door, he strode up to Sarah and

Mat.   Goal   Circ:direction circ:loc. Actor   Mat. Circ: direction
                                                expressive
Adj.clause Th. anaph. cataph.   anaph   anaph.   anaph

gently put his hands on her shoulders. She always felt reassured by the kind eyes

Circ:manner Mat. Goal Circ:direction Senser Circ:temp.Mental=>verbal Phen
Attitude   temp PV   attitude
Adj.Th. anaph. anaph.   anaph.   colloc:kind   cataph. attit

and big white beard of this gentle giant, but his massive frame was blocking her

Phenom   vs   Actor   Mat.
Attitude Attitude   Attitude attitude spatial PV
            anaph. Conj. anaph. colloc:giant colloc:mass anaph.

view of the doorway where three of Frank's mates were gently easing through

Goal   Circ.clause Actor Circ:manner Mat.   Circ:loc
                             Attitude+colloq attitude   attitude
Colloc:block anaph.   anaph   colloc:ease

a stretcher with Frank's limp body on it.

Goal   Circ:accomp circ:loc
Attitude
Colloc:body anaph.   anaph.

4. George didn't know how to break it to her that Frank had gone down the shaft

Senser Mental:cogn. Verbal Receiver Projection Actor Mat Circ:dir.Purp
   Neg.   *colloq.*   *Aspect*   *Reg:work*
S.Th.   cataph. anaph.   anaph. S.Th   colloc:pit

to check a minor accident and had been hit by a falling rock. "He's taken bad, love.

Mental:cogn. Phenom. Mat.:passive Actor Mat.=>Rel:attrib
Attitude   *Aspect*   *Colloq.*   *Affect*
Colloc: safety, accident   colloc.:rock   colloc:limp body

We'll just edge him into the bedroom and lay him on the bed. Then you can wash

Actor   Mat. Goal Circ:direction Mat. Goal Circ:dir. Circ:temp Actor Mat
person qualify colloq   *colloq*   *person*   *Modal*
anaph   colloc:ease anaph exoph   anaph   colloc. Adj.Th.

him and tend to that gash in his head. Charlie has gone runnin' for the doctor."

Goal   Mat. Goal qual.   Actor   Mat. Circ:purpose
  Colloq   *attitude temp PV*   *colloq.*
anaph.   exoph colloc: hit anaph. S.Th.   homoph.

The reason why our linguistic analysis of the narrative text seems so dense, of course, is that we are constantly choosing specific options as we speak or write. Our story might have begun: **Suddenly the young woman dozing by the fire jumped up.** In this version the Ideational changes include shifting the behavioural process of sleeping and the place where she did it to an embedded clause in the initial sentence, while the main process of the independent clause becomes material action, **jumped up**, as opposed to **awoke**. Interpersonally the meaning changes because the heroine, *Sarah*, is not named and we remain outside her consciousness through the objective temporal adverb, *suddenly*, as opposed to the more subjective *with a start*. The Textual meaning has also changed because the adverb 'suddenly' is given thematic prominence at the front of the clause and the deictic reference to 'the young woman' and 'the fire' create an assumed external context.

Anyone who has learned a second language to a high degree of fluency will know how complex is the variety of simultaneous choices that have to be made as we make our meanings for native speakers of that language.

The point about SF textual analysis, however, is that the analysis is only as comprehensive as a particular study requires, and for most purposes we can focus on the main tendencies of a text in each of the three functions (what some stylistics specialists have called 'a patterning of patterns'). We have to have the whole grammar at our disposal, of course, for recognising the choices that have been made in a particular instance or stretch of text.

Thus, focussing for a moment on the bold type of the lines of Ideational analysis immediately below the first paragraph of the story text, we may note that most of the processes involving Sarah are **Behavioural**, while most of the features of the scene in the room involve a passive **Material** process. Most of the *Interpersonal* features at this stage reflect the narrator's *attitude* to the scene or the conscious adoption of a literary register, though occasional colloquialisms also begin to get us inside Sarah's mind.

In the second paragraph there is a distinct shift to **Mental** processes of perception or cognition with an accompanying **projection** of what is perceived or known. As the point of view shifts to her subjective consciousness, we note that the colloquialisms intensify and the modal verbs (*needn't, wouldn't, might*) and comment adjuncts make us party to the debate going on in her head. Once she rouses herself to action, we get a string of **Material** processes which continue in the third paragraph with the actions of George and his workmates. Sarah's perception of her father-in-law is mostly carried by lexical items of appraisal (nouns, adjectives and adverbs: *kind eyes, gentle giant, massive frame*) which reassure us—and Sarah—prior to the shock of the news he imparts.

The final paragraph balances between the **Mental** and **Verbal** processes with their **projections** of George breaking the news and the **Material** processes of the accident itself and their plans for coping with it. George's direct speech remains in character with *colloquial* lexical choices and expressions of *attitude*.

When we reach this degree of precision in our multimodal study we may note how very differently we are positioned by, and respond to, a pictorial narrative and a verbal narrative.

While the painting *Breaking the News* can transmit instantly the drama of the action (including the uncertainty about the nature of 'the news'), the mood of the participants (which we infer through their stance and facial expression) and the practical and stylistic details of every item in the setting—all of which have to be spelled out quite laboriously in words, phrases, clauses and paragraphs—we can only imagine what the depicted people are thinking and saying. The pictorial text falls far short of the literary text in the transmission of thoughts, sensations, emotional reactions, expectations and plans. These are conveyed by a complex interplay of selections in all three metafunctions: shifts between **Mental, Verbal, Behavioural, Material** and **Relational** processes; shifts between *colloquial, literary, attitudinal and technical* registers, interacting with shifts in the *Modalities of certainty/uncertainty, past/present/*

future; even the sequencing, linking and referencing of units through the Textual function contributes to the creation of the web of empathy, engagement or alienation we get caught up in as we read a story. It also helps to control the pace of our involvement, which, of course, a painter can never control.

Narrative Structure

Narrative Structure is the dramatic trajectory of a story's action first theorised by Aristotle in his *Poetics* and most lucidly expounded by Boris Tomashevsky in his *Theory of Literature* (1925). It moves from its initial situation, through a complication, a *peripeteia*, or turning point, a denouement which represents some kind of reversal of the complication, to a closing situation. It is the mechanism by which the theme, which may be stated statically as some sort of contrast, is given dynamic form … In psychological terms, it is the way we are moved from recognition of a problem to involvement with it, from a stance where we can dispassionately view a situation through the intellect to a feeling that we have sympathetically experienced the situation and its outcome (O'Toole, 1982: 5).

As the title of our painting—and the narrative based on it—suggests, some 'news' is about to change an initial 'given' situation, the young woman's simple but happy family life. The present participle, 'breaking' pinpoints the peripeteia, or moment of transition, from that life to something unforeseeable. We cannot see whether 'Frank' is dead or just seriously injured, but the serious posture and gaze of his father prepares us for the worst. This is an incomplete narrative because there is no explicit resolution or concluding situation—but this is its appeal, because we have to construct the end of the story for ourselves.

The underlying central theme of a story is refracted through the trajectory (in this case, incomplete) of the narrative structure:

> But the image is further refracted by the workings of point of view, and the particular pleasure that reading provides seems to be due largely to the play with point of view … Shifts in point of view are manifested in features of the language of the text.
>
> (O'Toole, 1982: 37–38)

The shift from Sarah's experience of waking up to the objective narrator's description of the setting is conveyed mainly through lexical choices as marked in the analysis, while the shift back to her internal thought processes in the second paragraph involves a clear shift to modalised processes (*would be delayed, had to be there, she needn't rush, it wouldn't do any harm, she might boil*), comment adjuncts and colloquial lexis. The third paragraph combines objective description of George's entry with Sarah's appraisal of her father-in-law in the lexis describing him. Lastly, we shift to George's point of view through verbal aspect and his speech telling Sarah 'the news' in the short sentences of spoken dialogue in a working man's dialect.

Fable is the original sequence of events as they happened. We frequently have to reconstruct this as we go along from the shifts in sequence (flashbacks, anticipations, embedded narratives, etc.) and the shifts in pace and focus which constitute the **Plot**. If Fable is primarily temporal sequence, then Plot is primarily causal sequence—again, something we reconstitute as we read. The temporal changes in this story are strongly linked to point of view as characters' memories and plans punctuate the otherwise linear narrative.

Character and **Setting**, both crucial components of narrative, regulate not only the choice of lexical items (descriptions of Sarah and her room), but the components of processes (behavioural, mental, material) and the circumstances of time and place within which they take place.

As we have pointed out, the trajectory of the Narrative Structure in the story—as in the painting—is deliberately left incomplete:

> A. State 1: late afternoon calm → B. [mini-crisis (foreshadowing crisis): emergency hooter; no fire, no dinner] → C. Crisis: George rushes in → D. Peripeteia: George breaks the news → E. the nature of the news [masked] → F. Resolution: none [we can only imagine the change in the lives of Sarah and Emma].

Paragraph 1: Setting and Character

Behavioural processes, Passive Material P., circ: loc.; people and objects
Point of View: Verb aspect (previous actions); lexis colloquial or expressing attitude; literary metaphors

Paragraph 2: Plot and Point of View

Mental processes; Material processes modalised (ie delayed, hypothesised or negated); concessive and purpose clauses and adjuncts → Material processes (action)
Colloq. + attitude lexis; comment adjuncts.
Collocations of domesticity/ workplace

Paragraph 3: Plot and Point of View

Mental Pr. (Sarah) /Material Pr. (George and men); circ. of direction, manner and accomp.
Colloq. + attitude lexis; temporal + spatial adjuncts
Collocations stress size, strength and manner; anaphora for people and items already established.

Paragraph 4

Mental Pr. (shift to George); Frank as Goal of Mat. Prs).; circ: direction + purpose

Verb aspect (projection of Mental or Verbal Pr.); Colloq. + attitude lexis
Collocations of physical accident + nursing

Pedagogical Conclusions

I have tried to show that a flexible but consistent linguistic analytical model can illuminate the similarities and differences between texts of different genres and can help us understand the intentions of their authors. A pictorial semiotics based on the same model helps us both to 'read' a painting in its own right and to relate its Representational, Modal and Compositional structures to the equivalent semantic structures of a verbal text.

Comparing three genres of written text about the same event can show students of history, news media and literature the ways in which the event is framed, the author's 'take' on the event and his/her expectations of the reader, and the typical ways in which such genres are structured. Precise lexico-grammatical analysis points to a provisional interpretation of the 'meaning' of the account which in turn may prompt closer investigation of the details, so that we enter what some important German theorists like Hans-Georg Gadamer and Leo Spitzer termed 'the hermeneutic circle.' My own preference is for a 'hermeneutic spiral,' since the interpretive process is never closed off, but always expands as we return to a text and it yields more of its secrets. The point is that we have a linguistic model which can recognise and account for choices of words and grammatical structures that an author has made across three distinct functions and at various ranks of unit. Like learning a new language (for other than practical purposes of trade or tourism), this is an important dimension of mind training. If we remember the fascination that small children have with patterns of language in both sound and sequence, we will encourage them throughout their educational career to engage with the details of what they read.

This becomes even more important in our world of increasing 'multimodality.' It is not only in the art gallery, or reading the Sunday supplement, or responding to an advertisement involving both words and pictures, or opening a website that we need to sharpen our critical faculties. If we have a proven method and vocabulary for labelling the details of a visual text, we will be more astute thinkers and wiser citizens.

We should allow time to look properly at visual texts: why do we allow ourselves about a minute to take in a painting in a gallery, when we are prepared to devote forty-five minutes to a piece of classical music or a week or so to a novel? Perhaps because we have lacked a coherent and consistent language for discussing—or even thinking about—what we see before our eyes.

And then there is the issue of creativity in education. Students can learn to appreciate the creative element in how a writer or painter transmits their view of reality. But given a story-line (as John Longstaff was in 1887), they could attempt their own drawn, painted, cartooned, photographed or computer-generated visual version of that story-line. Or given a pictorial display (as I have been here), they could compose a verbal text in a pre-specified genre and observe the play of functional choices. With this kind of exercise they will be deploying both the left and right hemispheres of their brain—always a significant educational exercise.

12 Pushing Out the Boundaries

Designing a Systemic-Functional Model for Non-European Visual Arts: A Chinese Landscape Painting

Introduction

This chapter attempts to push out the cultural boundaries to explore whether a classical Chinese landscape painting can be usefully analysed using the S-F semiotic grammar, or whether the special preoccupation of Chinese painters, viewers and art theorists with the quality of the materials used and their application requires the kind of focus on the substance stratum we would normally reserve for the analysis of sculpture in the West.

This also raises questions about such distinctive features of the Chinese social semiotic as moral and aesthetic philosophies, the relation between painting, calligraphy and poetry, and the perception of the place in Chinese society of the artist by the public and artists themselves.

Published in a new journal, *Linguistics and the Human Sciences*. 2005. Volume 1.1, it was also conceived as a tribute to Michael Halliday, himself a scholar of Chinese language, literature and culture, whose linguistic and social semiotic model has led the way in opening up China to western linguists and in broadening the awareness of Chinese linguists about dominant tendencies in Systemic-functional linguistics and semiotics.

Analysis

The crucial factor was the Interpersonal function. Most art theory and critical practice over the centuries has focused on iconography, the literary or other *representational* content of a painting or sculpture. Since the 1920s Gestalt psychology forced a reappraisal of *compositional* elements such as part/whole relations, parallelism, proportion and framing in painting, but these were not related in a coherent theoretical way to what was represented. Of course, the teaching and study of perspective involved the relationship between the painting and its viewer as well as purely technical geometric mapping, but the recognition of *modalities* such as viewing angle, internal framing, the play of light and rhythm and the role of intermediaries in the foreground was not conceived as a distinct level of meaning in the visual arts.

188 *Painting*

Before Michael Halliday's radical trifunctional model was spelled out in the 1970s you could have said the same for language theory and critical practice. The referential (Experiential) functions of language were always the priority; both Prague School and Transformational linguists focused on particular (though different) aspects of word order (Textual); and although such Interpersonal things as modal verbs, polarity, lexical colouring and intonation all had their specialised treatment, they were not integrated into a coherent overall view of language. Roman Jakobson's (1960) attempt to distinguish six universal factors and functions in language use—including Emotive, Conative and Phatic functions, all of which involve interpersonal elements—were never explored in depth other than anecdotally by either Jakobson or his disciples. It was left to Halliday to show, in both his work on a child's language development and in adult registers, how these three functions are realised through particular lexicogrammatical and phonological systems and how they interrelate in actual texts and discourses.

One of Jakobson's functions which had to be taken into account by students of literary style who were using the Hallidayan model for analysing works of narrative prose and poetry, like myself, was the Poetic function, and we will have to consider the implications of this for the study of works of 'displayed art.' Meanwhile, in preparing for a seminar at Sydney University in 1986 demonstrating the power of a trifunctional model for the analysis of a semi-abstract Cubist painting, I attempted to tease out the systems from which painters choose their options in a 'grammar' of painting which viewers like ourselves share sufficiently to make possible 'readings' of a work.

Halliday's model has inspired a large number of vivid diagrams over the years (perhaps proving its multimodal potential!) and the one I have found most useful is the chart 'Functions and systems in language" (1973), (Chart 1).

Visual grammars (Chart 2) clearly need to have their categories relabelled to fit their semiotic specificity, so Halliday's Ideational function became 'Representational' in my model for painting; his Interpersonal became 'Modal'; and his Textual became 'Compositional'.

However, the concept of Rank Scale still remained important: intuitively we know that we do not focus on a whole painting at any one moment (except from a considerable distance), but home in on individual Episodes; within each Episode we distinguish individual Figures; and each Figure, human or non-human, consists of a number of Members. And there is scientific evidence from work on eye-scans to back up this intuition. All eighteen of the works I analysed in my book (2011) and others in this book have yielded insights from the interplay between features at various ranks. As Halliday made plain in introducing the concept of Rank (even before 'Scale and Category' grammar became Systemic), "To show that a system operates at a given rank is the first step in stating its relationship to other systems; likewise to assign an item to a given rank is stating the systematic and structural relations into which it may enter and those which it may embody into itself" (Halliday, [1966] 2002: 120). Further authority for my transfer of the concept of Rank to the visual mode came from the Renaissance art theorist Alberti, who, in 1435, proposed a scale very similar to mine for the analysis of painting.

Even the concept of Rank Shift appears to be applicable to the visual arts. A painting hanging on the wall in a depicted scene is an example of a unit at the top of the rank scale fulfilling the function of a unit lower on the scale, in this case often a Picture as a Member within an Episode. Some late Renaissance depictions of art patrons showing off the treasures they have commissioned consist almost entirely of rank-shifted units.

The first systemic choice through which the Representational function is realised in painting (top left-hand box of the chart) appears to be between Action/Scene/Portrayal. Action will usually involve a 'transitivity' relation between an Agent and a Patient, while representation of scenes or portrayals of sitters will be more like relational verbs in showing things as they are. *How* people and things are represented, however, depends on the selection of options in the Modal and Compositional functions. Three major systems in the Modal function are labeled Focus, Gaze and Modality. An important aspect of the painter's Interpersonal address to the viewer is how he or she uses Clarity of line, brightness of Light, vividness of Colour and Scale proportions to make a particular figure or group of feature of the context stand out. In other words, the traditionally recognised geometry of Perspective is just one of many systems which are fulfilling a Modal function of directing our focus. Similarly (but with different systemic choices) the artist may use the Gaze of a depicted person or the Eyework between two people; particular periods and schools of painting have favoured the inclusion of children or servants or animals in the foreground as Interediaries, either inviting eye contact with us or arousing our curiosity about the painting's main subject; they may construct a path for the eye to follow (in interior scenes and even abstracts as well as in landscapes); and they may use the play of rhythms (the periodic alignment of objects, light, or even brushwork) to draw us in. It was no accident that I renamed the Modal function the 'Engagement' function in the more popular presentation of my CD Rom (1999), attached to O'Toole (2011).

Apart from these direct forms of address to the viewer, there may be more generalised modalisations: we may recognise the depicted reality as Fantasy, or doubt its veracity through visual Irony. We may see some element as Symbolic or Intertextual, whereby the painter nudges us to recognise a resonance between his subject and that of other paintings or sets of ideas. At the rank of individual Members the artist may resort to Stylisation, may use the device of Chiaroscuro, or may use only part of a member or Figure (akin to literary Synecdoche) to remind us that what is *not* there may affect what *is*.

The systems which operate in the Compositional function include visual equivalents to Halliday's concept of Cohesion in the Textual function in language, so that at the rank of Member such devices as Reference, Parallelism, Contrast and Rhythm mimic lexical patterns in verbal texts. On the other hand, at higher ranks the concepts of Theme and Rheme, so applicable in a sequential clause of language are unsuited to the 'simultaneous syntagms' of painting, even if there is, as has been claimed, a consistent scanning path we all follow through a painting. Here a rich and ready-made source for my systemic model was the Gestalt theory of perception brilliantly applied to drawing and painting by Rudolf Arnheim (1954). This covers those relatively neglected issues of how a figure relates to its frame and the relations between horizontals, verticals and diagonals, while the kind of compositional skills which are taught in art school, like line, proportion, rhythm and colour cohesion are also given a more theoretical grounding when they are related to selected options in the Representational and Modal functions. The same Compositional systems are operative at the ranks of Episode and Figure, though they do not have to coincide with the options chosen at the rank of the whole Picture.

An important theoretical question which I have not managed to solve myself is the extent to which the headings in the boxes at each rank on the chart are clines rather than systems. I have argued that choices in the Representational function like Action/Scene/Portrayal are systemic, as are options in Gaze in the Modal function. On the other hand, Clarity, Light and Colour in the Modal function and Verticals, Horizontals and relative positions in the Gestalt are more a question of degree, or points on an almost infinite cline, not discrete options in a closed system. Of course, there are areas of language grammar, especially towards the lexical and phonological end of the rank scale where clines rather than systems are the norm, but we may have to allow for a greater degree of subjectivity in reading a visual message than a verbal one. This is not to excuse the lack of explicit theory about such issues in art history, criticism and teaching.

The problem of Jakobson's Poetic function can be solved in a Hallidayan framework, I think, by analysing its manifestations at the 'interlevel' of Register. Although it draws on the resources of the phonology and lexicogrammar, the Poetic function adds to the meaning through a 'patterning of patterns' from those systems. Thus rhyme and paronomasia (sound echoes) associate discrete and usually unrelated lexical items through matching sounds; metre associates distinct clause and group syntagms through rhythmic parallels; puns and metaphors create alternative semantic fields alongside the dominant field, and so on. I have argued in my S/F analysis of Rembrandt's painting *The Night Watch* that parallel orientations of arms and legs and muskets and pikes set up distinctive and significant patterns, while the visual pun involved in the 'three left hands' of Captain Banning Cocq creates a whole set of alternative semantic fields for the painting as a whole. (See Chapter 10 in this volume.)

We should remember that Jakobson's claims for a Poetic function among his six language functions (1960) were part of an eloquent and much-quoted argument that literary studies were inadequate without the close analysis of the material of literature, i.e., language, and, for that matter, conversely that linguistics itself is impoverished if it does not take into account the poetic uses of language. This was a timely message for literary students and linguists in 1958, when he proclaimed it, as it was in 1920 when he and other Russian Formalists first formulated it; I believe that similar arguments need to be made—and backed up by case studies—for the close semiotic analysis of the languages of the visual arts in our own day, when the assumptions and methods of art history and biographical studies of artists still hold sway.[1]

So far we have argued for 'pushing out the boundaries' of systemic functional grammar towards visual modes of communcation. A recurrent criticism of my attempts at a semiotics of art (not least by myself) has been the restriction of its applications to the Western art tradition, albeit stretching from Giotto (1304–1306) to my contemporary Nigel Helyer. Indian students have claimed that the model was too positivist to respond to the spiritual qualities of Indian religious painting, although, of course, written Indian mystical texts—even chanted mantras—are susceptible to linguistic analysis. Similarly, the much vaunted 'spiritual rhythm' or 'rhythmic vitality' of Chinese painting is, it seems, not accounted for simply by analysing the Representational, Modal and Compositional functions in a work. However, the majority of Western artists, even of non-religious themes, try to invest thir works with rhythmic vitality, and one is a little suspicious of the constant repetition in virtually every book on Chinese art of the first of the six Canons regarding spiritual rhythm in painting by Hsieh Ho, an art theorist in the sixth century!

There are several aspects of Chinese painting and culture that do need to be considered, such as the competing claims of Confucianism, Taoism and Buddhism as underpinning philosophies for artists at various periods, and the sheer length of Chinese painting culture from 600 BC to the present, and the dynasty as a defining factor in subject and style. On the other hand, there is the power of tradition and the almost universally respected virtues of copying and imitation of 'the masters,' unlike the constant search for innovation which motivates shifts in theme and style in Western art forms. The role of the artists in society, often a wealthy elite within—or deliberately apart from—an elitist political regime has to be recognised, as does the self-perception of the artist in relation both to the regime and a coterie of his friends and fellow-artists. The interplay between the arts in general and within a single text is crucial: a single scroll may combine painting and calligraphy as a vehicle for poems or proverbs or folktales or personal reminiscences,

My broad answer to these issues is that none of them affect the validity of the semiotic model as a set of analytical tools for analysing a Chinese painting, since they operate primarily at the level of the social semiotic. They have all been dealt with extensively by generations of art historians, both in China and the West, and they need to be reconsidered in relation to the semiotic analysis of specific texts. As with language in Halliday's schema, the social semiotic is what gets talked about, or painted, and the way its texts—written, spoken, painted or sculpted—are constructed and circulated. The social semiotic, then, is reconstructed from the semiotic practices of the painters, and a systemic-functional model of the language of painters can help with that task.The semiotic analysis will, as always, be enriched by philosophical, sociological and art-historical considerations, but they should not always precede and dominate the discussion.

I will return to the issue of the social semiotic after applying the systemic-functional framework to an analysis of a famous seventeenth century Qing Dynasty landscape painting, Gong Xian's *Landscape in the Manner of the Southern Masters* (refer to Colour Section), a hanging scroll, dated 1689.[2]

Representation

In the Representational function we have one of those towering views of craggy mountains, partly clothed in pines, for which the Southern Masters were famous. There are some bare trees in the mid-foreground and, in the extreme foreground, a rocky shore. There are two sets of buildings: in the mid-foreground beneath the bare trees stands a cluster of simple thatched huts, maybe of fisherfolk or farmers, and, some way up the mountain side—a grander, more classical, perhaps more public building with a domed roof and two rows of columns. No human beings are visible, which is fairly rare in Chinese landscapes—and this brings us already to the Modal function.

Modal Function

Very often the tiny figures standing on pathways, rocky outcrops, bridges or boats in even the vastest and least accessible mountain terrain are there both to 'represent' someone: a traveller, the painter, his poet friend, etc., and as an Intermediary, someone whose main function is to draw the viewer into the world of the painting. But no such figures are evident here. Nor, unlike many such paintings, are there any actual pathways on ether the mountain or the shore. But the very fact of framing the land with a rough but horizontal shoreline (the same distance from the bottom edge of the scroll-frame as the mountain peak from the top edge) establishes the viewer's relation to the scene (i.e., working just like Modality in the clause). We, the viewers, are not *on* the sea or lake, but at a height where we seem to look slightly *down* on the huts and slightly *up* at the domed building. There does not need to be, in reality, a high shoreline for us to stand on. As in many Western landscapes, the painter is using this device of viewing height and angle for purely Modal purposes. A Chinese scholar, Mary Tregear, has a very insightful discussion of the evolution of this technique:

> In the early period [of landscape painting, 10th–12th centuries] painters explored the possibilities offered by the manipulation of eye level.

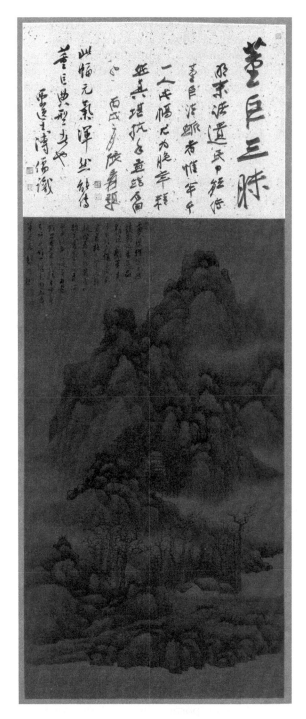

Plate 4 Gong Xian: *Landscape Scroll* (1682). Inks and colour wash
Honolulu Museum of Art

> Perhaps as a development from the vertically arranged narrative 'stills' of [scroll paintings in] previous centuries, a technique evolved of raising the eye level in a continuous upright composition so that successive eye levels are established. This allows the expression of great distance and height within a restricted format, avoiding vertiginous effects. Not only does a huge mountain not menace or overhang as one looks square at its face from a respectful distance, but chasms and many receding valleys can also be expressed comfortably within the same frame.
>
> (Tregear, 1980: 107)

(We hardly need to point out here that a Hallidayan visual semiotics allows one to see the place of a technical feature like this within the whole grammar of painting.)

Although no actual pathways are depicted, Gong Xian has provided *paths for the eye* with a series of horizontal V-shaped inlets or patches of mist in the gullies, drawing our gaze towards the huts, the bare branches of the front trees and the dense lushness of the midground trees. The building among these trees has no fewer than four such pointers: two to its right, one on the left, and one (vertically) from the upper left-hand side of the mountain—immediately, we may also note, beneath the right-hand column of the calligraphy. And there is even a bush or secondary peak in this cleft, visually (i.e., Modally) underscoring this connection.

Two sets of relationships are becoming apparent as we pursue this analysis of systems in the Modal function: the dialogue between the two sets of buildings, and the dialogue between the painted image and the accompanying and related inscription. The buildings contrast in type of structure, the grouping of their elements (at the rank of Figure within each building Episode on the Rank Scale, in their class connotations, the trees surrounding each of them and their nearness (hence relatability to the viewer)).

Composition

This is a relevant moment to introduce the Compositional function: the domed building is in the dead centre of the painting geometrically; its vertical columns are echoed by the fenestration of the lower section (which is also aligned with the dome) and by the trunks of the pine trees in front and below. The dense pine trees cluster round it, both protecting it in that harsh rocky landscape (Representationally) and revealing it to our view (Modally).[3] The building, which is probably a temple (Rep.) is vertically arranged (Comp.) and is approached with the eye (Mod.) vertically from above (via the calligraphy and the cleft in the mountain) and from below (via the most salient outcrop of rocks on the shore and the mist-lit space between two of the tallest bare trees). This latter space is then echoed, as our eye moves up towards the temple, by a proportionally matching space between the two tallest leafy pines. As we have seen, the temple is also indexed horizontally by the wedges of mist, and it is viewed face-on, orthogonally to the picture-surface, from the position that Gong Xian has constructed for us as viewers. In terms of both Modal and Compositional systems it is also framed, or cradled (I use the emotive metaphor deliberately), by the stillest area of the painting, which is itself surrounded by the vigorous rhythms of the most dramatic rock formations.[4]

The peasant huts, on the other hand, are off-centre, only indexed horizontally by the inlet and, at a shallow diagonal, by the long line of rocks from the shore in the left foreground. They are thatched, not domed, and bunched rather than grouped, below a quite threatening line of tall wintry trees, whose rapid, jerky rhythms are in stark contrast with the slower rhythms of the rock formations and the stable verticals of the classical building and its soft pine trees. In a flight of fancy we might see the low-browed windows of the outer huts as a pair of eyes offering at least the visual metaphor of a 'gaze' to the viewer.[5]

Calligraphy

Then there is the visual dialogue we have noted between the central building and the calligraphic inscription. I have argued in my discussion of a painting by students of Malevich (1920–1921) (O'Toole, 2011: Chapter 6) that the combination of painted image and written inscription (iconic vs symbolic signs in C. S. Peirce's terms; or neuropsychologically right vs left hemispheres) always creates a dialogue, even conflict for the viewer. The tension between the visual and verbal codes, however close their messages, is Modal in its challenge. But written messages in paintings are rarely close like those in illustrations of stories, and the relation may be positively cryptic: take the fragments of words from newsprint on Cubist collages; take the verbal exhortation 'Arrange a "Red Gift Week" Everywhere and All Over' in the Malevich poster; take even the captions in the magnified comic-strip images of Pop Art. Take this Chinese landscape: the inscription slants slightly at the bottom to leave breathing space for the jutting rock. Mary Tregear, however, makes an interesting link between the moving eye level in the image itself which we discussed earlier and the influence of calligraphy; and this rather contradicts my claims about the conflict between painted and verbal messages, at least as far as Chinese painting is concerned:

> The moving eye level was allied to a control of the surface composition by judgements of balance of line and tone close to that developed in the composition of calligraphy and entailing a fine understanding of the surface tension which holds a painting in its frame.
> (Tregear, 1980: 107).

The calligraphic text above Gong Xian's landscape needs to be interpreted as well as deciphered. As Jonathan Hay says in a detailed historiographical study of this painting:

Gong Xian's dense inscription interweaves issues of social status, style and artistic lineage, but it is the last aspect that is most relevant here. Gong's opening words confirm the modern art-historically informed view of the painting's antecedents: "In painting, one must make an orderly arrangement of the principles of the Song and the Yuan; afterwards, these may be distributed freely and [one's painting] will be of the untrammeled class." Yet the final part of the inscription puts the painting in a rather different light: Mengduan and Qinan in later years used Ni and Huang for amusement, but for basic fundamentals they relied on Dong and Ju. And these have truly been my own masters! I write this at the conclusion of this work on silk in order to set forth the intentions of my brush. Gong Xian, in the *jisi* year [1689] at the time of the 'grain-rains' [late spring].

(Hay, 1994: 189–191)

For a Western social semiotic it is intriguing that the Chinese painter includes in his calligraphic image both a theoretical justification for his style and a claim for a particular lineage of antecedents. Even more striking, as Hay points out, are the political implications of who he names and does not name in this lineage:

By defining a southern, orthodox tradition as a geographically southern tradition, Gong Xian was asserting the place of the south, and especially Jiangnan, as the cultural centre of the Chinese nation, in contrast to north China—which had fallen to the Manchus first, which had supplied the vast majority of early collaborators, and where the Qing capital was now located. Narrowly art historical as it seems, Gong's inscription is equally a political statement: he is refusing to align China's cultural centre with its political centre, and he is doing so within a month of Kangxi's visit to Nanjng as the new Son of Heaven coming south to bring Jiangnan fully into the orbit of Beijing … Gong's panting depicts a landscape which is in its own way lush and rich: the uncompromisingly barren trees around the foreground homestead seem almost out of place, left over from another landscape. The painting, in short, proffers a vision of a calm and peaceful nation.

(Hay, 1994: 191–192)

As so often under modern totalitarian regimes, painting is used as the only possible, though highly coded, form of opposition in troubled times.

The Substance of a Painting

To return from these broader issues of the social semiotic to our analysis of the visual text, the other outstanding feature of Gong Xian's image is the quality of the brushwork. Compositionally, he has used the dense texture of small trees and bushes to soften and yet emphasise the outlines of rocks and crags. If you half close your eyes—which is often a good thing to do when you are letting a painting do its work visually—the landscape becomes a series of thick black lines outlining the rock formations. This is very different from the meticulously detailed brushwork of the dead tree branches and pine foliage, or the calligraphy of the inscription (which, of course, also belongs in a tradition). Even the edges of the thatched roofs of the homestead are shaded with the same brush strokes, a very rare kind of modeling in Chinese painting compared with Western styles of realism.

Brushwork in the Chinese traditions of calligraphy and painting involves a complex interplay of technical factors: the quality and age of the brush; the density and colour of the ink; the porosity of the paper—all become semiotically significant in their own right. When the graphic substance (brush + ink + paper) becomes as semantic as the subject represented, the modal involvement of the viewer, and the geometry of the composition, then we need the other dimension of semiosis which is familiar to systemic-functional linguists. We need the tristratal model of Meaning—Grammar—Graphology to account for what is going on: Meaning is realised primarily through formal options in the 'Grammar' of painting, to be sure, but it is also realised *directly*, without the intrusion of grammar, in the Substance of texture, line, calligraphy—the work of a particular brush texture making particular shapes of strokes with ink of a particular blackness and density on a paper of a particular porosity. This is something akin to the visual, graphological meanings in concrete poetry, although that art form looks quite one-dimensional beside the rich graphological meanings of the Chinese masters of landscape. Perhaps, indeed, it is more akin to the *phonological* play with the substance of sound in the patterning of lyric poetry in all cultures.

I want to finish by disclaiming a possible implication in the title of this chapter. I have not designed a semiotic model for non-European visual arts. I have contributed to pushing out the boundaries of Halliday's model for the analysis of language towards a trifunctional semiotic model for analysing painted, or sculpted, or built texts which I know many students have found useful.[6] But the model, like Halliday's SF Grammar, is a universal one. Particular systems may dominate in the realisation of each of the functions in any one visual culture, and each system may be realised in particular culturally characteristic forms and patterns, but these will be discovered by applying the model as it stands to a painting or sculpture or building within any culture. The social semiotic we discover or elaborate through the analysis of many texts will also differ radically from culture to culture and from period to period, but the procedures whereby we build up our picture of the social semiotic by the accumulated analyses of and comparisons between many texts will remain much the same. The painted responses of an artist from a protected elite to threats or insecurities in a new totalitarian regime are comparable between the Qing Dynasty and that of Chairman Mao, or Hitler or Stalin or the Taliban, and can be explored as usefully in a 1682 painting as one in 2004.

Notes

1. This theme is is pursued with some vigour in Chapter 5 of O'Toole (2011: 119–130), entitled 'Why semiotics? The role of semiotics in relation to art history, criticism and teaching.'
2. The painting, done in ink and slight colour on silk is 99.5 × 60 cm. and hangs in the Honolulu Academy of Arts in Hawaii. I am grateful to the Academy for letting me use their reproduction of the painting.
3. I am not breaking any procedural rules by jumping from function to function here. One may proceed by analysing each function more or less exhaustively in turn, and that will certainly clarify the distinctive systems of each function. On the other hand, as with language texts, whether poetic or non-poetic, we often find that the most interesting parts of the text—what we might call 'semantic hot-spots'—involve the close interplay of all three semantic functions. I am sure that the domed temple is one of these.
4. A very similar device can be found in the 'halo' of foliage around the head of Venus and the light framing the foliage itself in Botticelli's *Primavera* (see once again O'Toole (2011; Chapter 1) and the extended analysis in the accompanying CD Rom.
5. This fancy is not really very far-fetched or unique. In my analysis of an Australian painting *The Gatekeeper's Wife* (1966) by Russell Drysdale (O'Toole, 2011, Chapter 6) I found a similar, even more glaring, metaphor of windows as Gaze. In the case of Gong Xian's *Landscape*, this flight of fancy has already been taken by one very rigorous historian of Chinese art.
6. See Kay L. O'Halloran (ed.) (2004) for some recent applications in a range of visual modes.

13 Exploiting Famous Paintings
The Canon Colour Wizz Photocopier and Picasso's *Girl Before a Mirror*

Introduction

The interplay of the pictorial and the verbal elements of a magazine advertisement has become a favourite subject for multimodal analysis in recent decades. The selection and placing of the words in relation to the image, together with the possibilities they open up for verbal and visual puns and other options in intertextuality, tell us a great deal about current fashions in advertising and the state of the social semiotic in this area of discourse. We, as viewers/readers are being constructed by the advertising industry as consumers of monetary, utilitarian, aesthetic and—particularly—erotic values.

Canon Australia in this colour advertisement published in *The Australian Weekend Magazine* of 2–3 May 1992 were clearly well aware of the erotic appeal of both the painting of a young woman gazing at herself in a mirror by one of the most consciously erotic of French painters and of the words of the advertiser's copy to arouse the reader and motivate him/her to invest in their product.

Analysis

Since the focus of this section of *The Hermeneutic Spiral* is on the analysis of paintings, we will start with an SF analysis of Picasso's painting as if it was on a gallery wall. We will then attempt a linguistic analysis of the accompanying advertising text (Plate 5 in the Colour Section) and finally will consider the rich interplay of visual, verbal and design texts.

Representational Function

I have warned students of painting and my colleagues in seminars not to be too focused on the title on the wall beside a painting, as this distracts us from examining properly the non-representational elements of its modality and composition and makes us feel that the title is all we need to know to interpret it. The pinkish-white profile of the girl on the left side of the canvas looks real enough and her white arm stretching across the frame and glass

Plate 5 Pablo Picasso: *Girl Before a Mirror* (1936) and the Canon Colour Wizz Photocopier

The Australian Magazine, 2–3 May 1992

of the mirror to grasp the right side of its frame is slim, curved and highly stylised, appearing to stroke or embrace her reflected image. Her other arm, almost plant-like in its organic delicacy, reaches up to touch the support of the frame. The two arms emanate from a small green circle which seems to represent her shoulder, seen head-on, and this is where the Cubist deconstruction of the female body begins, for just below that green circle are two closely overlapping white circles—the nearer one with an upwardly protruding nipple—which can only be breasts. Spontaneously we check to the reflection in the glass of the mirror (right) and find two slightly smaller white circles, one with a nipple pointing outwards towards the viewer, the other screened by green and white striped material whose pattern is picked up by the girl's underclothes. These are linked below her body to a larger white circle, which appears to be the reflection of her right knee, seen head-on.

As our gaze shifts from the circle of the girl's head through the green circle of her shoulder and the white circles of her breasts and their reflection to the right knee, it becomes clear that the Representational function at Picture rank needs to be interpreted at the rank of Members. This process reaches a conclusion with the little curved line between the thighs which can only be the cleft of her vagina. However, this cleft is only perceptible through clothing if the pubic hair beneath has been shaved, so by having it so clearly and prominently displayed, Picasso is foregrounding the sexual pleasure that this girl's body holds for him.

Now the display of genital parts of both women's and men's bodies has been subject to centuries of suppression in Western culture to the extent that representations of male genitals were often cut off and replaced by fig-leaves and the female cleft was smoothed over in sculptures and paintings and airbrushed out in nude photographs, until the emancipation of the representation of both sexes, led by Picasso and many artists in the twentieth century. To pun a linguistic term, until the 1930s the representation of the genitals of both sexes was a 'marked option' and their obliteration was the norm.

The green and white circles of the shoulder of the subject on the left and the right knee of her reflection are clearly external views, as are the breasts in both images and the vaginal cleft of the reflection, but the belly of the original girl is displayed in profile and as if it was an x-ray of the distended womb and birth canal. It is as if the right-hand view of the woman's body in the mirror was that of an external viewer (i.e., Picasso), while the internal view on the left engages with the young woman's own sense of her own body, and, perhaps, the likely fruit of their lovemaking. The separation and repositioning of different organs was, of course, made possible by Cubism, but in many ways it reconstructs the experience of love-making, where the active partner focuses on and arouses one fetishised erogenous zone at a time.

John Berger reminds us in the remarkable *Success and Failure of Picasso* (Berger, 1965: 154–162) that the most active period of Picasso's long life and career was between 1931 and 1943. He had been aroused sexually and creatively from a period of low inspiration when he fell in love with

Marie-Thérèse Walter. This young woman was the inspiration for more than 50 paintings and dozens of sketches by Picasso—including *Girl Before a Mirror* (1936)—which represent the peak period of his painting and remain the most popular (and expensive) of his works even today. Whether the model was nude or partially clothed, the tell-tale cleft is usually clearly marked in this series.

At the base of the lower left half of the painting the thick black line of the x-rayed vagina curves around the front of the empty circle of her womb, almost parallel with her distended belly and precisely opposite the vaginal cleft of her mirror image. Compositionally, it appears to be linking the moment of orgasm with the promise of conception. Clearly, in an image as complex as this it is as necessary to note the crossing of the vertical functional boundaries on our chart (Representation/ Composition) as it is to note simultaneously the interplay of Members at Episode rank.

In the upper half of Picasso's painting the relationship between the face of the girl and its mirror-image appears to be more straightforward: the pinkish-white profile of the girl is reflected in the red and grayish profile of her reflection almost precisely opposite. Now we all know that our reflection in a mirror is not identical with our face in life as others see it, but the contrast here comes as a shock. Marie-Thérèse's face is both a white female profile with her right eye gazing sideways *at us* and a bright yellow disk with her left eye facing forward to the mirror. And while the left image is suffused with light (framed by her blonde hair and a beam (halo?) of white light interrupting the pattern of the wallpaper), the image she sees (or Picasso sees, and we see) is altogether darker and more threatening. The golden sun of the girl's half-face has become a red, hook-nosed and grey-tinged half-moon (framed by concentric arcs of the orange mirror-frame, a blue shawl and green scarf). Above her nose and forehead sits a small green blob, which, biographers tell us, is a very fashionable tiny pill-box hat. My theory is that this part of the painting is a kind of *memento mori* in the long tradition of *Vanity* paintings, where a person (most frequently a beautiful woman) in the prime of life is depicted with their reflection as an old crone, or even a skeleton. For all his erotic fascination with his beautiful blonde mistress, Picasso fears the social vanity of the pill-box hat on the old crone's face. Perhaps this is why the vaginal cleft—a childish or youthful image—is so unambiguously part of the mirror-image (albeit screened—and accentuated—by underclothing), whereas the face and naked white belly belong to the girl's side of the painting.

Composition

We have already discussed the division of the painting as a whole into roughly four equal quarters, with the faces of the girl and her mirror image at the left and right at the top, and the sexual parts left and right at the bottom. However, there is so much play with pattern and colour at the ranks of Figure and Member that we are challenged to account for some of the variety of shapes.

The background to the mirror scene has two dominant wallpaper patterns:

1. on the top left around the girl's head: red squares containing a green circle within a green grid;
2. around the base of the mirror: yellow squares containing a green circle within the green grid;
3. behind the girl's back: yellow squares containing a green dot within a red grid.
4. The other recurring pattern involves horizontal black stripes, representing a bathing suit down her back from shoulder level to the bottom;
5. its continuation in red stripes on black around her breasts, and black stripes on brown; beyond her white belly in front;
6. the horizontal stripes are then resumed on the front of the mirror-image, but now they are green on white across the curves of her belly and cleft.

This latter area has three large "petal shapes" in red, green stripes and dark blue, while smaller such shapes occur in green around the girl's chin and cheek and in purple pointing upwards towards the face of the reflection. It is hard to rationalise systemically these combinations of shape and colour, except where they highlight significant body parts. It was recognised at this stage of Picasso's career, however, that he experimented with contrasts of complementary green and red colours. In the act of painting the choice of paint colour may have been intuitive rather than deliberate.

Language and Design of the Advertisement

The image of Picasso's painting is framed above and below by two broad red strips (the only reds in the design apart from the brand-name 'Canon,' below right). The strips, like banners, carry the headlines: 'Natural, lifelike colours.' and 'At a totally unreal price.' These are both Moodless clauses (i.e., containing no verb, like many newspaper and advert headlines), simply announcing a fact. However, 'Natural' and 'lifelike' hardly describe the facts or the 'colours' in the painting they are announcing. The image of the girl's face in the mirror is a distortion of her natural age and personality, and its colours are gloomy and brooding—not at all the bright extravert face of the original.

The second red banner, below the painting, is either an in-joke, (since most readers of *The Australian Magazine* in 1992 and most potential purchasers of a Canon Colour Wizz digital photocopier will be aware that the price of the *painting* runs into hundreds of millions in any currency: 'unreal,' indeed!). Thus the 'totally unreal price' must be pointing forward to the claims about the copier itself in the orange 'facts' box below: 'less than $10,000' and 'neat little price.' The Experiential truth of the headlines is modalised (in moodless clauses!) by the ambiguity of their reference.

The Interpersonal function implicit in the adjectives 'lifelike' and 'totally unreal' is intensified in the 'facts' box below by the rhetorical question: 'A Canon Colour Copier for less than $10,000?'—Another moodless clause mirroring the disbelief of the reader, but immediately answered by a double affirmative: 'It's hard to believe, but it's true. The copywriter now launches into a song of praise with highly patterned sentence structures:

'The Colour Wizz *has* Canon's digital technology (1) and bubble-jet printing (2), which *means* crisp (1), vivid (2) copies.': Two relational clauses (verbs italicised) each with double features of the machine and results.

The central sentence of this 'song' addresses the reader directly with 3 modalised transitive clauses:

> *You can link it ... to use as a printer and scanner (1) ... you can use it to liven up your documents and presentations (2), you can even make colour overhead transparencies with it (3).*

Note that these uses have doubled virtues leading to the final triumphant *even* triple achievement.

This song of praise winds up with two almost rhyming relational clauses:

> *And to match its neat little price,*
> *the Canon Wizz comes in a neat little size.*

It will not escape the attentive connoisseur of advertisements that *neat little price (purse)* is an affectionate pun on the colloquial term for the female vulva. Also that it refers back to *unreal price*, which is the phrase in the advert adjacent to Picasso's depiction of the girl's vaginal cleft.

The advert finishes with an imperative *call 008 023 026*, which strengthens the modality of the direct address *You can* in the main paragraph.

The Canon logo in the bottom right hand corner matches the bright red of the banner headlines and mimics with red, yellow and blue rapid paint strokes some of the dominant colours of the painting. The rapidity of these brush strokes represents the speed of this model of copier: COLOUR WIZZ.

Conclusion

Our summary of the formal and semantic relationships between Picasso's painting and the design of the advertizing text surrounding it suggests that the Canon copywriters were very sensitive interpreters of Picassos intentions in *Girl Before a Mirror*. They had done their homework more thoroughly and in greater detail than most art critics.

Plate 1 Frank Hinder: *Flight into Egypt* (1952). Oil and tempera on hardboard

State Art Collection, Art Gallery of Western Australia
Gift of the Friends of the Art Gallery, 1953
Photographer: Bo Wong

Plate 2 Rembrandt: *Night Watch* (1642).
Oil on canvas. Rijksmuseum, Amsterdam

Plate 3 John Longstaff: *Breaking the News* (1887). Oil on canvas

State Art Collection, Art Gallery of Western Australia
Purchased with funds from the Hackett Bequest Fund, 1933
Photographer: Bo Wong

Published with permission of the Art Gallery of Western Australia.

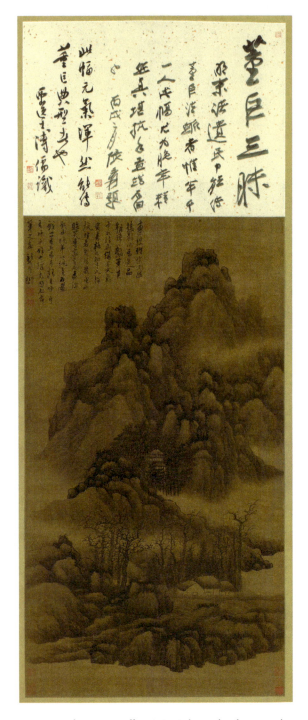

Plate 4 Gong Xian: *Landscape Scroll* (1682). Inks and colour wash
Honolulu Museum of Art

Plate 5 Pablo Picasso: *Girl Before a Mirror* (1936) and the Canon Colour Wizz Photocopier

The Australian Magazine, May 2–3, 1992

Part 5

Architecture and Language

14 The Presentation of Self in Everyday Architecture and Language

1. Introduction

The title of this paper is a tribute to the great American social psychologist Erving Goffman who pioneered the study of human behaviour in terms of spatial relations and discourse, but was writing too early in the 1960s to benefit from the precise analytical tools of SF linguistics and multimodal studies.

In analysing the opening scene of an episode of the British TV comedy *Fawlty Towers* we can "freeze" both the architecture of a small seaside hotel—without resort to elaborate draughtsmanship—and the dialogues which take place there. We can also follow the dynamic interaction of speech and spaces.

As Goffman showed, the relation between "regions" of built space and the language and behaviour they generate constitute a "performance," not as a piece of staged or filmed entertainment as in this TV show, but as a transaction between performers and their audiences in everyday situations. A performer's choice of a "frontstage" or "backstage" room, a corridor, the desk in a hotel lobby, or even a telephone matches and often governs their choice of Interpersonal, Experiential and Textual semantic functions in their discourse.

Chart 3 (in the Chart Section) represents my attempt (O'Toole, 2011) to apply M.A.K. Halliday's chart (Halliday, 1973) of Functions and Systems in language (Chart 1) to the study of architecture. I believe that his labels for the semantic functions are appropriate for the semiotic functions of buildings.

The **Experiential** function comprises the practical function of units at each rank, often incorporated in the name we give them. Thus a hotel is a Residential, but Public building; at the rank of Floor it comprises Entry, Reception, Dining, Administration/Office and—upstairs—Bedrooms and Bathrooms.

The **Interpersonal** function realises the building's orientation and style and the power relations between its users, the stance, as it were, of its owners towards the world.

The **Textual** function includes its relations of size, colour, verticality and texture to its neighbourhood, the connections it offers between rooms (e.g.,

208 Architecture and Language

Figure 14.1 Fawlty Towers Exterior

corridors, doorways) and between floors (e.g., stairs) and the colour and finish of its surfaces.

If we look at Fawlty Towers from the outside (Figure 14.1)—which viewers normally only do in the opening title sequence—we see a fairly large suburban residence with central portico (for entry and exit), bay windows (for light and views) and chimneys to remove smoke from fireplaces. Interpersonally, it stands imposingly on a mound some 2 metres high ("an Englishman's home is his castle"), the portico has a certain grandeur (as well as keeping visitors dry as they approach the door), and the larger, symmetrical bay windows are on the front face (façade) of the building. The white stucco finish with black trim around the windows and door offers an updated (early 20th century) Edwardian version of the black-and-white timbered style of Tudor architecture, so beloved of tradition-loving English architects and their clients. The unstuccoed and rather neglected looking chimneys are too tall, like Basil Fawlty, and lend the building an air of disorganisation at the top.

Figure 14.2 is an architectural plan of the ground floor of the hotel with the Foyer and Reception area, where most of the action in this episode takes

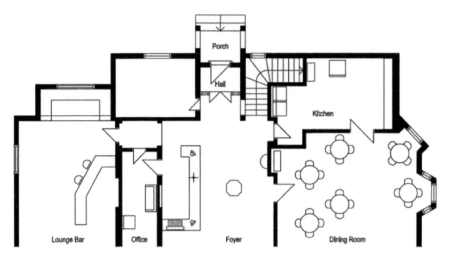

Figure 14.2 Plan

place. The plan is useful in fixing the relative positioning and scale of the various rooms, but their dynamic relations become much clearer when we record the behaviour and speech of Basil and Sybil and their guests, as in the series of clips from the first 9 minutes of the episode "The Hotel Inspectors," which follow in Section 3.

With buildings, as with language texts, it is important that we take note of the operation of the three functions of meaning at every rank of unit. Just as most single lexical words in language have an Experiential content, and may have an Interpersonal force and may be contributing to Textual cohesion, so at the lowest rank in our Architecture chart such Elements in a Room as tables, desks or counters—and even such "properties" (as they would be called in the theatre) as a telephone, a key or a map may carry Interpersonal or Textual meanings as well as their Experiential meaning. This will become clear when we look at the interplay of architecture and language in the following sections.

2. The Goffman Connection

I have chosen to analyse a short section of an episode from the 1970s BBC comedy show *Fawlty Towers* partly because it illustrates so clearly the interplay of speech and space, partly because it is still considered one of the funniest situation comedies ever made, and partly because it illustrates so well the theory and situations described in Erving Goffman's first book, *The Presentation of Self in Everyday Life* (1965). Goffman, a Canadian, had done the

210 *Architecture and Language*

field research for his PhD in the Shetland Islands off the coast of Scotland. He had set out to study the extent to which people in catering establishments like hotels and restaurants—even in a very isolated community—"perform" their roles as managers, waiters, cooks according to the expectations of their clientele, their colleagues and audiences, varying them according to the "region" of the establishment where they are performing: "on stage" serving at table or in reception, and "off stage" relaxing with colleagues or their families in less public regions.

It is not clear whether John Cleese or his Canadian wife, Connie Booth, while writing the scripts for *Fawlty Towers* in the early 1970s were directly influenced by Goffman, but we know that Cleese was a keen student of social psychology and he would be likely to know Goffman's book, which was published in the U.K. by Penguin Books in 1969. In any case "interaction ritual" was a hot topic in academia and the quality media at that time. *Fawlty Towers* is a beautiful illustration of all Goffman's categories of person, place and behaviour; exaggerated, of course, but that is why it is so funny.

In all his writing Goffman pays attention to the spaces where interaction happens and to the language which people use to enact and describe their roles, but he did not have a linguistic model adequate to account for the subtlety of their play with and breaking of conversational rules.

I hope to show how an appropriate linguistic model and a related architectural model, both developed from Halliday's systemic-functional semiotics, can clarify the interplay between speech and space (hopefully, without spoiling the jokes!).

3. Direct and Indirect Speech Acts

[*Note: The capital letters in brackets in this text refer to moments in the dialogue which are marked sequentially in the left margin of the script.*]

Early in this scene at the reception desk at Fawlty Towers [I] Basil needs a pen to draw a map of the town centre for Mr Hutchison:

BASIL: I mean there are no **pens** here! (EXCLAM.)
(*Sybil hands him a cardboard box … She shakes it. It rattles*)
BASIL: Well, what are they doing in there? (INTERROG.)
SYBIL: I put them there. (DECLAR.)
BASIL: Why? (INTERROG.)
SYBIL: Just sign there, Mr Walt. (IMPER.) Because you're always losing them, Basil. (DECLAR.)

In terms of a systemic analysis all these utterances are clear, relevant and economical:

> Interpersonally, all four Mood choices occur: an Exclamation by Basil—an Interrogative by Basil—a Declarative by Sybil—an Interrogative by Basil—an Imperative and a Declarative by Sybil;

- Experientially, it is "pens" that are being talked about: their existence—their location—as Goal in the location—and the reason for their being in that location;
- Textually, the pens are referred to as "they" and "them" and their location by "here" (in the hotel)—"in there" and "there" (in the box), while the new guest has to sign "there" (the register), all exophoric references to the physical context.
- Despite Basil's annoyance at this stage, all of these utterances are contextually relevant and grammatically appropriate. A Hallidayan analysis tells us precisely how they are making meaning.

This kind of conversational cooperation is rather rare in *Fawlty Towers*; as Sybil says to Basil later in the episode, "Cooperation—that's a laugh. The day **you** cooperate you'll be in a wooden box. I've never heard such rudeness." [O] Most frequently Basil and his interlocutors make inappropriate choices of Mood, of Experiential topic and of Textual theme and cohesion to assert their power or make fun of their interlocutor. In other words, they are making "indirect speech acts," or flouting Grice's Maxims of Quality, Quantity, Relevance and Manner. In 1969, the philosopher Paul Grice proposed these four conversational maxims to explain the link between utterances (which may be perfectly grammatical) and what is understood from them:

1. Maxim of Quality: only say what you believe to be true, or have evidence for;
2. Maxim of Quantity: make your contribution as informative as is required for the current purposes of the exchange, and not more so;
3. Maxim of Relevance: make your contribution relevant to the interaction, or indicate where it is not;
4. Maxim of Manner: avoid prolixity, ambiguity and confusion.

This line of thought has been further developed by the philosopher John Searle (1975) in his theory of direct and indirect speech acts, by Penelope Brown and Stephen Levinson (1987) as "Politeness Theory" and by Geoffrey Leech in his "Politeness Maxims." These contributions in Pragmatics help us to understand what kind of supplementary meanings over and above the linguistically coded ones are being made by Basil and Sybil Fawlty and the new guest, Mr Hutchison.

Mr Hutchison mainly flouts the maxims of Quantity and Manner. His first utterance is in a pseudo-Shakespearean style [E]: "Fear not, kind sir, it matters not one whit" (which Basil thinks he has mis-heard). He then goes on with a prolix announcement about going into the town which turns into a kind of thesaurus entry [F]: "some sort of transport, some hired vehicle, that is, to get me to my first port of call." This simple request for a taxi has become—as Basil suggests—"an announcement." The prolixity continues in most of his following requests for a phone call to be made, a diagram to be drawn and the drawing to be interpreted. These, however, are punctuated by short and quite aggressive replies by Hutchison to Basil's questions [**G**]:

> "In a nutshell.... At two o'clock, please ... I never use the telephone if I can avoid it. [Why not?] The risk of infection ... [what's wrong with the map?] It's got curry on it ... [Look, just *listen*.] No, I just want a diagram.... Well, I'd rather have the diagram if it doesn't put you out. [It does put me out.] Well, I'd like it all the same."

When Mr Hutchison returns from the lounge a few minutes later, he launches into a long announcement about a TV programme he wants to view that evening [**S**]. Most of this flouts the maxims of Quantity, Relevance and Manner and induces Basil to ask: "I'm sorry, are you talking to me?" and then "Why don't you talk properly?"[**T**]

There is even more hidden meaning in this last question than can be accounted for with Grice's maxims. Any student of English dialects (or British citizen in general) will recognise that Hutchison speaks with a Manchester accent, that he has the air of a businessman (probably a travelling salesman, that most despised, yet vital, of hotel guests for snobbish hoteliers like Basil Fawlty, who himself speaks with the "received pronunciation" of Oxford, Cambridge and the Royal Family). His peremptory replies and demands are consistent with this job and accent, but the long and flowery speeches are totally inappropriate in social terms, as Basil sees it.

Halliday discusses the relation between dialect and register in his paper "Language and Social Man (Part I)":

> Our language is also determined by who we are; that is the basis of dialect, and in principle a dialect is with us all our lives—it is not subject to choice. In practice, however, this is less and less true, and the phenomenon of 'dialect switching' is widespread. Many speakers learn two or more dialects, either in succession, dropping the first when they learn the second, or in coordination, switching them according to the context of situation. Hence the dialect comes to be an aspect of the register. If for example the standard dialect is used in formal contexts [like checking in at a hotel, M.O'T] and the neighbourhood one in informal contexts, then one part of the contextual determination of linguistic features is the determination of choice of dialect.
>
> (Halliday, 1978: 34–35)

Basil's question "Why don't you talk properly?" [**T**] (asked in quite an angry tone of voice) is not, then, just a protest about Hutchison's brusque demands, or his flouting of the Gricean maxims of Quantity, Relevance and Manner, but about a businessman of "Northern" proletarian background presuming to talk the language of Shakespeare ("Fear not, kind sir, it matters not one whit.") He responds, therefore, by parodying Hutchison's prolixity [U]: "It is not possible to reserve the BBC2 channel from the commencement of this televisual feast until the moment of the termination of its ending."

As we shall see shortly, the verbal anger is also realised "architecturally" as physical conflict.

Basil's speciality is sarcasm, which we might define as rechannelled anger. When directed at Mr Hutchison, it flies right over his head (another sign of Basil's social and intellectual superiority?); when directed, as often, at Sybil, she takes no notice at all because she knows she is the superior partner in both their hotel and their marriage. Basil flouts the maxim of Quality by not telling the truth, but with an aggressive barb which tells **us** the truth about their relationship—which is belied by the affectionate terms he uses to address her [B]:

> Actually, I'm quite busy in here, dear ... are you very busy out there? ... So I'll stop work and come and help out there, shall I? ... [C] Darling, when you've finished, why don't you have a nice lie-down?. I'm so sorry to have kept you waiting, sir. I had no idea my wife was so busy ... [D] Oh dear, what happened? Did you get entangled in the eiderdown again? ... Not enough cream in your éclair? Hmmm? Or did you have to talk to all your friends for so long that you didn't have time to perm your ears? ... [M] I would find it a little easier to cope with some of the cretins we get in here, my little nest of vipers, if I got a smidgeon of co-operation from you. [N]

Basil's other indirect speech act is fawning on the guests he feels he needs to be nice to—either because he feels they are of his social class, like Mr Walt, or because they are permanent guests at Fawlty Towers like The Major and the elderly ladies, Miss Tibbs and Miss Gatsby—and the survival of the hotel probably depends on them.

Much of the comedy of this episode revolves around play with the code of language itself—what Roman Jakobson called the "Metalingual function." Basil reads the inscription "PENS" on the box Sybil has shown him as "BENS" and involves Mr. Walt, the newest guest, in backing his reading [H]. This paves the way for Mr Hutchison's confusion over the abbreviation for "Post Office" ("P.Off") on Basil's hand-drawn plan of the town centre, which he reads as "Boff" ("the name of a locale, you know, the name of a district" [J]). As usual, Basil compounds the misunderstanding by consulting Mr Walt again and concluding triumphantly "P.Off!" [K]—which the audience, like Mr Walt, construe as mildly insulting: "Pee off!"

When Manuel appears, the code becomes multimodal:

BASIL: Manuel, would you take these cases to Room 7, please.
MANUEL: *Que?*

214   *Architecture and Language*

Despairing of Manuel ("He's from Barcelona, you know.") getting the message, [L] Basil holds up a drawing of a suitcase, then one of a vertical arrow, then a large number 7. Manuel, not to be outdone, holds up a card of his own saying 'OK'—and gets the biggest laugh from the studio audience.

We have shifted from language functions to spatial functions.

4. Direct and Indirect Space Acts

As we showed in our first section and on our plan, the spaces in a hotel have "direct," experientially designated functions: Reception is for receiving and signing in guests; Office is for administration; Lounge Bar is for relaxing; Dining Room is for serving meals, etc.

However, the episode opens with Sybil on the phone at the Reception desk gossiping with a woman friend while she has her breakfast, while Basil is sitting at the desk in the office trying to read the newspaper and have a cigarette. They have both usurped the official spaces for "indirect space acts." The architectural arrangement is such that Basil cannot get his moment of peace and quiet because of the loud and raucous phone conversation and, because Sybil controls the matchbox, he has to try to light the match she gives him on the surface of the desk [B]: his indirect space act is not a success. Sybil, however, is the real boss in the hotel and whichever region she happens to plant herself in, she "owns." The end of the reception desk is not now available for "Reception," as it has become her breakfast table, and she has to summon Basil to deal with a new guest, and the hotel phone is taken over for a conversation which is nothing to do with the hotel. In fact, the telephone, which is an element of the architecture, becomes a channel for the "Projection" of a quite different world, the sexual adventures of one of Sybil's and Audrey's friends with a series of tradesmen [A]. Sybil, however, can handle more than one issue at a time, so at the desk she can at least be polite to Mr Hutchison as she gossips on the phone, and when she joins Basil in the Office (to file her nails) it turns out that her conversation with Audrey did after all involve the hotel because she had been told about three hotel inspectors in town [P]. She delivers this bombshell as she moves purposefully from the Office, across the Reception, to the Kitchen. The news leaves Basil architecturally unanchored as he first chases after Sybil, then moves to telephone his friend Bill from the desk [Q].

The other telephone on the Reception desk now takes on its indirect function as a weapon between Basil and Mr Hutchison, who has returned from the Lounge and rings the bell on the counter for attention [R]. Basil claims he cannot attend to the new request because he is on the telephone, but Mr Hutchison's indirect space act is to put his finger on the receiver rest ("Well, you haven't finished dialing yet, have you?"), cutting Basil off

[S]. Basil's reaction is to slam the receiver down, but Mr Hutchison gets his finger away just in time. This clever bit of slapstick is repeated a few moments later as Basil refuses to introduce the scheme of reserving a TV channel for his guest. The TV, of course, is another element of the architecture (in the guest's room) which projects the world outside (the revolt of the leader of the Blackfoot Indians in the 1860s) into the tightly defined world of the hotel. Similarly, the map of the town centre (with curry on it) [G] and the plan Basil draws to replace it serve the same logical function spatially as conjunctions or inverted commas would serve in what Halliday defines as linguistic projection.

"This Is a Hotel, Basil, Not a Borstal"

Sybil is referring to two very different kinds of institution, with different architectural layout, different social purposes and different human relations. A borstal was a kind of juvenile detention centre established in Britain from 1908 to 1982 to house and retrain young offenders and keep them out of the adult prison system. It was dominated by security desks and the inmates lived in locked cells. The "hosts," of course, were prison officers. By a nice coincidence, borstals were much in the British public eye by the 1970s when *Fawlty Towers* had its first run on TV: the poet and playwright Brendan Behan had staged his very popular play *Borstal Boy* in 1958; Erving Goffman published his *Asylums* (which includes prisons among its social institutions) in 1961; and the singer Donovan had referred to an escaped borstal boy running away to Torquay (the town where Fawlty Towers is supposed to be).

Basil has been complaining to Sybil (in the private space of the Office) about the "cretins" and "yobboes we get in here" [N]. She knows Basil is a "control freak"—although she is the one person he can't control—and wants him to show a little courtesy to the guests. Previously, Basil had turned the central architectural structure, the Reception Desk, into a kind of barrier between opponents for both verbal and physical competition—in fact a "Rejection Desk." It is very typical, however, that, once he is aware that Mr. Hutchison could be a hotel inspector, he starts to fawn over him, encourages him to have lunch before the official time and assures him (in the public space of the hotel lobby): "O, goodness, we don't worry about things like that here. No fear—I mean, this is a hotel, not a Borstal."

Throughout this short episode there is a constant interplay between the systemic choices in language and the systemic choices in architecture and the flaunting of rules for both.

In the light of the performances of Basil and Sybil Fawlty and Mr Hutchison, perhaps we should rephrase the title of this paper as "Giving Oneself Away in Everyday Architecture and Language."

Table 14.1 The Hotel Inspectors

	LANGUAGE	LANGUAGE <-> ARCHITECTURE	ARCHITECTURE
A	*Morning at Fawlty Towers. In the office, Basil is reading a newspaper. At the reception desk, Sybil is on the phone. She laughs—machine-gun plus seal bark.*	Pretentious name "Towers"; "Fawlty" upper class. Vulgar laugh	English suburban house Foyer with Reception desk. <u>Out</u> to Lobby and Entrance. <u>Up</u> to Guest rooms.
Sybil	I know ... well, it all started with that electrician, didn't it... a real live wire he was, only one watt but plenty of volts as they say... *She laughs again. The noise rattles Basil, who puts a cigarette in his mouth and looks in vain for a match.*	Private gossip in public space (S. invades privacy of B's office retreat	Phone as connector (Cf Stairs & Lobby)
Sybil	Well, anything in trousers, yes ... or out of them, preferably. *(she laughs)* Yes ... um ... no, just lighting up, go on ... I know, I'd heard that, with her mother in the same room. *Basil comes out and takes the matches; she takes them back from him and gives him just one. Basil is disgruntled but spots a guest coming and slips smartly back into the office.*	Gossip projects external register and electricity/sex metaphors into staid interior). Smoking as private, "escapist" act. Sexual innuendo as public joke.	S's creature comforts—tea, cake, cigarettes among Reception paraphernalia—register, phones, typewriter.
Sybil	No, no, of course I won't, go on. *(the new arrival, Mr Hutchison, stops at the desk; Sybil sees him)* Basil!	Retreat to "Private" space	
Basil	*(in the office)* Yes, dear?		
Sybil	Oh no! ... Who saw them? ... Basil!	Private/public culture clash epitomised	Desk resumes its official function
B Basil	*(trying to strike his match on the desk)* Yes, dear?		
Sybil	Could you come and attend to a gentleman out here, dear? *(to phone)* nineteen?!	Letting the building get in the way	Contact vs architecture (Phone = contact despite arch.)
Basil	What, you mean out where you are, dear?		
Sybil	Well, the last one was only twenty-two ... he was!		
C Basil	Actually, I'm quite busy in here, dear ... are you very busy out there?		
Sybil	I'm on the telephone, Basil. *(to Mr Hutchison)* My husband will be with you in a moment.	"Busy" games people play. (Eric Berne)	
Hutchison	Thank you.	Telephone as virtual escape	
Basil	So I'll stop work and come and help out there, shall I?		

Fawlty Towers, First series, first broadcast on 10.10.1975, BBC 2 (As appears in Cleese and Booth, 1988)

				Phone as weapon
R	Hutchison	Could you do that in a moment, please? I'm on the telephone.		B turns, irritated at interruption Remembers to be polite
	Basil			
	Hutchison	Well, you haven't finished dialing yet, have you? *(he puts his finger on the receiver rest, cutting Basil off; Basil slams the receiver down; Hutchison gets his finger away just in time)* Now listen … there is a documentary tonight on BBC2 on Squawking Bird, the leader of the Blackfoot Indians in the late 1860s. Now this commences at eight forty-five and goes on for approximately three-quarters of an hour.		Phone as distraction
	Basil	I'm sorry, are you talking to me?	Insistent sound and gesture *(no words)*	
S	Hutchison	Indeed I am, yes. Now is it possible for me to reserve the BBC2 channel for the duration of this televisual feast?	Polite request (Modalised imperative)	Phone as weapon
	Basil	Why don't you talk properly?	Blunt response	
	Hutchison	I beg your pardon?	Argument becomes physical	
	Basil	No, it isn't.		
	Hutchison	What?		
T	Basil	It is not possible to reserve the BBC2 channel from the commencement of this televisual feast until the moment of the termination of its ending. Thank you so much. *(he starts to re-dial, but Hutchison puts his finger on the rest again.)*	Elaborate formal announcement	
	Hutchison	Well, in that case, may I suggest you introduce such a scheme?	TV as projection of larger world	
U	Basil	No. *(he brings the receiver down hard, missing the finger by a whisker)*	B, overpolite, ignores announcement H grandiose	
	Hutchison	I'd just like to tell you that I have a wide experience of hotels and many of those of my acquaintance have had the foresight to introduce this facility for the benefit of their guests.	Register and style = dialect and class Polite query Rude refusal	
	Basil	*(unimpressed)* Oh, I see, you have a **wide** experience of hotels, have you?	B's elaborate refusal parodies. H's style	
	Hutchison	Yes, in my professional activities I am in constant contact with them.		
	Basil	*(dialing again)* Are you really. Are you. *(he stops; he has registered a potential connection between Hutchison and 'hotel inspector')*		
	Hutchison	Well, then, is it possible for me to hire a television for me to watch the programme in the privacy of my own room?	Polite request (modal)	
	Basil	*(playing for time)* … I beg your pardon?	Elaborate explanation = threat	

"Images sourced from Davies, J.H. (dir.), Cleese, J. and Booth, C. (scr.). 2001. *The Complete Fawlty Towers*. UK: BBC Worldwide."

Screenshot 14.1 "Fear not, kind sir, it matters not one whit."

Screenshot 14.2 "I never use the telephone if I can avoid it."

Screenshot 14.3 "No, I just want a diagram."

Screenshot 14.4 "Manuel, would you take these cases to Room 7, please?"

Screenshot 14.5 "Manuel will show you to your room ... If you're lucky."

Screenshot 14.6 "And if anybody wants me, I shall be in the lounge."

Screenshot 14.7 "There are some hotel inspectors in town."

Screenshot 14.8 "Well, you haven't finished dialing yet, have you?"

Acknowledgements

I would like to acknowledge the help of Geoff Warn, a practising architect, in drawing the floor plan of Fawlty Towers and sharing with me the rich play with architectural forms in this episode.

My son, Janek, has given invaluable help on many occasions in downloading relevant clips from the DVD of *Fawlty Towers* and integrating them into this paper. We still enjoy laughing together even after many viewings.

References

Abrams, M.H. 1957. *A Glossary of Literary Terms*. New York: Holt, Rinehart & Winston.
Andrew, Joe and Chris Pike (eds.). 1974–2006. *Essays in Poetics*. UK: Keele University.
Arnheim, R. 1954. *Art and Visual Perception: A Psychology of the Creative Eye*. London: Faber & Faber.
Atkin, Ronald H. 1974. *Mathematical Structure in Human Affairs*. London: Heinemann.
———. 1981. *Multidimensional Man*. Harmondsworth: Penguin Books.
Auden, W.H. 1950. *Collected Shorter Poems, 1930–1944*. London: Faber and Faber Ltd. p. 19.
Barthes, R. 1975. "Introduction à l'analyse structurale des récits." *Communications*, 8: 1–27.
Baxendall, M. 1972. *Painting and Experience in Fifteenth Century Italy*. Oxford: Clarendon Press.
Berger, John. 1965. *Success and Failure of Picasso*. Harmondsworth: Penguin Books.
Brown, P. and S. Levinson. 1987. *Politeness: Some Universals in Language*. Cambridge: Cambridge University Press.
Butcher, S.H. 1932. *Aristotle's Theory of Poetry and Fine Art*. 4th edition. London: Macmillan, Section X: 71.
Chatman, Seymour. 1969. "New Ways of Analyzing Narrative Structure." *Language and Style*, 2: 1–36.
Chekhov, A.P. 1954–1957. "The Student" in *Sobraniye sochinenii v 12 tomakh*. Vol. 7. Moscow: 366–369.
Cleese, John and Connie Booth. 1988. *The Complete Fawlty Towers*. London: Methuen.
Crowley, Frank. 1980. *A Documentary History of Australia, 3: Colonial Australia 1875–1900*. London & Melbourne: Thomas Nelson.
Davies, J.H. (dir.), Cleese, J. and Booth, C. (scr.). 2001. *The Complete Fawlty Towers*. UK: BBC Worldwide.
Eisenstein, S. 1949. *Film Form* (trans. Jay Leyda). New York: Harcourt Brace.
———. 1964. "*Stachka 1924*: k voprosu o materialisticheskom podkhode k forme" (On the problem of a materialist approach to form). in Il'in, L.A. (ed.) *Izbrannye sochineniya* (Selected Works). Vol. 1. Moscow: Iskusstvo, 109–116.
Fowler, R. 1975. *Style and Structure in Literature: Essays in the New Stylistics*. Oxford: Basil Blackwell.
Goffman, Ervin. 1961. *Asylums*. London: Penguin Books.
———. 1965. *The Presentation of Self in Everyday Life*. London: Penguin Books.

224 References

Gombrich, E. 1972. "Botticelli's Mythologies" in *Symbolic Images: Studies in the Art of the Renaissance*. London: Phaidon.

Gong Xian. 1682. *Landscape Scroll*. Honolulu Museum of Art.

Gooding, Jan. 1985. "Frank Hinder's *Flight into Egypt*." Visitors' Pamphlet. Art Gallery of Western Australia.

Halliday, M.A.K. 1966. "Descriptive Linguistics in Literary Studies" in *Patterns of Language*. London: Longman.

———. 1971. "Linguistic Function and Literary Style" in Seymour Chatman (ed.) *Literary Style: A Symposium*. New York: Oxford University Press, 330–365.

———. 1973. "The Functional Basis of Language" in M.A.K. Halliday *Explorations in the Functions of Language*. London: Edward Arnold.

———. 1975. *Learning How to Mean: Explorations in the Development of Language*. London: Edward Arnold.

———. 1978. "Language and Social Man (Part 1)" in *Language as Social Semiotic: The Social Interpretation of Language and Meaning*. London: Edward Arnold: 8–35.

———. 1985. *An Introduction to Functional Grammar*. 2nd edition. London: Edward Arnold.

Hay, J. 1994. "The Suspension of Dynastic Time" in J. Hay (ed.) *Boundaries in China*. London: Reaktion Books: 171–197.

Hinder, Frank. 1952. Personal correspondence. Art Gallery of Western Australia.

Hrushovski, B. 1974. "A Unified Theory of the Literary Text" in Z. Ben Porat and B. Hrushovski *Structuralist Poetics in Israel*. Institute for Poetics and Semiotics. Tel Aviv: Tel Aviv University: 13–23.

———. 1976. *Segmentation and Motivation in the Text Continuum of Literary Prose: The First Episode of War and Peace: Papers on Poetics and Semiotics*. Vol. 5. Tel Aviv: Tel Aviv University.

Jakobson, Roman. 1960. "Linguistics and Poetics" in Thomas A. Sebeok (ed.) *Style in Language*. Bloomington: Indiana University Press.

Joyce, James. 1954. "Two Gallants" in *Dubliners*. London: Cape.

———. 1944. *Stephen Hero*. T. Spencer (ed.). London: Cape.

Kreitler, H. and S. Kreitler. 1972. *Psychology of the Arts*. North Carolina: Duke University Press.

Kress, G. and T. Van Leeuwin. 1996. *Reading Images: The Grammar of Visual Design*. London & New York: Routledge.

Leech, Geoffrey N. 1983. *Principles of Pragmatics*. London: Longman.

Lévi-Strauss, Claude. 1960. "L'analyse morphologique des contes russes." *International Journal of Slavic Linguistics and Poetics*, 3.

Litz, A. Walton. 1969. "Two Gallants" in C. Hart (ed.) *James Joyce's Dubliners: Critical Essays*. London: Faber, 62–71.

Lotman, Yu.M. 1968. "Problema khudozhestvennogo prostranstva v proze Gogolya." *Trudy po russskoi i slavyanskoi filologii*, 11: 5–50.

———. 1977. *The Structure of the Artistic Text* (trans. Ronald Vroon). Michigan Slavic Contributions 7. Ann Arbor: University of Michigan.

O'Halloran, K.L. 2004. *Multimodal Discourse Analysis: Systemic-Functional Perspectives*. London & New York: Continuum.

O'Halloran, K.L. and B.A. Smith (eds.). 2011. *Multimodal Studies: Exploring Issues and Domains*. London & New York: Routledge.

O'Toole, L. Michael. 1982. *Structure, Style and Interpretation in the Russian Short Story*. London & New York: Yale University Press.

———. 2011. *The Language of Displayed Art*. 2nd edition. London & New York: Routledge.

——— and Ann Shukman (eds.). 1975–1982. *Russian Poetics in Translation*. 12 volumes. UK: University of Essex Press. (Now available online through Amazon.)

Oulanoff, H. 1966. *The Serapion Brothers: Theory and Practice*. The Hague: Mouton.

Panofsky, Erwin. 1939. "Iconography and iconology" in Introduction to *Studies in Iconology: Humanistic Themes in the Art of the Renaissance*. New York: Oxford University Press, 3–31.

Parker, Trey and Matt Stone. 2002. *South Park*. Episode 609 of the animated TV cartoon: *Free Hat*. Director: Tony Nugnes.

Poe, E.A. 1965. *Complete Works*. Vol. 13. New York: A.M.S. Press, 153.

Propp, V.I. 1928. *Morfologiya skazki*. Leningrad: Ak Nauk.

Pudovkin, V.I. 1928. "S.M. Eizenshtein (Ot Potemkina k Oktyabryu)" in Zhizn' iskusstva.

Scheglov, Yu.K. 1968. "Opisaniye struktury detektivnoi novelly" in *Preprints for the International Symposium on Semiotics*. Warsaw: International Symposium of Semiotics.

Searle, John. 1975. "Indirect Speech Acts" in P. Cole and J.L. Morgan (eds.) *Syntax and Semantics, Speech Acts*. New York: Academic Press: 59–82.

Shklovsky, Viktor. 1925a. "Novella tain" ("The Mystery Story") in *O teorii prozy*. Moscow: Federation.

———. 1925b. *O teorii prozy*. Moscow: Federation.

Spitzer, Leo. 1948. "Linguistics and Literary History," Princeton: University of Princeton Press, pp. 1–40.

Taylor, Richard (ed.). 1982. "The Poetics of Cinema" in L.M. O'Toole and Ann Shukman (eds.) *Russian Poetics in Translation*. Vol. 9. UK: Essex University Press. (Now available on-line through Amazon.)

——— and Ian Christie (eds.). 1988. *The Film Factory: Russian and Soviet Cinema in Documents 1896–1939*. London: Routledge & Kegan Paul.

Tindall, William York. 1960. *A Reader's Guide to James Joyce*. London: Thames and Hudson.

Tregear, Mary. 1980. *Chinese Art*. London: Thames & Hudson.

Turgenev, I. 1852. "Bezhin lug" *A Sportsman's Sketches*. St. Petersburg: Sovremennik.

Tynyanov, Yu.N. 1927. "Oda kak oratorskii zhanr" Translated in L.M. O'Toole and A. Shukman (eds.) *Poetika III*, Leningrad: 102–128. (Now available online through Amazon.)

Uspensky, B.A. 1970. *Poetika kompozitsii*. Moscow: Ak Nauk (trans. *The Poetics of Composition*. 1974. Berkeley: University of California Press).

van Dijk, T.A. 1971. *Some Aspects of Text Grammar*. The Hague: Mouton.

Wind, E. 1958. "Botticelli's 'Primavera' " in *Pagan Mysteries of the Renaissance*. 2nd edition. New York: Barnes & Noble.

——— and Yu K. Scheglov. 1967. "Strukturnaya poetika—porozhdayuschaya poetika." *Voprosy Literatury*, 1: 73–89.

Index

AGWA 140
Alberti 142
American New Criticism 50
Andrew, Joe 34
architecture functions 207; combined meanings of spatial features 207; "on stage" 207; regions of buildings 207
Aristotle 7
Arnheim, Rudolf 190
art 139; art analysis 140; art teaching 140; semiotics of art 142; three functions in painting 159
Atkin, Ron 75
Auden, W.H. 144

Bakhtin, M 93
Barthes, R 47
Booth, Connie 210
borstal 215
Botticelli 141
brain hemispheres' response to pictorial/verbal text 178
Bruegel 144–8
Bulli mine disaster 5; historian's account 171; journalist's account 172; literary retelling 172; painting 175
Butt, David 139

catharsis 14
centrifugal/centripetal 18
character (Char) 2; as dimension of NS 16; juxtaposition of chars 24, 62
Chekhov, Anton 9
Chinese art 187; calligraphy 190; Chinese religions and art 190; painting landscape 188
Chinese dynasties, art and politics 196
Christian drama 14
Cleese, John 210

cohesion 26; grammatical/lexical/phonological 26
colour theories 148; colour matching in advert copy 204
Conan Doyle, Sir Arthur 54
Cubism 144–7; deconstruction of bodies 201

dialect speech 212
digital/computer generated imagery 97
dimensions of analysis 13
dispositional sequence 37
dominant 75, 153
Dubliners 34; Dublin setting 41

Eisenstein 109
epilogue 19
epiphany 40
episode in visual art 160; episodes in *The Night Watch* 164–6
Essays in Poetics 7
explication de texte 2
expressiveness devices (ED) 63

fable 7; dispositional sequence 36
facial reflection 203
family relations (Joseph) 79
Firth, J.R. 26
focus 145
foregrounding 155–6
frame 146
free indirect speech 45
French Structuralists 50
Frost, Robert 2
functional poetics 74
functions 141; functions in language 141; functions in painting 189

gaze 146
generative poetics 52

genital suppression in art 201; the marked option 201
gestalt 149
Gleason, James 153
Goffman, Erving 207
Gong Xian 5; calligraphy 196; landscape scroll 192; graphology in Chinese painting 197; the social semiotic 190
Gooding, Jan 141, 153
Grice, Paul 211; conversational maxims 211
Gurbanov, V.V. 28; sentence length in Chekhov 28

Halliday M.A.K. 1; dialect and register 212; language functions 139; language in social context 26
Helyer, Nigel 139
hermeneutics 1; hermeneutic spiral 4; hermeneutic process 5; hermeneutics and art intuition 35, 54; generation of text 53
Hinder, Frank 4, 140
historical account 5
Hodge, Bob 137
Hrushovski, Benjamin 47
humour 95; clashing registers 95; youth idiom 95

illumination 148
imaginative function 154–5
indirect speech acts 210; parody 213; sarcasm 213
interaction ritual 210
intermediaries 146, 192
interplay of language and architecture 5
intertextuality 147; in adverts 199
inverse relations 77
irony 146
irrational vs reason 54

Jakobson, Roman 188; factors and functions in communication 189; metalingual function 213; poetic function 154
Joyce, James 43

Kreitler and Kreitler 154
Kress, Gunther 137

lexicogrammar 4
light 145

lighting 160
linguistic realisations of narrative functions 178
Longstaff, John 5
Lubbock, Percy 23
Lucas, George 95

Martin, James 139
matrix arrays 77
mental process 3
metahierarchy 78
metre: iambic, anapaest 3
modality 2; in advert 204; modal function in painting 190; negative modality 74
Multidimensional Man 76
multimodality in adverts 199
musical structure in film 105

narrative structure (NS) 2; components of NS 17; generative grammar of NS 50; in painting 74
negativity 3
Neo-Formalist Circle 34; collective analysis 35
newspaper report 5
Nightline and TV interviews 98

O'Toole: three functions in painting 159
Oulanoff 12

Panofsky: iconography vs iconology 161
parallels 149
pastiche 73
patterns of colour 203
patterns of style 26
peripeteia 18
Petrovsky 14, 16–21
philological circle 1
physical sensation 24
Picasso, Pablo 5
Pike, Kenneth 163; particle – field wave theory 164; Halliday version 164
plot 7
Poe, E.A. 17
poetic function 190
point of view (PV) 2; limited PV 58; PV and irony 23; PV and sentient centre 16; PV and irony 23; shifts in PV in written narrative
Porter Institute, Tel Aviv 75

Index   229

portraiture in Netherlands 161
pragmatics 211
Prague School Structuralists 7, 50
projections of space 214
proletkult: opposition to Formalists 51
prologue 19
Propp 16; constituent structure of narrative 52; Levi-Strauss critique 18
puns: verbal 203; visual 166

rank scale 141–3
rank shift 189
realization 141–3
reductionism 47
register 153, 212
relative clauses 144
religious art 152
remastered film classics 95
Rembrandt 4
rhyme scheme 3
Rijksmuseum 4
Russian Formalists 5
Russian Poetics in Translation 7
Russian short story 7
Russian Structuralist Poetics: revival of Formalist principles 50

satire 93; satire as intertextuality 97
scale 145
Scheglov, Yurii 50
Searle, John 211
security/adventure oxymoron 63
self-reflexive jokes 98
semantic metafunctions: Experiential/Interpersonal/Textual 4
sensation/thought 17
sequence 149, simultaneous syntagm in art
sets in topology 77; cover sets 78
setting 2; Russian/biblical Dublin and circularity 41; settings as distractors 62
Shklovsky, Viktor 5; Sherlock Holmes detection plot 53
Shukman, Ann 7, 50

Singapore: University 93; Singapore culture 105
social semiotic 141–5; in adverts 199
sound 24
South Park 97
space in narrative 85
Spielberg, Stephen 95
Spitzer 1
structuralism and analytical consistency 37
stylistics 9
Sydney University 137
symbolism 38
syntagmatic functions/paradigmatic indices 158
systems vs clines 190

tense 3
terminology 12
theme 14
Threadgold, Terry 139
time 85; Newton vs Einstein 87
Tindall 40
Tomashevsky 14
topology 75
traffic 77; forces which warp the geometry 78
tragedy 14
transitivity 143; material/behavioural/mental/verbal process 182
Treagar, Mary 193; eye-level and perspective
Turgenev, Ivan 30
Tynyanov, Yuri 167

Van der Eng, Jan 158
van Dijk, Teun 48
virtual sound effects 160
voyeurism 39

Warn, Geoff 134, 222
words in paintings 196; Chinese scrolls 197; Cubism, Pop Art 196

Zholkovsky, Alexander 50

PGMO 04/05/2018